RESEARCH METHODOLOGY AND INTELLECTUAL PROPERTY RIGHTS

As per new 2022 CBSC scheme of Visvesvaraya Technological University
(For 5th Semester common for all Branch)

Prof. Kailas Shrikant Pathade
Assistant Professor
Department of Mechanical Engineering
VSM's Somashekhar R. Kothiwale Institute of Technology,
NIPANI-591237

To my dearest daughter, Shreesha,

Your innocent smile, joyful laughter, and boundless energy bring light to my life every day. This book is a testament to the love and inspiration you give me. I dedicate this work to you, hoping that you will one day follow your dreams with the same passion and curiosity that guided me in creating this book.

You are my greatest motivation, and I look forward to the countless journeys we will embark on together.

With all my love,
Kailas Pathade

PREFACE

Research is the cornerstone of innovation and progress, particularly in engineering, where curiosity meets practical application. This book, ***Research Methodology and Intellectual Property Rights***, is designed to equip 5th-semester engineering students of Visvesvaraya Technological University with the essential tools and knowledge to navigate the research landscape effectively. Whether it's conducting literature reviews, understanding intellectual property, or mastering technical reading, this book is a comprehensive guide to enhancing theoretical understanding and practical research skills.

This book's idea emerged from my academic experiences and role as a PhD scholar. Over time, I noticed that while students are taught the technical aspects of engineering, they often need help with research methodology, which is equally crucial for their academic and professional careers. This book aims to fill that gap, offering a structured approach to research with real-world applications, examples, and ethical considerations.

Writing this book has been a rewarding yet challenging journey. One of the biggest challenges was ensuring the content remained accessible and academically rigorous. The goal was to strike a balance between introducing fundamental concepts like the **Objectives of Engineering Research** or **Ethics in Research**—and covering more complex topics, such as **Patents**, **Copyrights**, and **Geographical Indications**. Organizing the material logically and coherently, ensuring that it builds on prior knowledge while introducing new, advanced topics, was an intricate process.

The content is organized into five comprehensive modules:

- ❖ **Module 1** introduces the basics of research, types of research misconduct, and ethics in research practice.
- ❖ **Module 2** delves into literature review, technical reading, and how to effectively search and analyze bibliographic databases like Web of Science and Google Scholar.
- ❖ **Module 3** focuses on intellectual property, covering essential aspects like patents and their legal framework.
- ❖ **Module 4** explores copyrights and trademarks, focusing on their protection, infringement, and relevance in engineering research.
- ❖ **Module 5** highlights industrial designs and geographical indications, with real-life case studies illustrating how these concepts apply to innovation.

This book is an academic resource and a practical guide designed to make the research process less daunting and more systematic. Each chapter has been carefully tailored to the needs of 5th-semester engineering students, ensuring that the material is both relevant and engaging. In addition, I've included ethical discussions and case studies to emphasize the importance of integrity in research, a quality that is often overlooked in academia.

I hope this book provides all students clarity, direction, and motivation on their academic journey.

With best regards,
Kailas Pathade
October 2024

ज्ञानेन तु तदज्ञानं येषां नाशितमात्मनः ।

तेषामादित्यवज्ज्ञानं प्रकाशयति तत्परम् ॥

: श्रीकृष्ण, श्रीमद्भागवत गीता, अध्याय 5 श्लोक 16

ACKNOWLEDGMENTS

The journey of writing this book, ***Research Methodology and Intellectual Property Rights***, has been both challenging and deeply rewarding. I could not have completed this work without the guidance, support, and encouragement of many individuals, to whom I am deeply grateful.

First and foremost, I would like to express my heartfelt thanks to my colleagues, both teaching and non-teaching staff, at **VSM's Somashekhar R. Kothiwale Institute of Technology, Nipani**. Your support and camaraderie have been invaluable throughout this process.

I sincerely appreciate **Prof. Rakeshkumar G**, Head of the Mechanical Department at **VSM's Somashekhar R. Kothiwale Institute of Technology, Nipani**, for his continuous motivation and support.

I am equally thankful to **Prof. B. K. Karoshi**, Principal of **VSM's Somashekhar R. Kothiwale Polytechnic, Nipani**, for his insightful guidance and encouragement, which played a pivotal role in shaping this book.

A special thanks to **Dr. Umesh Patil**, Principal of **VSM's Somashekhar R. Kothiwale Institute of Technology, Nipani**, and **Dr. Siddagouda Patil**, CEO of **Vidya Samvardhak Mandal (VSM), Nipani**, for their leadership and belief in my work. Your support has provided the foundation for this book's creation.

I am deeply grateful to **Sahakar Ratna Shri. Chandrakant Anna Kothiwale**, Chairman of **Vidya Samvardhak Mandal (VSM), Nipani**, and **Shri. R. Y. Patil**, Vice-Chairman of **Vidya Samvardhak Mandal (VSM), Nipani**, for their unwavering support and encouragement. I also wish to thank all the **Directors of Vidya Samvardhak Mandal (VSM), Nipani**, for fostering an environment conducive to academic and professional growth.

I would also like to acknowledge my PhD guides, **Dr. Mandar Sapre** and **Dr. Shahid Tamboli** from **Symbiosis University, Pune**, for their invaluable advice, mentorship, and academic insight that significantly contributed to the successful completion of this book.

Lastly, but most importantly, I am profoundly thankful to my wife, **Dhanashree**, and my parents for their endless patience, understanding, and support during this journey. To my family and friends, thank you for being my source of strength and encouragement and constantly reminding me to persevere.

This book would not have been possible without each of you. I am deeply grateful for your contributions.

With sincere appreciation,

Kailas Pathade

SYLLABUS

RESEARCH METHODOLOGY & INTELLECTUAL PROPERTY RIGHTS			
Course Code:	BRMK557	CIE Marks	50
Teaching Hours/Week (L: T:P: S)	2:2:0:0	SEE Marks	50
Total Hours of Pedagogy	25	Total Marks	100
Credits	03	Exam Hours	03

Module-1

Introduction: Meaning of Research, Objectives of Engineering Research, and Motivation in Engineering Research, Types of Engineering Research, Finding and Solving a Worthwhile Problem.

Ethics in Engineering Research, Ethics in Engineering Research Practice, Types of Research Misconduct, Ethical Issues Related to Authorship.

Module-2

Literature Review and Technical Reading, New and Existing Knowledge, Analysis and Synthesis of Prior Art Bibliographic Databases, Web of Science, Google and Google Scholar, Effective Search: The Way Forward Introduction to Technical Reading Conceptualizing Research, Critical and Creative Reading, Taking Notes While Reading, Reading Mathematics and Algorithms, Reading a Datasheet.

Attributions and Citations: Giving Credit Wherever Due, Citations: Functions and Attributes, Impact of Title and Keywords on Citations, Knowledge Flow through Citation, Citing Datasets, Styles for Citations, Acknowledgments and Attributions, What Should Be Acknowledged, Acknowledgments in, Books Dissertations, Dedication or Acknowledgments.

Module-3

Introduction to Intellectual Property: Role of IP in the Economic and Cultural Development of the Society, IP Governance, IP as a Global Indicator of Innovation, Origin of IP History of IP in India. Major Amendments in IP Laws and Acts in India.

Patents: Conditions for Obtaining a Patent Protection, To Patent or Not to Patent an Invention. Rights Associated with Patents. Enforcement of Patent Rights. Inventions Eligible for Patenting. Non-Patentable Matters. Patent Infringements. Avoid Public Disclosure of an Invention before Patenting. Process of Patenting.

Process of Patenting. Prior Art Search. Choice of Application to be Filed. Patent Application Forms. Jurisdiction of Filing Patent Application. Publication. Pre-grant Opposition. Examination. Grant of a Patent. Validity of Patent Protection. Post-grant Opposition. Commercialization of a Patent. Need for a Patent Attorney/Agent. Can a Worldwide Patent be Obtained? Do I Need First to File a Patent in India? Patent Related Forms. Fee Structure. Types of Patent Applications. Commonly Used Terms in Patenting. National Bodies Dealing with Patent Affairs. Utility Models.

Module-4

Copyrights and Related Rights: Classes of Copyrights. Criteria for Copyright. Ownership of Copyright. Copyrights of the Author. Copyright Infringements. Copyright Infringement is a Criminal Offence. Copyright Infringement is a Cognizable Offence. Fair Use Doctrine. Copyrights and Internet. Non-Copyright Work. Copyright Registration. Judicial Powers of the Registrar of Copyrights. Fee Structure. Copyright Symbol. Validity of Copyright. Copyright Profile of India. Copyright and the word 'Publish'. Transfer of Copyrights to a Publisher. Copyrights and the Word 'Adaptation'. Copyrights and the Word 'Indian Work'. Joint Authorship. Copyright

Society. Copyright Board. Copyright Enforcement Advisory Council (CEAC). International Copyright Agreements, Conventions and Treaties. Interesting Copyrights Cases.

Trademarks: Eligibility Criteria. Who Can Apply for a Trademark. Acts and Laws. Designation of Trademark Symbols. Classification of Trademarks. Registration of a Trademark is Not Compulsory. Validity of Trademark. Types of Trademark Registered in India. Trademark Registry. Process for Trademarks Registration. Prior Art Search. Famous Case Law: Coca-Cola Company vs. Bisleri International Pvt. Ltd.

Module-5

Industrial Designs: Eligibility Criteria. Acts and Laws to Govern Industrial Designs. Design Rights. Enforcement of Design Rights. Non-Protectable Industrial Designs India. Protection Term. Procedure for Registration of Industrial Designs. Prior Art Search. Application for Registration. Duration of the Registration of a Design. Importance of Design Registration. Cancellation of the Registered Design. Application Forms. Classification of Industrial Designs. Designs Registration Trend in India. International Treaties. Famous Case Law: Apple Inc. vs. Samsung Electronics Co.

Geographical Indications: Acts, Laws and Rules Pertaining to GI. Ownership of GI. Rights Granted to the Holders. Registered GI in India. Identification of Registered GI. Classes of GI. Non-Registerable GI. Protection of GI. Collective or Certification Marks. Enforcement of GI Rights. Procedure for GI Registration Documents Required for GI Registration. GI Ecosystem in India.

Case Studies on Patents. Case study of Curcuma (Turmeric) Patent, Case study of Neem Patent, Case study of Basmati patent. IP Organizations in India. Schemes and Programmes.

Assessment Details (both CIE and SEE)

The weightage of ***Continuous Internal Evaluation (CIE) is 50%*** and for ***Semester End Exam (SEE) is 50%***. The minimum passing mark for the ***CIE is 40%*** of the maximum marks ***(20 marks out of 50)***. A student shall be deemed to have satisfied the academic requirements and earned the credits allotted to each subject/ course if the student secures not less than ***35% (18 Marks out of 50)*** in the semester-end examination (SEE), and a minimum of ***40% (40 marks out of 100)*** in the sum total of the CIE (Continuous Internal Evaluation) and SEE (Semester End Examination) taken together.

Continuous Internal Evaluation:

Three Unit Tests each of 20 Marks (duration 01 hour)

1. First test at the end of 5 th week of the semester
2. Second test at the end of the 10 th week of the semester
3. Third test at the end of the 15 th week of the semester

Two assignments each of 10 Marks

4. First assignment at the end of 4 th week of the semester
5. Second assignment at the end of 9 th week of the semester
6. At the end of the 13th week of the semester Group discussion/Seminar/quiz any one of three suitably planned to attain the COs and POs for 20 Marks (duration 01 hours)

The sum of three tests, two assignments, and quiz/seminar/group discussion will be out of 100 marks and will **be scaled down to 50 marks** (to have less stressed CIE, the portion of the syllabus should not be common /repeated for any of the methods of the CIE. Each method of CIE should have a different
syllabus portion of the course).

CIE methods /question paper is designed to attain the different levels of Bloom's taxonomy as per the
Outcome defined for the course.

CONTENTS

Module 5

"If we knew what it was we were doing, it would not be called research, would it?"

: Albert Einstein

Module - 1

Chapter 1:
INTRODUCTION

INTRODUCTION

Research is the driving force behind innovation and progress in engineering, enabling the development of new technologies, existing processes, and the solution of complex problems. This chapter introduces the fundamental concepts of engineering research, beginning with its meaning and the objectives it aims to achieve, such as advancing technology and improving industry practices. It also explores the motivations that inspire engineers to pursue research, from solving pressing issues to pushing the boundaries of technological possibilities. The various types of engineering research, from fundamental to applied, are discussed to provide a clear understanding of the diverse approaches within the field. Finally, the chapter emphasizes the importance of identifying and solving worthwhile problems, ensuring that research efforts are impactful and meaningful to the engineering discipline.

1.1. MEANING OF RESEARCH

Research[1] is the systematic effort to gather, analyze, and interpret the problems confronted by humanity. Research aims to expand the understanding of a particular subject, whether in the sciences, humanities, social sciences, or other fields. Research can also be defined as ***a thinking process and scientific method of studying a problem and finding a solution.***

Research can be defined in multiple ways as follows,

- ➢ "A systematic effort to gain new knowledge."
- ➢ Research is a careful and detailed study of a specific problem, issue, or area of knowledge to discover new information or understand existing information better.
- ➢ It involves a systematic and scientific approach to investigation, where the goal is to discover something unknown or gain a deeper understanding of something known.
- ➢ Research is driven by the curiosity to explore, understand, and explain the world around us, making it a fundamental tool for acquiring knowledge and contributing to the advancement of various fields.

Perspectives on the Meaning of Research by Renowned Scientists

Different scientists have defined and interpreted the research concept in various ways, each offering unique insights based on their fields of expertise. Here are some notable perspectives:

1. **Albert Einstein:**

   Einstein viewed research as a pursuit of truth and understanding, driven by curiosity. He famously said, ***"The important thing is not to stop questioning. Curiosity has its own reason for existence."*** For Einstein,

---

[1]*Research: A detailed and careful study of something to find out more information about it.*

research was about exploring the unknown and challenging existing knowledge to uncover deeper truths about the universe.

2. **Marie Curie:**

Marie Curie, a pioneer in radioactivity research, considered research a rigorous and systematic approach to uncovering new knowledge. She emphasized perseverance in research, stating, ***"I was taught that the way of progress was neither swift nor easy."*** Her perspective highlights the importance of dedication and persistence in the research process.

3. **Isaac Newton:**

Newton, a key figure in the scientific revolution, saw research as a way to understand the natural world through observation and experimentation. He described his work as ***" If I have seen further it is by standing on the shoulders of Giants."*** indicating that research builds upon the findings of predecessors to achieve greater understanding and discovery.

4. **Richard Feynman:**

Feynman, a theoretical physicist, viewed research as an adventure into the unknown, where the goal is not just to discover facts but to understand them deeply. He said, ***"The first principle is that you must not fool yourself—and you are the easiest person to fool."*** Feynman's view underscores the importance of skepticism and critical thinking in the research process.

5. **Karl Popper:**

Popper, a philosopher of science, defined research as a process of conjecture and refutation. He believed that scientific research progresses through the formulation of hypotheses that are rigorously tested and potentially falsified. According to Popper, "***Research is not about proving theories correct but about eliminating incorrect ones.***"

6. **Stephen Hawking:**

Hawking described research as the pursuit of understanding the fundamental principles that govern the universe. He said, ***"My goal is simple. It is a complete understanding of the universe, why it is as it is, and why it exists at all."*** For Hawking, research was about seeking a comprehensive theory that explains the workings of the cosmos.

1.1.1. KEY ASPECTS OF RESEARCH:

- ➢ **Problem Identification**: Research begins with a clear problem. Understanding the problem is crucial because it helps to focus the research efforts and prevents getting lost in excessive information. The research question, which stems from the problem, defines the research project, which is an organized set of activities designed to reach conclusions and ultimately solve the problem.
- ➢ **Building Knowledge:** The purpose of research is to connect various areas of existing knowledge and to add original contributions to it. Research involves more than just gathering information; it is about generating new insights that are systematic and relevant to the current world. There must be a balance between what is achievable within the research timeline and the contribution it will make.

1.2. RESEARCH FLOW CYCLE

The fig. 1.1 is the research cycle with four key stages, showing how the process moves in a circular and iterative manner. Below is a detailed explanation of each step and how they are interconnected:

1. **Practical Problem**
    - ➢ **Definition**: The research process begins with identifying a **practical problem**. This could be an issue, gap, or challenge that exists in a specific field and needs to be solved.
    - ➢ **Importance**: Understanding the problem is crucial because it provides the foundation for the entire research process. The problem is the motivation behind the research, and everything that follows is focused on addressing or solving this problem.

2. **Research Question**
   - ➢ **Definition**: Once the practical problem is identified, the next step is to formulate a **research question**. This is a focused question that defines the scope of the research and specifies what the researcher aims to find out or solve.
   - ➢ **Connection**: The research question is **motivated** by the practical problem. It translates the problem into a manageable and researchable form.
3. **Research Project**
   - ➢ **Definition**: A **research project** is the set of activities or investigations designed to answer the research question. This includes designing experiments, collecting data, and analyzing findings.
   - ➢ **Connection**: The research project is **defined** by the research question. The methods and activities chosen are based on how the question can be answered or addressed.
4. **Result or Answer**
   - ➢ **Definition**: The research project leads to a **result or answer**. This could be a solution to the practical problem or new insights into the research question.
   - ➢ **Connection**: The result or answer from the research project **helps to solve** the practical problem identified at the start of the cycle.

Cycle Nature
   - ➢ The diagram emphasizes that research is often cyclical. Once an answer or result is achieved, it may lead to new practical problems, which in turn restart the cycle with new research questions and projects.
   - ➢ **Iterative Process**: Research is rarely a linear process. New findings often raise additional questions, requiring further exploration, thus feeding back into the research cycle.

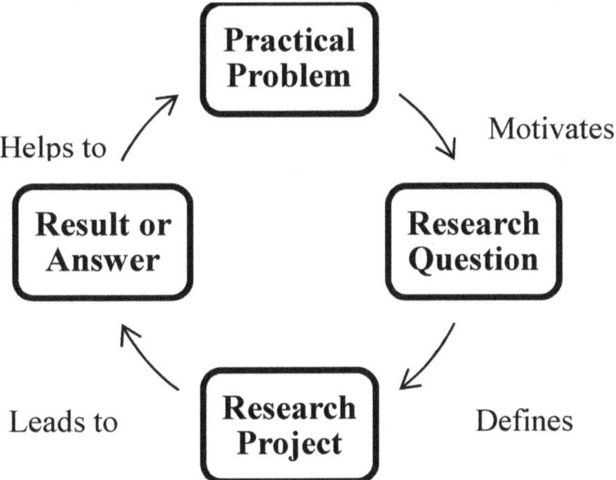

Fig. 1.1. Research Flow Cycle[1]

1.3. BASIC STEPS IN RESEARCH

The basic steps in research typically follow a systematic process to ensure that the investigation is thorough and yields reliable results. Here are the key steps as illustrated in Fig. 1.2.

1. **Problem Identification and Definition**: Clearly define the research problem. This step involves understanding the nature of the problem, its scope, and its significance. A well-defined problem is crucial for guiding the research process.
2. **Literature Review:** Before proceeding with the research, it is essential to review existing literature to understand what has already been studied and identify gaps in the current knowledge. This helps in refining the research problem and developing a theoretical framework.
3. **Formulating Research Questions or Hypotheses**: Based on the problem and the gathered information, formulate specific research questions or hypotheses. These guide the investigation and help focus on critical aspects of the problem.

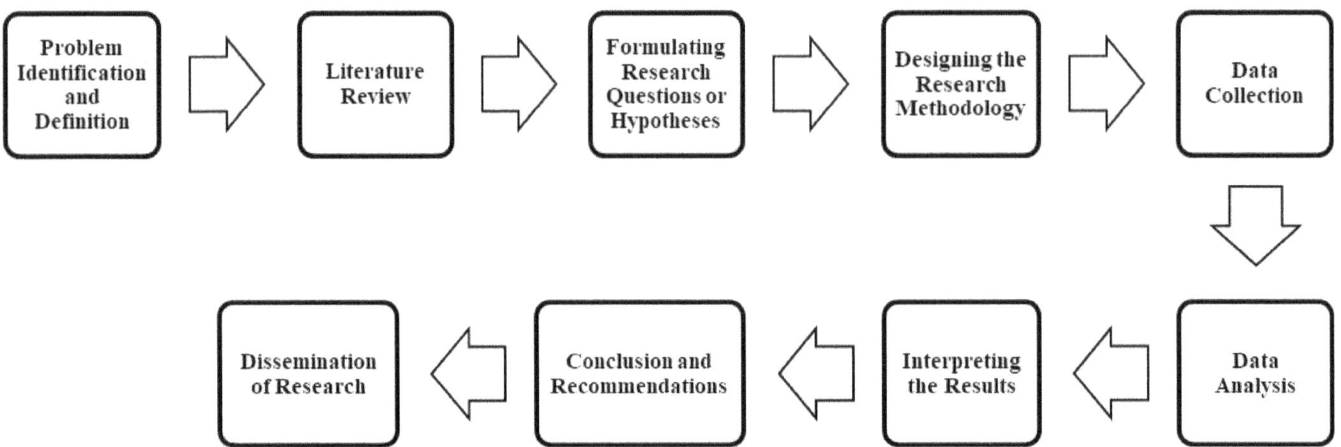

Fig. 1.2. Research Flow Cycle

4. **Designing the Research Methodology**: Develop a plan for investigating the problem. This includes selecting the research design (e.g., experimental, correlational, case study), choosing appropriate data collection methods (e.g., surveys, experiments, interviews), and determining the sampling strategy.

5. **Data Collection**: Collect data relevant to the problem using the methods identified in the research design. This data is the foundation for analyzing the problem and testing the hypotheses.

6. **Data Analysis**: Analyze the collected data to identify patterns, relationships, or trends that provide insights into the problem. Statistical analysis, thematic analysis, or other relevant methods may be used depending on the nature of the data.

7. **Interpreting the Results**: Interpret the findings from the data analysis in the context of the research problem. Determine whether the results support or refute the hypotheses and how they contribute to understanding or solving the problem.

8. **Conclusion and Recommendations**: he researcher summarizes the findings, draws conclusions, and provides recommendations for future research or practical applications.

9. **Dissemination of Research**: Finally, the research findings are shared with the academic community, industry, or public through publications, presentations, or reports, contributing to the body of knowledge.

This approach ensures a systematic and thorough investigation of the research problem, leading to well-founded solutions and contributions to the field.

1.4. AIMS OF ENGINEERING RESEARCH

Engineering research is a systematic inquiry aimed at discovering new knowledge, developing innovative technologies, and solving complex problems within the field of engineering.

1. **Discovering New Information:** Engineering research aims to discover new information or confirm existing knowledge through systematic investigation and analysis.

2. **Innovation and Development:** To develop new technologies, tools, processes, or materials that can be utilized in various engineering fields to solve real-world problems.

3. **Problem Solving:** To address specific engineering challenges by finding efficient, cost-effective, and sustainable solutions.

4. **Optimization of Processes and Systems:** To improve the efficiency, reliability, and performance of existing engineering processes, systems, and products.

5. **Technological Improvement:** To enhance existing technologies, making them more efficient, sustainable, and user-friendly.

6. **Sustainability and Environmental Impact:** To develop engineering solutions that are environmentally friendly and contribute to sustainability by reducing resource consumption and minimizing waste.

1.5. OBJECTIVES OF ENGINEERING RESEARCH

The objectives of engineering research can be broadly categorized into several key areas, each contributing to the overall progress and innovation in engineering disciplines. Understanding these objectives is crucial for researchers as they guide the direction and purpose of their investigations.

1. **Advancement of Knowledge:** One of the primary objectives of engineering research is the advancement of knowledge within the field. This involves exploring new concepts, theories, and methodologies that push the boundaries of what is currently known.

2. **Solving Specific Problems:** The primary objective is to find solutions to specific engineering problems, which involves identifying the research problem and formulating hypotheses to test potential solutions.

3. **Enhancing Reliability and Validity:** Research strives to enhance the reliability and validity of findings by maintaining objectivity and using scientific methods to ensure that results are accurate and reproducible.

4. **Developing Theories and Models:** Another key objective is to develop new theories and models to explain engineering phenomena and predict outcomes under various conditions.

5. **Optimizing Designs and Processes:** Engineering research often focuses on optimizing designs and processes to improve efficiency, reduce costs, and enhance performance. This includes using techniques like finite element analysis and topology optimization.

6. **Improving Material Quality:** Research aims to improve the quality of materials used in engineering applications, which can lead to better performance and durability of engineering products.

7. **Ensuring Safety and Compliance:** Ensuring that engineering solutions are safe and comply with regulatory standards is critical. This involves rigorous testing and validation of designs and processes.

8. **Innovation and Development of New Technologies:** Engineering research seeks to advance technological innovation by exploring new technologies and methodologies that can lead to developments.

9. **Facilitating Practical Applications:** Engineering research aims to facilitate the practical application of findings, ensuring that theoretical discoveries can be translated into real-world solutions that address current engineering challenges.

10. **Contribution to Societal Needs:** Engineering research also aims to contribute to societal needs by addressing issues that have a direct impact on the public. This includes research in areas such as renewable energy, healthcare technology, and sustainable development. Example: Development of photovoltaic cells have been driven by the need to find sustainable energy solutions to combat climate change.

11. **Educational Development and Knowledge Dissemination:** Research in engineering also plays a crucial role in education, both in terms of advancing the curriculum and training the next generation of engineers. The research contributes to textbooks and academic papers that are used in engineering education.

12. **Economic Growth and Industrial Competitiveness**: Engineering research contributes to economic growth by fostering industrial innovation and competitiveness. Research-driven advancements in technology and processes can lead to the creation of new industries, enhancement of existing ones, and improvement of national and global economic performance.

13. **Sustainability and Environmental Protection:** With increasing global awareness of environmental issues, engineering research is increasingly focused on sustainability and environmental protection. This objective involves developing technologies and processes that minimize environmental impact, reduce waste, and promote the efficient use of resources.

1.6. MOTIVATION IN ENGINEERING RESEARCH

1. **Intrinsic Motivation:** Intrinsic motivation refers to the internal drive that compels individuals to engage in research out of curiosity, passion, or the desire for personal fulfillment. In engineering research, intrinsic motivation often stems from a deep interest in a particular problem or the satisfaction derived from solving complex challenges. Researchers who are intrinsically motivated are more likely to pursue innovative approaches, persist through setbacks, and contribute original ideas to the field.

2. **Extrinsic Motivation:** Extrinsic motivation, on the other hand, involves external incentives that encourage individuals to engage in research. These incentives can include financial rewards, recognition, career advancement, and the potential for patents or commercial success. In engineering research, extrinsic motivation often plays a significant role, particularly in applied research where the outcomes can lead to marketable products or solutions.

3. **Challenge of Solving Unsolved Problems:** The desire to face and overcome the challenge of solving unsolved problems is a significant motivator. Researchers are often intrigued by practical issues and are motivated to find effective solutions.

4. **Service to Society:** Engineering researchers are motivated by the desire to contribute to society. Their work often aims to address societal needs and improve the quality of life through technological advancements.

5. **Respect and Recognition:** The pursuit of respectability and recognition within the scientific community and society at large is another motivating factor. Achieving breakthroughs and contributing valuable knowledge can earn researchers significant respect.

6. **Curiosity and Desire for New Knowledge:** Curiosity about new things and the desire to understand causal relationships drive many researchers. This curiosity leads to the exploration of new ideas and the development of innovative solutions.

7. **Personal and Professional Goals:** Engineering researchers are often motivated by a combination of personal and professional goals. Personal goals might include the desire for intellectual growth, personal satisfaction, or the pursuit of a lifelong passion. Professional goals could involve achieving tenure, advancing in one's career, or contributing to the scientific community. For many professionals, research is a source of livelihood and a means of professional growth. It provides opportunities for career advancement and personal development through continuous learning and discovery.

8. **Government and Employment Directives:** External factors such as government directives and employment conditions can also motivate research. These factors may compel researchers to focus on specific areas of interest or address particular problems.

9. **Impact on Technological Innovation:** The potential to drive technological innovation and make significant contributions to the field of engineering is a powerful motivator. Researchers are inspired by the possibility of creating new technologies that can transform industries and society.

10. **Building Knowledge Reservoirs:** The need to build up an infrastructure for creating new knowledge and developing a knowledge reservoir is a crucial motivator. This knowledge can be applied for socio-economic and cultural development, providing material well-being for societies.

11. **Impact on Society and the Environment:** Many engineers are motivated by the potential impact of their research on society and the environment. Engineering research often addresses pressing global challenges, such as climate change, resource scarcity, healthcare, and infrastructure development. The opportunity to contribute to solutions that improve quality of life, promote sustainability, or enhance public safety can be a powerful motivator.

12. **Curiosity and Intellectual Rigor:** Researchers are often part of a community characterized by curiosity, cooperation, and intellectual rigor. The collaborative environment and the pursuit of fundamental questions about nature and technology drive their motivation.

1.7. TYPES OF ENGINEERING RESEARCH

Engineering research can be broadly categorized into several types, each with its own methodologies, objectives, and outcomes. Following are the different types of research.

i. Fundamental (Pure or Basic) Research
ii. Applied Research
iii. Exploratory or Formulative Research
iv. Descriptive Research

v.   Diagnostic Study
vi.   Evaluation Studies
vii.   Action Research
viii.   Experimental Research
ix.   Analytical study or statistical Method
x.   Historical Research
xi.   Surveys
xii.   Case Study

i.   Fundamental (Pure or Basic) Research

Fundamental Research, also known as Pure Research or Basic Research, is a type of research that is conducted to increase our understanding of fundamental principles and phenomena. It is driven by curiosity and a desire to expand knowledge for its own sake, without necessarily aiming for immediate practical applications.

Fundamental Research is theoretical and exploratory, focusing on the discovery and explanation of basic scientific principles and theories. It seeks to answer questions about how and why things happen, often laying the groundwork for further applied research.

Aim: The primary aim of Fundamental Research is to expand our understanding of the underlying principles that govern the natural world, society, or any field of study. It seeks to contribute to the general body of knowledge and may lead to the development of new theories or frameworks.

Focus: Fundamental Research focuses on exploring basic concepts and theories that can help explain phenomena. It is often conducted without any immediate concern for practical outcomes, but the knowledge gained can eventually lead to significant practical applications in the future.

Examples: Social Sciences: Exploring the origins of human behavior, social structures, or cultural norms to build theories that explain societal dynamics.

ii.   Applied Research

Applied Research is a type of research conducted to solve specific, practical problems or address real-world challenges. It involves the application of existing knowledge and theories to develop new products, processes, or technologies that can directly benefit society or industry.

Applied Research is goal-oriented and focuses on finding solutions that have immediate practical applications. Unlike Pure Research, which seeks to expand knowledge without concern for its practical utility, Applied Research is motivated by the desire to address specific issues and produce tangible outcomes.

Aim: The primary aim of Applied Research is to apply existing knowledge to create new technologies, improve existing products, or solve pressing problems in various fields such as healthcare, engineering, education, and business. It often bridges the gap between theoretical knowledge and practical implementation.

Focus: Applied Research focuses on real-world problems and challenges. Researchers engaged in Applied Research typically work on projects with clearly defined objectives, such as improving healthcare patient outcomes, enhancing manufacturing processes' efficiency, or developing new educational tools to improve learning outcomes.

Examples: Development of a New Drug: Researchers working to develop a new medication for treating a specific disease are engaged in Applied Research. They apply existing knowledge of biology, chemistry, and pharmacology to create a drug that can be tested for safety and efficacy in clinical trials.

iii. Exploratory or Formulative Research

Exploratory or Formulative Research is conducted to explore a problem or issue when it is not well understood or clearly defined. It is the initial step in the research process and is often used to gain insights, identify patterns, and formulate hypotheses that can be tested in subsequent studies.

This type of research is flexible and open-ended, allowing researchers to explore a wide range of possibilities without the constraints of predefined hypotheses. It is typically qualitative in nature and may involve interviews, focus groups, or literature reviews.

Aim: The primary objective of Exploratory Research is to gain a deeper understanding of a problem, identify variables that may be relevant, and develop a theoretical framework or hypothesis that can guide further research.

Focus: Exploratory Research focuses on discovery and hypothesis generation. It is particularly useful when little is known about the problem or when researchers are venturing into new areas of study.

Examples: Exploring Consumer Behavior: A company may conduct exploratory research to understand why customers are not purchasing a new product, leading to insights that can inform marketing strategies.

iv.   **Descriptive Research**

Descriptive Research is a type of research that aims to describe the characteristics, behaviors, or phenomena under study. It accurately represents the subject matter, often through data collection and analysis.

This type of research is concerned with "what is" rather than "why." It describes the current state of affairs and is often used to provide a snapshot of a particular phenomenon or population.

Aim: The primary aim of Descriptive Research is to provide a detailed, factual account of a situation, event, or group. It helps in understanding the "who," "what," "where," "when," and "how" of a subject.

Focus: Descriptive Research focuses on providing a comprehensive and accurate portrayal of a particular phenomenon. It does not attempt to explain causality but rather to describe the characteristics or behaviors observed.

Examples: Market Research: A company may conduct descriptive research to understand the demographics and purchasing behavior of its customers.

v.   **Diagnostic Study**

A diagnostic study is research that identifies the causes or factors contributing to a particular problem or condition. It seeks to diagnose the underlying issues that need to be addressed.

Nature of Diagnostic Study: This type of research is problem-focused and aims to uncover the root causes of a specific issue. It is often used in medical, psychological, and organizational contexts.

Aim: The primary objective of a Diagnostic Study is to identify the underlying causes of a problem, enabling researchers or practitioners to develop targeted interventions or solutions.

Focus: Diagnostic Studies focus on understanding the "why" behind a problem. They seek to identify the factors or conditions contributing to the issue and provide insights into how it can be resolved.

Examples: Medical Diagnosis: A study aimed at identifying the causes of a specific health condition, such as heart disease, by analyzing patient data and risk factors.

vi.   **Evaluation Studies**

Evaluation Studies are research conducted to assess the effectiveness, efficiency, and impact of a program, policy, or intervention. They provide feedback that can be used to improve the program or inform decision-making.

Evaluation Studies are practical and outcome-oriented. They focus on determining whether a program or intervention has achieved its intended goals and what factors have influenced its success or failure.

Aim: The primary objective of Evaluation Studies is to objectively assess a program's performance, identifying areas of success and opportunities for improvement.

Focus: Evaluation Studies focus on measuring outcomes, assessing the processes involved, and determining the impact of a program or intervention. They are often used to inform policy decisions or improve program implementation.

Examples: Educational Program Evaluation: An evaluation study might be conducted to assess the effectiveness of a new teaching method in improving student performance.

vii. **Action Research**

Action Research is a participatory research approach involving researchers and participants collaborating to solve a problem or improve a situation. It is iterative, with planning, action, observation, and reflection cycles.

Action Research is practical and focused on bringing about change. It is conducted in real-world settings and involves active participation from those affected by the problem being studied.

Aim: The primary aim of Action Research is to generate knowledge while simultaneously solving a problem or improving a situation. It emphasizes collaboration and empowerment of participants.

Focus: Action Research focuses on the process of change and improvement. It is typically used in educational, organizational, and community settings where participants are directly involved in the research process.

Examples: Educational Improvement: Teachers may engage in action research to improve classroom practices by implementing new teaching strategies and observing their effects on student learning.

viii. **Experimental Research**

Experimental research involves the manipulation of one or more independent variables to observe their effect on one or more dependent variables. Controlled conditions and random assignment of participants characterize it.

This type of research is quantitative and aims to establish cause-and-effect relationships. It is often conducted in laboratory settings where variables can be tightly controlled.

Aim: The primary aim of Experimental Research is to determine whether a cause-and-effect relationship exists between variables by controlling for extraneous factors and isolating the variables of interest.

Focus: Experimental Research tests hypotheses by manipulating variables and observing the outcomes. It is beneficial in the natural sciences, psychology, and medicine.

Examples: Drug Testing: Researchers may conduct an experiment to test the efficacy of a new drug by randomly assigning participants to either the treatment group or a placebo group and comparing the outcomes.

ix. **Analytical Study or Statistical Method**

An Analytical Study or Statistical Method involves using mathematical and statistical techniques to analyze data and test hypotheses. It is focused on identifying patterns, relationships, and trends within data sets.

Analytical Studies are quantitative and involve rigorous data analysis. They are often used to make inferences, predict outcomes, and validate theories.

Aim: The primary objective of an Analytical Study is to understand the relationships between variables and make predictions based on statistical analysis. It is used to test hypotheses and validate theories with empirical data.

Focus: Analytical Studies focus on the analysis of data to uncover patterns, trends, and relationships. They are commonly used in fields such as economics and social sciences.

Examples: Economic Forecasting: Economists may use statistical methods to analyze historical data and forecast future economic trends, such as inflation rates or GDP growth.

x. **Historical Research**

Historical Research involves the study of past events, individuals, or periods to understand their significance, causes, and consequences. It relies on the analysis of historical records, documents, and artifacts.

This type of research is qualitative and interpretative, focusing on understanding the context and meaning of historical events. It often involves the reconstruction of past events based on available evidence.

Aim: The primary aim of Historical Research is to gain a deeper understanding of the past, to explain the causes and effects of historical events, and to provide insights that can inform current and future decisions.

Focus: Historical Research focuses on the analysis and interpretation of historical data. It seeks to understand the context in which events occurred and explain why things happened the way they did.

Examples: History of a Social Movement: Researchers may study the civil rights movement by analyzing historical documents, speeches, and photographs to understand its impact on society.

xi. **Surveys**

Surveys are a research method that collects data from a sample of individuals through questionnaires, interviews, or observations. They are used to gather information about a population's attitudes, opinions, behaviors, or characteristics.

Surveys are quantitative and are designed to collect data that can be analyzed statistically. They are often used to generalize about a population based on the responses of a sample.

Aim: The primary objective of a Survey is to collect data that can be used to describe characteristics or behaviors of a population, test hypotheses, or inform decision-making.

Focus: Surveys focus on gathering data from a large number of respondents. They are often used in market research, public opinion polling, and social science research.

Examples: Customer Satisfaction Surveys: Companies may conduct surveys to assess customer satisfaction with their products or services, gathering data that can be used to improve customer experience.

xii. **Case Study**

A Case Study is an in-depth investigation of a single individual, group, event, or situation. It is a qualitative research method that provides a detailed and comprehensive understanding of the subject under study.

Case Studies are qualitative and exploratory, focusing on the detailed examination of a specific case within its real-life context. They are often used in social sciences, education, and business research.

Aim: The primary aim of a Case Study is to gain a deep understanding of the subject under study, to explore the complexities and nuances of the case, and to generate insights that can inform theory and practice.

Focus: Case Studies provide a holistic view of the subject, considering various factors and their interactions. They are particularly useful for exploring new or complex issues in depth.

Examples: Business Case Studies: A company might conduct a case study to analyze a successful marketing campaign, examining the strategies and outcomes.

1.8. THREE BROAD CATEGORIES OF DEVELOPING AND ACCESSING KNOWLEDGE IN RESEARCH

Developing and accessing knowledge through research is broadly categorized into three overlapping categories:

1. **Observation:** Observation is a fundamental way of gathering information from a source. This could involve direct observation in a laboratory, measurements, or even surveys. In engineering research, observation often includes data collection, such as measuring the time it takes for a firmware routine to run. Processing observational data is essential for understanding phenomena. **Examples**: Measuring things in a laboratory, conducting surveys among groups of people, Tracking the time, it takes for software or firmware to run.

   Processing: The observational data may require further processing, leading us to the second category: **models**.

2. **Models:** Models provide simplified descriptions of complex systems, often through mathematical equations or statistical relationships. These models help explain the interactions between variables or phenomena and serve as an abstract way to understand the observed data.

   Types: Statistical relationships, Figures and diagrams, Mathematical equations.

   Purpose: Models help us understand observed phenomena by abstracting them into simplified forms.

Example: An equation that describes the relationship between attributes or the behavior of a system or device.

3. **Processes, Algorithms, and Procedures:** This category involves structured methods of doing things to achieve a desired outcome. These include algorithms, procedures, or reference designs that guide researchers in achieving specific goals.

   Examples: Algorithms that perform tasks, Procedures followed to reach a result, Reference designs that guide how things are arranged or done.

These three categories are interconnected, and each helps build knowledge systematically. The Fig. 1.3. illustrating the interrelation between three key components: Model, Observation, and Process. Each circle represents a different aspect of a research framework or methodology.

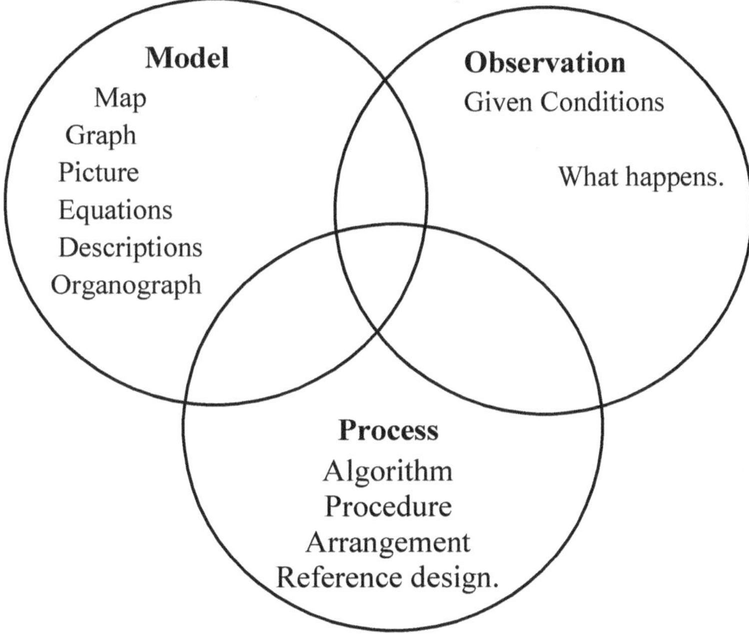

Fig. 1.3. Research Flow Cycle

Components of the Image:
- The circle labeled "Model" includes elements like Map, Graph, Picture, Equations, Descriptions, and Organograph.
- The circle labeled "Observation" focuses on "Given Conditions" and "What happens."
- The circle labeled "Process" contains terms such as Algorithm, Procedure, Arrangement, and Reference design.

Important Results and Conclusions:
- The intersection between Model and Observation suggests that theoretical frameworks (models) are tested against empirical data (observations) to validate hypotheses.
- The overlap between Model and Process indicates that theoretical models inform the design of processes, algorithms, and procedures.
- The intersection of Observation and Process highlights how observations influence and refine processes and algorithms in practice.
- The central area where all three circles overlap represents a comprehensive approach where models are designed and refined based on both observations and procedural implementations, leading to robust and effective solutions.

This diagram effectively encapsulates the dynamic interplay between theory, observation, and practical application in research, emphasizing the importance of integrating these components for successful outcomes.

1.9. FINDING AND SOLVING A WORTHWHILE PROBLEM

1. **Starting with a Research Problem**
   - A researcher may start with problems given by a **supervisor** or ones suggested by others.
   - Research might also involve **rethinking a theory** or gathering ideas from a group of papers recommended by the supervisor.
   - The challenge for research scholars lies in **finding a suitable problem** to start their research.
   - Developing skills for identifying problems is essential but often **not formally taught**.

2. **Initial Identification of the Research Problem:**
   - Once a **vague idea**[2] of the problem is identified, the next step is to conduct a **literature survey and technical reading** to confirm its worth.
   - However, before the survey begins, an **initial spark** is needed. This spark could come from:
     - ❖ An oral presentation followed by **questions or self-reflection**.
     - ❖ Developments in other fields that might provide a **tool or method** that has implications for the researcher's subject.

3. **Attributes of a Worthwhile Research Problem:**

   A valuable research problem often has one or more of the following characteristics:
   - i. **Non-intuitive[3] or counter-intuitive[4]**: Even experts in the field might find the problem unexpected.
   - ii. **Anticipated by the research community**: A problem that researchers have been expecting or waiting to be solved.
   - iii. **Simplification of a central theory**: Simplifying complex aspects of the existing theory.
   - iv. **New result**: Discovering something that could start a **new subject** or field.
   - v. **New or improved method**: Creating a **better method** for something with practical applications.
   - vi. **Stopping further work**: Solving a problem so well that it **closes an area** of research.

4. **Conviction in the Worthiness of the Problem:**
   - The researcher must be convinced that the problem is **worth solving**. This conviction drives **best efforts**.
   - Not all problems need to be major; even **small problems** can contribute to **significant advancements** when solved effectively.

5. **Tackling Hard Problems:**
   - Some problems are **universally hard** and open, with **deep connections** to other concepts.
     - ❖ Most researchers may not work on such problems in their lifetime.
     - ❖ The decision to tackle a **hard problem** involves weighing the **time investment** against the likelihood of success, which is often low.
     - ❖ Even if the problem isn't solved, there may be **partial results** that contribute to the dissertation.

6. **Pólya's Four-Step Procedure for Problem Solving:**

   George Pólya (1887–1985) proposed a systematic procedure for solving problems, which is useful for engineering researchers[2]:
   - i. **Understand the Problem:**
     - Restate the problem in your own words.
     - **Visualize** the problem by drawing figures or diagrams.
     - Check if additional information is needed.
   - ii. **Formulate a Strategy:**
     - Begin by exploring different approaches to solve the problem or a simpler version of it.

---

[2] *Vague idea: An idea that is not clear or distinct*
[3] *Non-intuitive: Something is not easy to learn or understand, or not based on intuition*
[4] *Counter-intuitive: Does not happen in the way you would expect it to*

    ➤ Look for **patterns** or insights that might lead to the solution.

iii. **Execute the Plan:**
   - Implement the solution strategy. If it fails, start over with a new approach.
   - Repeated attempts can lead to a **flash of insight** or a new idea.

iv. **Reflect on the Solution:**
   - Reflect on what worked and what didn't.
   - This reflection is an **investment** for solving future problems.

7. **Importance of Problem-Solving in Engineering Research:**
   - Problem-solving is central to **engineering research**.
   - It requires a combination of understanding, strategy, execution, and reflection.
   - Researchers need to continually refine their approach as they progress through their careers.

1.10. COMPARISON OF RESEARCH TYPES

1. Table 1.1. Descriptive Research Vs Analytical Research

Feature	Descriptive Research	Analytical Research
Objective	To describe and document phenomena	To analyze, interpret, and explain phenomena
Purpose	Provides a detailed account of the characteristics of a population, event, or situation	Seeks to uncover and understand the underlying reasons, causes, and effects
Approach	Observation, surveys, case studies, documenting current status	Critical analysis, hypothesis testing, statistical methods
Outcome	Provides detailed descriptions of the subject	Provides insights, explanations, interpretations, and predictions
Focus	What, where, and how something happens	Why and how something happens, often involving in-depth exploration
Examples	Population census, case studies, market research	Crime rate analysis, economic impact studies, cause-effect relationships
Data	Can be both qualitative and quantitative	Often quantitative, but can include qualitative data for deeper analysis
Time Frame	Often shorter-term, focused on current or recent situations	Can be long-term, involving complex data analysis and interpretation
Methodology	Collects data without changing the environment or variables	Analyzes data to test hypotheses or explain relationships

2. Table 1.2. Applied Research Vs Fundamental (Basic) Research

Feature	Applied Research	Analytical Research
Objective	To solve practical, real-world problems	To expand knowledge without immediate practical application
Purpose	Focuses on practical application and improving processes or solving specific issues	Aims to understand fundamental principles and theories
Approach	Problem-solving, intervention-based, often uses empirical methods	Exploration, theoretical, hypothesis-driven
Outcome	Provides direct solutions that can be implemented	Expands understanding of concepts and theories
Focus	Specific, real-world problems and applications	General, broad areas of inquiry and knowledge expansion

Examples	Developing a new medical treatment, improving manufacturing processes	Exploring the behavior of particles in quantum mechanics, studying the origin of the universe
Time Frame	Short to medium term, focused on immediate application	Long term, may not have immediate or practical use
Data	Often empirical, can be qualitative or quantitative	Mostly theoretical or experimental, may involve quantitative data
Benefits	Provides immediate, practical benefits to society or industry	Contributes to a deeper understanding of fundamental phenomena

3. **Table 1.3. Quantitative Research Vs Qualitative Research**

Feature	Quantitative Research	Qualitative Research
Objective	To quantify data and generalize results from a sample to a population	To understand experiences, opinions, and motivations in depth
Purpose	Focuses on numerical data to establish patterns, relationships, or trends	Focuses on exploring meanings, insights, and understanding behaviors
Approach	Structured, using instruments like surveys, experiments, or statistical tools	Unstructured or semi-structured, using interviews, observations, or content analysis
Outcome	Provides statistical analysis, patterns, and generalizable conclusions	Provides detailed, narrative insights and in-depth understanding
Data	Numerical data (e.g., percentages, averages, frequencies)	Non-numerical data (e.g., words, images, interviews, observations)
Analysis	Uses statistical methods like correlation, regression, or hypothesis testing	Uses thematic analysis, narrative analysis, or content analysis
Examples	Surveys with closed-ended questions, controlled experiments, market statistics	Case studies, in-depth interviews, focus groups, ethnographies
Sample Size	Typically larger to allow for statistical generalization	Typically smaller, focused on deep exploration of specific cases
Time Frame	Often shorter, depends on data collection and statistical analysis	Often longer, as it involves more detailed, in-depth study
Flexibility	More rigid and structured, follows a fixed process	More flexible and open-ended, can evolve during the research process

Questions

1. Define the term research and explain the research flow cycle with a Relevant diagram.
2. Define engineering research and list its aims and objectives.
3. What are the factors that motivate you to do engineering research? Briefly explain
4. What are the three broad categories of developing and accessing knowledge in research? Explain with a diagram.
5. Discuss the different types of engineering research. Clearly point out the differences between all of them with examples.
6. Compare descriptive research versus analytical research with examples.

"Ethics is knowing the difference between what you have a right to do and what is right to do."

: Potter Stewart

Module - 1

Chapter 2:
ETHICS IN ENGINEERING RESEARCH

INTRODUCTION

In the field of engineering research, ethical considerations hold a significant position in steering researchers towards practices that are both responsible and open. This chapter explores the vital role of ethics in engineering research, highlighting the importance of maintaining integrity throughout the research process. It analyzes the ethical principles that govern practices within engineering research, ensuring that researchers conform to standards that cultivate trust and credibility in their scholarly endeavors. In addition, the chapter evaluates different types of research misconduct, including fabrication, falsification, and plagiarism, which critically jeopardize the validity and reliability of research results. Moreover, it considers ethical issues related to authorship, highlighting the essential need for clarity and justice in attributing contributions to research publications. Through this discussion, students will gain a comprehensive understanding of the ethical considerations essential to conducting and publishing engineering research responsibly.

2.1. ETHICS IN ENGINEERING RESEARCH

Ethics[5] in engineering research refers to the moral principles and professional standards that guide engineers in conducting research and applying their findings. Ethical considerations are crucial to ensure that the research process and outcomes are beneficial to society, respectful of individuals' rights, and conducted with integrity. As engineering projects often have significant implications for public safety, environmental sustainability, and societal well-being, the ethical dimension of engineering research cannot be overstated.

2.1.1. IMPORTANCE OF ETHICS IN ENGINEERING RESEARCH

1. **Public Safety and Welfare**: Engineering research often leads to developing new technologies, infrastructures, and systems that directly impact public safety. Unethical practices, such as data manipulation or cutting corners in research, can lead to catastrophic failures, resulting in loss of life, environmental damage, and financial loss. For example, the unethical practices in the construction of the Hyatt Regency walkway in Kansas City led to its collapse in 1981, resulting in 114 deaths.

2. **Environmental Impact:** Engineers are responsible for considering the environmental implications of their research. Ethical research should prioritize sustainability and minimize harm to the environment. The Bhopal gas tragedy in 1984 is a stark reminder of the consequences of neglecting environmental ethics, where the release of toxic gas from a pesticide plant caused thousands of deaths and long-term environmental damage.

---

[5] *Ethics: The study of what is morally right and wrong in human behaviour*

3. **Integrity and Accountability:** Ethical research requires honesty and transparency in data collection, analysis, and reporting. Fabrication, falsification, and plagiarism are severe ethical breaches that undermine the credibility of engineering research. The Volkswagen emissions scandal, where the company manipulated emissions data, illustrates the importance of maintaining integrity in research and development processes.

4. **Social Responsibility:** Engineering research should aim to address societal challenges and contribute to the betterment of humanity. Ethical considerations include ensuring that research benefits are distributed equitably and that vulnerable populations are not exploited. For instance, developing accessible technologies for persons with disabilities is an ethical imperative that aligns with social responsibility.

5. **Legal and Professional Obligations**: Engineers are bound by legal and professional codes of conduct, such as the ASME (American Society of Mechanical Engineers) Code of Ethics and the IEEE (Institute of Electrical and Electronics Engineers) Code of Ethics. These codes provide guidelines for ethical behavior, including responsibilities to the public, employers, clients, and the profession.

2.1.2. ETHICAL CHALLENGES IN ENGINEERING RESEARCH

1. **Conflicts of Interest**: Researchers may face situations where personal, financial, or professional interests conflict with their duty to conduct unbiased research. Managing conflicts of interest is critical to maintaining the trustworthiness of the research process.

2. **Intellectual Property and Plagiarism**: Protecting intellectual property rights and ensuring proper attribution of ideas and findings are essential ethical practices. Plagiarism, whether intentional or unintentional, is a serious violation of academic integrity.

3. **Human and Animal Rights**: Research involving human subjects or animals must adhere to strict ethical standards to protect their rights and well-being. Informed consent, confidentiality, and humane treatment are fundamental principles in such research.

4. **Data Privacy and Security**: With the increasing reliance on digital technologies in engineering research, ensuring data privacy and security has become a significant ethical concern. Researchers must take measures to protect sensitive data from unauthorized access or breaches.

5. **Bias and Discrimination**: Ethical research practices demand avoiding bias and discrimination in all aspects of the research process. This includes ensuring diversity in research teams, avoiding biases in data interpretation, and addressing any potential discriminatory outcomes of the research.

2.1.3. ETHICAL GUIDELINES AND FRAMEWORKS

1. **ASME Code of Ethics**: The ASME Code of Ethics provides engineers with a framework for ethical decision-making, emphasizing responsibilities to the public, the profession, and clients. It encourages engineers to act with integrity, uphold professional standards, and consider the broader societal impacts of their work.

2. **IEEE Code of Ethics**: The IEEE Code of Ethics highlights the importance of honesty, fairness, and respect for others in engineering practice. It also emphasizes the need to avoid conflicts of interest and prioritize the public's safety, health, and welfare.

3. **Belmont Report (1979)**: Primarily focused on biomedical research, the Belmont Report also provides ethical principles that apply to engineering research. It outlines three core principles: respect for persons, beneficence, and justice, which can guide ethical decision-making in research involving human subjects.

2.2. ETHICS IN ENGINEERING RESEARCH PRACTICE

Ethics in engineering research practice is a critical component of the engineering profession, ensuring that research activities are conducted responsibly, transparently, and with a commitment to the welfare of society. Ethical research practices protect public safety and the environment and uphold the integrity of the engineering profession. Understanding the ethical dimensions of engineering research is essential as researchers prepare to contribute to developing technologies and systems that will shape the future.

2.2.1. CORE PRINCIPLES OF ETHICAL RESEARCH PRACTICE

1. **Integrity[6] and Honesty**: Integrity in research practice involves the commitment to truth and transparency in all aspects of research. This includes accurately reporting data, acknowledging limitations, and giving proper credit to the work of others. Honesty in research also means avoiding *fabrication, falsification, and plagiarism (FFP)* practices that can severely undermine the credibility of research findings.
   Example: The Sokal Affair (1996) is a notable example of a physicist deliberately submitting a nonsensical article to a cultural studies journal, exposing the dangers of intellectual dishonesty in research.

2. **Respect for Intellectual Property[7]**: Engineering research often builds on the ideas and findings of others. Respecting intellectual property means properly citing sources, acknowledging contributions, and avoiding the unauthorized use of others work. This principle is vital in fostering innovation and collaboration in the engineering community.
   Example: The legal disputes between Apple and Samsung over smartphone design patents highlight the importance of respecting intellectual property in engineering research and development.

3. **Confidentiality and Data Protection**: Researchers often handle sensitive information, whether it involves proprietary technology, personal data, or corporate secrets. Ethical research practice requires that this information be protected against unauthorized access or disclosure.
   Example: The Cambridge Analytica scandal (2018) demonstrated the ethical implications of mishandling personal data, leading to significant breaches of privacy and trust.

4. **Responsible Publication and Peer Review**: Ethical research practice includes the responsible publication of research findings. This involves choosing appropriate venues for publication, avoiding duplicate submissions, and participating in the peer review process. Peer review is a critical component of research ethics, ensuring that research is rigorously evaluated before it is shared with the broader community.
   Example: The retraction of numerous papers from prominent journals due to unethical research practices, such as data manipulation or ghostwriting, illustrates the importance ethics in research publication.

5. **Social Responsibility and Impact**: Engineering research should aim to address societal needs and contribute positively to the community. Ethical researchers consider the broader implications of their work, including potential social, environmental, and economic impacts. This principle encourages engineers to develop solutions that are sustainable, equitable, and beneficial to all stakeholders.
   Example: The development of renewable energy technologies, such as solar panels and wind turbines, reflects the ethical commitment to addressing climate change and reducing reliance on fossil fuels.

6. **Human and Animal Welfare**: When engineering research involves human subjects or animals, it is essential to prioritize their welfare. This includes obtaining informed consent from human participants, ensuring the humane treatment of animals, and adhering to ethical guidelines established by relevant authorities.
   Example: The ethical controversy surrounding animal testing in engineering and biomedical research underscores the need for careful consideration of alternatives and adherence to ethical standards.

2.2.2. ETHICAL DECISION-MAKING IN ENGINEERING RESEARCH

1. **Identifying Ethical Issues**: The first step in ethical decision-making is to identify potential ethical issues that may arise during the research process. This could involve conflicts of interest, possible harm to the public or environment, or issues related to intellectual property.

---

[6]*Integrity: The quality of being honest and having strong moral principles*
[7]*Intellectual property (IP) is a category of property that includes intangible creations of the human intellect.*

2. **Evaluating Options**: Once an ethical issue is identified, researchers must consider their options, considering the potential consequences of each course of action. This involves weighing the benefits and risks to various stakeholders, including the public, the environment, and the research community.
3. **Seeking Guidance**: Researchers should seek guidance from ethical frameworks, professional codes of conduct, and, when necessary, institutional review boards (IRBs) or ethics committees. These resources provide valuable insights into how to navigate complex ethical dilemmas.
4. **Making Informed Decisions**: After evaluating options and seeking guidance, researchers must make informed decisions that align with ethical principles. This may involve taking actions that prioritize public safety, protect intellectual property, or ensure the integrity of the research process.
5. **Reflecting on Outcomes**: Ethical decision-making is an ongoing process that requires researchers to reflect on the outcomes of their decisions. This reflection helps researchers learn from their experiences and apply ethical principles more effectively in future research.

2.3. TYPES OF RESEARCH MISCONDUCT

Research misconduct refers to unethical practices that violate the standards of scientific integrity and honesty in the research process. Such misconduct can undermine the credibility of research findings, damage the reputation of individuals and institutions, and ultimately harm society. Understanding the types of research misconduct is essential. This section explores the various forms of research misconduct, providing examples and highlighting the importance of ethical research practices.

1. **Fabrication**

   Definition: *Fabrication involves making up data or results and recording or reporting them as if they were real.* This type of misconduct is one of the most severe, as it introduces completely false information into the scientific record, potentially leading to incorrect conclusions and decisions.

   Example: A famous case of fabrication occurred in the field of physics when Jan Hendrik Schön, a researcher at Bell Labs, was found to have fabricated data in numerous published papers. His fraudulent work initially gained significant attention for its groundbreaking claims in nanotechnology, but it was later retracted when the misconduct was discovered.

   Impact: Fabrication can lead to wasted resources, as other researchers may base their work on false data. It also damages the scientific community's credibility and can have broader societal implications if the fabricated research influences public policy or technological development.

2. **Falsification**

   Definition: *Falsification involves manipulating research materials, equipment, processes, or data to produce a desired outcome.* Unlike fabrication, which involves creating data, falsification involves altering or misrepresenting actual data to fit a preconceived hypothesis or to make the results appear more favorable.

   Example: In 2015, the case of Dong-Pyou Han, a former biomedical researcher, highlighted the issue of falsification. Han added human antibodies to rabbit blood samples to falsely indicate that his HIV vaccine research was more successful than it actually was. This misconduct led to significant setbacks in HIV research and the loss of millions of dollars in research funding.

   Impact: Falsification undermines the integrity of the research process, leading to false conclusions and potentially harmful applications. It can also damage public trust in science and research institutions.

3. **Plagiarism**

   Definition: *Plagiarism is the act of using another person's ideas, processes, results, or words without giving proper credit.* This form of misconduct violates intellectual property rights and academic integrity. It includes both literal copying and paraphrasing without proper attribution.

   Example: A well-known case of plagiarism involved Rajendra K. Pachauri, the former head of the Intergovernmental Panel on Climate Change (IPCC). He was accused of plagiarizing large sections of his novel Return to Almora from various sources, raising questions about the ethical standards of prominent scientific figures.

Impact: Plagiarism not only disrespects the original creators but also diminishes the credibility of the plagiarist. It can lead to severe penalties in academic settings, including retraction of published work, loss of reputation, and expulsion from academic programs.

4. **Conflict of Interest[8]**

   Definition: *A conflict of interest occurs when researchers have a financial, personal, or professional interest that could influence the outcome of their research.* While not misconduct in itself, failing to disclose a conflict of interest or allowing it to affect the research process is unethical.

   Example: The case of Dr. Charles Nemeroff, a prominent psychiatrist, illustrates the impact of undisclosed conflicts of interest. Dr. Nemeroff should have reported millions of dollars in income from pharmaceutical companies while researching their products. This lack of transparency raised concerns about the impartiality of his research findings.

   Impact: Undisclosed conflicts of interest can lead to biased research outcomes, reduce public trust in research, and potentially result in harmful consequences if the research informs public policy or clinical practice.

5. **Misrepresentation**

   Definition: *Misrepresentation involves presenting data, results, or methods in a misleading way to make the research appear more significant, novel, or successful than it actually is.* This can include selective reporting of results or exaggerating the implications of the findings.

   Example: The "cold fusion" controversy in the late 1980s, where researchers Stanley Pons and Martin Fleischmann claimed to have achieved nuclear fusion at room temperature, is an example of misrepresentation. The results could not be replicated, and the original claims were eventually discredited, leading to a loss of credibility for the researchers involved.

   Impact: Misrepresentation can lead to false scientific knowledge, misguide further research, and result in poor decision-making in both public policy and industry.

6. **Violation of Ethical Guidelines in Human and Animal Research**

   Definition: *Conducting research that violates ethical guidelines for human and animal subjects is a serious form of misconduct.* This includes failing to obtain informed consent, inadequate care for animal subjects, or exposing participants to unnecessary harm.

   Example: The Tuskegee Syphilis Study, conducted between 1932 and 1972, is a notorious example of unethical human research. African American men were misled and denied treatment for syphilis in order to study the disease's progression, resulting in significant harm and deaths. This study violated numerous ethical principles, including informed consent and the duty to protect participants from harm.

   Impact: Violations of ethical guidelines can cause harm to participants, lead to legal consequences, and damage the reputation of the research institution. Such misconduct also undermines public trust in research and the scientific community.

2.4. ETHICAL ISSUES RELATED TO AUTHORSHIP

Authorship in academic and scientific research is a recognition of the contributions made by individuals to a research project. It is not only a matter of professional credit but also carries responsibilities related to the integrity and accountability of the research. Ethical issues related to authorship arise when these contributions are not accurately or fairly represented. Understanding these ethical concerns is crucial for maintaining the credibility of the research process and ensuring that all contributors are appropriately recognized.

---

[8]*conflict of interest: a situation in which a person is in a position to derive personal benefit from actions or decisions made in their official capacity.*

1. **Guest Authorship (Honorary or Gift Authorship)**

   Definition: *Guest authorship occurs when individuals are listed as authors despite not making significant contributions to the research.* This may be done to enhance the prestige of a paper by including a well-known researcher or as a favor to colleagues.

   Ethical Issue: Guest authorship misrepresents the actual contributions to the research, inflating the academic credentials of individuals who did not earn them.

   Example: In some cases, senior faculty members may be added as authors on papers written by their students or junior colleagues without contributing significantly to the research. This practice, often seen as a way to enhance the paper's credibility, is unethical.

   Impact: Guest authorship undermines the integrity of academic publishing and can lead to unjust allocation of credit, affecting promotions, funding, and professional reputation.

2. **Ghost Authorship**

   Definition: *Ghost authorship occurs when someone who has contributed significantly to the research or writing of a manuscript is not listed as an author.* This often happens in cases where companies or professional writers draft papers for researchers, who then publish the work under their own names.

   Ethical Issue: Ghost authorship conceals the true contributors to the work and can lead to conflicts of interest, mainly if the ghostwriter is affiliated with a corporation that has a stake in the research outcomes.

   Example: Ghostwriting is expected in the pharmaceutical industry, where companies hire writers to draft articles later published under academic researchers' names. This practice is deceptive and undermines the transparency of the research process.

   Impact: Ghost authorship can result in the dissemination of biased or unreliable research, harming the credibility of the published work and misleading the scientific community and the public.

3. **Order of Authors**

   Definition: *The order of authors typically reflects the level of contribution each author has made to the research. The first author usually has made the most significant contribution, while the last author is often the senior researcher or group leader.*

   Ethical Issue: Disputes can arise over the order of authors, particularly when the contributions need to be clearly defined or agreed upon in advance. Manipulating the order to favor specific individuals or failing to accurately represent contributions is unethical.

   Example: A common ethical issue is when a senior researcher demands to be listed as the first author despite having contributed less than junior researchers. This can lead to conflicts and resentment within the research team.

   Impact: Disputes over authorship order can strain professional relationships, reduce collaboration, and lead to the unfair allocation of credit, affecting career progression and recognition.

4. **Contributorship and Accountability**

   Definition: *Contributorship involves specifying each author's role in the research process.* This approach, which is encouraged by many journals, helps clarify the contributions of each author and holds them accountable for their specific part of the work.

   Ethical Issue: When roles are not clearly defined, it becomes difficult to hold individuals accountable for their contributions, leading to potential ethical violations such as data manipulation or failure to fulfill responsibilities.

   Example: A paper that lists multiple authors without specifying who was responsible for the data analysis may obscure who is accountable if issues arise with the analysis. This lack of clarity can lead to ethical lapses being overlooked or unresolved.

   Impact: Clearly defined contributorship promotes transparency, ensures that credit is appropriately assigned, and enhances the accountability of all authors involved.

5. **Criteria for Authorship**

   Definition: Authorship should be based on a significant intellectual contribution to a research project. According to guidelines from organizations such as the International Committee of Medical Journal Editors (ICMJE), authorship requires:

   > ➢ Substantial contributions to the conception or design of the work, or the acquisition, analysis, or interpretation of data.
   >
   > ➢ Drafting the work or revising it critically for important intellectual content.

   Ethical Issue: Ethical concerns arise when individuals who do not meet these criteria are included as authors or when those who do meet the criteria are excluded.

   Example: A situation where a senior researcher insists on being listed as an author on all papers produced by their lab, regardless of their actual contribution, constitutes an unethical claim to authorship.

   Impact: Improper assignment of authorship can lead to disputes, undermine the value of academic contributions, and distort the record of who is responsible for the research.

6. **Authorship Disputes**

   Definition: *Authorship disputes arise when there is disagreement over who should be listed as an author or the order in which authors should be listed. Such disputes often occur due to unclear communication, differing expectations, or perceived injustices.*

   Ethical Issue: Disputes can lead to the exclusion of deserving contributors or the inclusion of undeserving ones. These conflicts can delay the publication of research and harm professional relationships.

   Example: A common scenario is when a student and a supervisor disagree on the order of authorship, with the student feeling they should be first author due to their significant contribution, while the supervisor believes their guidance warrants first authorship.

   Impact: Authorship disputes can cause significant stress and conflict within research teams, potentially leading to the breakdown of collaborations and a negative impact on the careers of those involved.

7. **Authorship in Collaborative Research**

   Definition: *Collaborative research often involves multiple institutions, disciplines, and researchers, making the assignment of authorship more complex. Clear guidelines and agreements are essential to avoid ethical issues in such collaborations.*

   Ethical Issue: In large collaborative projects, the contributions of individuals can be overlooked, or disagreements can arise over the relative contributions of different teams or researchers.

   Example: The Human Genome Project involved numerous researchers and institutions, necessitating clear agreements on how authorship would be assigned to ensure that all contributors were fairly recognized.

   Impact: Effective collaboration requires transparent and fair authorship practices. Establishing clear guidelines can avoid disputes, hindering collaboration, and result in the unfair allocation of credit.

Questions

1. List the different types of research misconduct and provide a brief explanation for each one.
2. What are the key ethical issues related to authorship? Explain each one.
3. What is the meaning of ethics and why is it important in the practice of engineering research?
4. Write a note on the following research misconduct (i) Falsification (ii) plagiarism.
5. What ethical considerations and responsibilities should be considered when determining authorship in Engineering research?
6. Explain Fabrication, Falsification and Plagiarism related to Engineering research.

"Literature allows us to be open, to listen, and to be curious."

: Tracy K. Smith

Module - 2

Chapter 3:
LITERATURE REVIEW AND TECHNICAL READING

INTRODUCTION

This chapter will explore the essential skills needed for effective literature review and technical reading, which are crucial in engineering research. The topics covered will guide us in understanding how to navigate new and existing knowledge, utilize bibliographic databases like Web of Science and Google Scholar, and develop effective search techniques. The chapter will also introduce critical and creative reading principles, focusing on conceptualizing research, understanding complex mathematical concepts, and interpreting datasheets—all fundamental aspects of academic and technical success.

3.1. LITERATURE REVIEW AND TECHNICAL READING

A literature review is a critical and in-depth evaluation of previous research on a particular topic. It involves the systematic identification, evaluation, and synthesis of existing literature to establish a foundation for further research. In engineering, a literature review not only demonstrates the researcher's knowledge of the field but also highlights gaps in the existing research that can be addressed by the study. Technical reading, on the other hand, refers to the process of comprehensively understanding and analyzing technical documents, such as research papers, standards, patents, and technical reports, which are essential for conducting a literature review.

3.1.1. OBJECTIVES OF A LITERATURE REVIEW

The primary objectives of a literature review in engineering research include:

1. **Identification of Gaps**: By evaluating existing literature, researchers can identify gaps or areas where further research is needed.
2. **Avoiding Duplication**: A thorough literature review ensures that the research does not duplicate existing studies unless it's a replication study with a different approach or context.
3. **Establishing Theoretical Frameworks**: Literature reviews help to develop or refine theoretical frameworks by linking existing theories with empirical evidence.
4. **Methodological Insights**: Reviewing literature provides insights into methodologies that have been previously employed, allowing researchers to choose the most appropriate methods for their studies.
5. **Supporting Arguments**: A literature review provides the necessary evidence to support the research question, hypothesis, or argument being proposed.
6. **Contextualization[9]**: It places the current study within the broader spectrum of existing research, helping to clarify how the research question or hypothesis fits into the larger academic conversation.

---

[9] *Contextualization: The process of considering something in relation to the situation in which it happens or exists*

3.1.2. STEPS IN CONDUCTING A LITERATURE REVIEW

1. **Defining the Research Question:** The first step in a literature review is to define a clear and concise research question. This helps to focus the search for relevant literature.
2. **Searching for Literature:** Literature search involves identifying relevant sources. Common databases include IEEE Xplore, Scopus, Web of Science, and Google Scholar. Keywords, Boolean operators, and advanced search techniques should be used to refine the search.
3. **Evaluating Sources:** Once the literature is gathered, each source should be critically evaluated for its relevance, quality, and credibility. Criteria include the publication date, peer-review status, and the impact factor of the journal.
4. **Synthesizing the Literature:** This step involves organizing the literature into themes, trends, and patterns. It may involve creating a conceptual framework that links various studies.
5. **Writing the Literature Review:** The synthesis of literature is then written in a structured format, often including an introduction, main body, and conclusion.
6. **Citing Sources:** Proper citation is essential to avoid plagiarism and to acknowledge the work of others. Citation styles like IEEE, APA, or MLA are commonly used in engineering.

3.1.3. TECHNICAL READING STRATEGIES

Technical reading is more intensive and analytical compared to general reading. Some strategies for effective technical reading include:

1. **Skimming and Scanning**: Quickly going through the document to get a general idea of the content, focusing on headings, abstracts, conclusions, and figures.
2. **Active Reading**: Engaging with the text by asking questions, making notes, and summarizing key points. This helps in better retention and understanding of complex material.
3. **Understanding Terminology**: Technical documents often contain specialized terminology. It is essential to familiarize oneself with these terms to fully understand the content.
4. **Analyzing Figures and Tables**: In engineering documents, a significant amount of information is conveyed through figures, tables, and charts. Analyzing these elements is crucial for a comprehensive understanding of the document.
5. **Critical Thinking**: Technical reading requires evaluating the validity of the information presented. This involves questioning the methodology, analyzing the data, and considering alternative interpretations.

3.1.4. IMPORTANCE OF LITERATURE REVIEW AND TECHNICAL READING IN ENGINEERING

In engineering education and practice, the literature review and technical reading are vital for several reasons:

1. **Foundation for Research**: A well-conducted literature review provides a solid foundation for research by identifying what has already been done and where the research can contribute new knowledge.
2. **Innovation and Problem-Solving**: By understanding existing solutions and their limitations, engineers can innovate and develop new solutions to existing problems.
3. **Professional Development**: Regular engagement with current literature and technical documents helps engineers stay updated with the latest trends, technologies, and standards in their field.
4. **Effective Communication**: A deep understanding of technical literature enables engineers to communicate their ideas more effectively in their own research papers, reports, and presentations.

3.2. NEW AND EXISTING KNOWLEDGE

In engineering research, knowledge is the cornerstone upon which innovations, discoveries, and technological advancements are built. The process of knowledge generation is twofold, encompassing both existing knowledge, which refers to the accumulation of what is already known, and new knowledge, which represents the contributions that add to this body of understanding.

3.2.1. EXISTING KNOWLEDGE

Existing knowledge refers to the collection of facts, theories, and principles established and validated over time. This body of knowledge is stored in various forms, including textbooks, journals, patents, standards, and digital databases, and is disseminated through academic courses, conferences, and professional practice.

Sources of Existing Knowledge

1. **Textbooks and Reference Books**: These are foundational resources that provide structured knowledge on specific subjects. For example, engineering thermodynamics, materials science, or circuit analysis textbooks present established principles and methodologies.

2. **Journals and Conference Proceedings**: Peer-reviewed journals and conference papers are primary sources of existing knowledge in engineering. They document research findings, case studies, and reviews that have undergone rigorous scrutiny by experts in the field.

3. **Patents**: Patents contain detailed descriptions of innovations that have been granted legal protection. They are valuable sources of technical information and design processes.

4. **Standards and Codes**: Standards, such as those from the IEEE, ISO, or ASTM, define accepted practices, materials, and specifications in engineering. They are based on existing knowledge and provide a benchmark for quality and safety.

5. **Databases and Digital Libraries**: Resources like IEEE Xplore, Scopus, and Google Scholar aggregate vast amounts of existing knowledge, making it accessible for research and learning.

Role of Existing Knowledge in Research

1. **Foundation for New Research**: Existing knowledge serves as the groundwork for new research. It informs researchers of what has already been done, allowing them to build upon it or challenge existing theories.

2. **Problem Identification**: By studying existing knowledge, researchers can identify gaps, inconsistencies, or areas where further exploration is needed. This is crucial for defining research questions or hypotheses.

3. **Methodological Guidance**: Established research methodologies and techniques, documented in existing literature, guide new research. Researchers often adopt or adapt these methods to suit their specific studies.

4. **Benchmarking and Validation**: Existing knowledge provides benchmarks against which new findings can be compared. It also aids in validating new results, ensuring that they are consistent with known principles or highlight legitimate deviations.

3.2.2. NEW KNOWLEDGE

New knowledge represents the novel insights, discoveries, or innovations that contribute to the existing body of knowledge. It is generated through original research, experimentation, and creative problem-solving. In engineering, new knowledge often manifests as new technologies, materials, processes, or theories.

Characteristics of New Knowledge

1. **Originality**: New knowledge must be original, offering insights that have not been previously documented. This could be a new theory, a novel application of existing technology, or the discovery of a previously unknown phenomenon.

2. **Validation and Verification**: New knowledge must be rigorously tested and validated to ensure its accuracy and reliability. This involves experimentation, peer review, and replication of results.

3. **Contribution to the Field**: New knowledge should contribute to the advancement of the field, providing value either by solving a problem, improving efficiency, or offering a new perspective.

4. **Dissemination**: New knowledge is typically disseminated through publications in peer-reviewed journals, presentations at conferences, patents, or through the development of new products or technologies.

Process of Creating New Knowledge

1. **Identifying Research Gaps**: The process begins with a thorough review of existing knowledge to identify gaps or areas that require further investigation.
2. **Formulating Research Questions**: Based on identified gaps, researchers formulate research questions or hypotheses that their study aims to address.
3. **Experimentation and Analysis**: New knowledge is generated through experiments, simulations, and data analysis. This process often involves iterative testing and refinement.
4. **Documentation and Publication**: Once validated, new knowledge is documented and published, allowing it to be shared with the broader scientific and engineering communities.
5. **Impact and Application**: New knowledge is applied in practical contexts, such as in the development of new products, processes, or technologies. Its impact is assessed through its adoption and integration into existing systems or practices.

Relationship Between New and Existing Knowledge

The relationship between new and existing knowledge is symbiotic. New knowledge builds upon the foundation of existing knowledge, while existing knowledge evolves through the integration of new discoveries and innovations. This dynamic interplay drives progress in engineering and other fields.

1. **Continuity**: New knowledge often extends or refines existing theories, leading to a more comprehensive understanding of a subject.
2. **Innovation**: Breakthroughs in new knowledge can challenge existing paradigms, leading to significant shifts in understanding or practice.
3. **Learning and Education**: For engineering students, understanding existing knowledge is crucial for learning, while engaging in research projects can contribute to the generation of new knowledge.

3.3. ANALYSIS AND SYNTHESIS OF PRIOR ART BIBLIOGRAPHIC DATABASES

In the field of engineering and technology, prior art refers to all the knowledge that existed before a given invention or innovation, including patents, publications, and other publicly accessible documents. Understanding and analyzing prior art is crucial for innovation, as it helps to ensure that new ideas are original and do not infringe on existing intellectual property. Bibliographic databases are invaluable tools in this process, providing comprehensive records of published research, patents, and technical documents.

Importance of Analyzing Prior Art

The analysis of prior art is a critical step in the research and development (R&D) process. It serves multiple purposes:

1. **Avoiding Redundancy**: By analyzing prior art, researchers can avoid duplicating work that has already been done, thereby saving time and resources.
2. **Ensuring Novelty**: In patent applications, proving the novelty of an invention is essential. Analyzing prior art helps to establish that an invention is indeed new and non-obvious.
3. **Identifying Research Gaps**: Prior art analysis allows researchers to identify gaps in existing knowledge, which can be addressed by new research.
4. **Strategic Planning**: Companies and researchers use prior art analysis to plan their R&D activities strategically, ensuring that they focus on areas with the potential for innovation and minimal competition.

Bibliographic Databases

Bibliographic databases are organized collections of references to published literature, including journal articles, conference papers, patents, and books. These databases often include abstracts, keywords, and other metadata, making it easier for researchers to find relevant prior art.

Types of Bibliographic Databases

1. **Patent Databases**: These databases, such as the United States Patent and Trademark Office (USPTO) and the European Patent Office (EPO), contain records of patents and patent applications. They are essential for conducting prior art searches in the context of intellectual property.
2. **Academic Databases**: Databases like IEEE Xplore, Scopus, and Web of Science contain peer-reviewed journal articles, conference papers, and other scholarly documents. They are crucial for analyzing the academic and theoretical foundations of prior art.
3. **Technical Standards Databases**: Organizations like IEEE, ISO, and ASTM maintain databases of technical standards, which are important references in engineering research.
4. **Citation Databases**: These databases, such as Google Scholar and CrossRef, track citations between publications, helping researchers to understand the influence and relevance of prior work.

3.4. WEB OF SCIENCE

Web of Science is one of the most comprehensive and widely used bibliographic databases in academic research. It is maintained by Clarivate Analytics and covers a vast array of disciplines, including engineering, natural sciences, social sciences, and humanities.

Key Features

1. **Multidisciplinary Coverage**: Web of Science covers over 34,000 journals across 256 disciplines, making it one of the most comprehensive sources of scholarly information.
2. **Citation Tracking**: It offers robust citation tracking tools, allowing researchers to trace the impact of specific articles through the number of times they have been cited.
3. **Impact Factor Analysis**: Web of Science is the source for the Journal Citation Reports (JCR), which provides the impact factor of journals, a crucial metric in evaluating the significance of research publications.
4. **Advanced Search Capabilities**: It provides advanced search options, including Boolean operators, citation reports, and the ability to search by author, institution, or funding agency.

Advantages

1. **Quality and Reliability**: Web of Science includes only high-quality, peer-reviewed journals, ensuring that the content is reliable and authoritative.
2. **Comprehensive Citation Data**: Its detailed citation analysis helps researchers understand the influence of their work and the work of others in the field.
3. **Interdisciplinary Research**: Its multidisciplinary nature facilitates cross-disciplinary research, enabling connections between engineering and other fields like materials science, environmental science, and physics.

Example Use Case

An engineering student researching the latest advancements in nanotechnology could use Web of Science to locate seminal papers, track citation trends, and identify key researchers and institutions in the field. By analyzing citation patterns, the student could also determine which research topics are gaining momentum and which ones have reached saturation.

3.5. GOOGLE

Google is the world's most popular search engine. While not a traditional bibliographic database, it plays a significant role in academic research due to its extensive indexing of web content. Google provides access to a wide array of information, including grey literature, technical reports, conference papers, and other non-peer-reviewed sources.

Key Features

1. **Broad Search Scope**: Google indexes a massive amount of content from across the internet, including academic and non-academic sources.

2. **Accessible Interface**: Its simple and intuitive interface makes it easy for users to find information on almost any topic quickly.
3. **Integration with Other Google Tools**: Google integrates with other services like Google Books, Google Patents, and Google Scholar, providing additional avenues for accessing academic content.

Advantages

1. **Wide Reach**: Google's vast index allows users to find information that may not be available in traditional academic databases, including unpublished studies, conference presentations, and technical reports.
2. **Real-Time Information**: It provides access to the most current information, including recent news, blog posts, and other forms of grey literature that might be relevant to ongoing research.

Limitations

1. **Lack of Peer-Review**: Not all content indexed by Google is peer-reviewed, which means that researchers must critically evaluate the credibility of the sources they find.
2. **Overwhelming Volume of Results**: The sheer volume of information can be overwhelming, making it challenging to sift through and find relevant academic content.

Example Use Case

An engineering student working on a project related to renewable energy could use Google to find the latest news articles, government reports, and white papers that might not yet be available in academic journals.

3.6. GOOGLE SCHOLAR

Google Scholar is a freely accessible search engine that indexes scholarly articles, theses, books, conference papers, and patents. It is a specialized version of Google that focuses on academic content.

Key Features

1. **Comprehensive Indexing**: Google Scholar indexes a wide range of scholarly materials, including peer-reviewed papers, theses, books, preprints, and patents.
2. **Citation Tracking**: It provides basic citation tracking, showing how many times a paper has been cited and by whom.
3. **Related Articles**: Google Scholar suggests related articles, helping researchers discover additional relevant literature.
4. **Personalized Profiles**: Researchers can create profiles to track their publications, citations, and h-index.

Advantages

1. **Free Access**: Google Scholar is freely accessible to anyone, making it a valuable resource for students and researchers without access to subscription-based databases.
2. **User-Friendly Interface**: Its simple and intuitive interface allows for quick searches and easy navigation.
3. **Wide Range of Content**: It covers a broad spectrum of academic disciplines, making it useful for interdisciplinary research.

Limitations

1. **Variable Quality**: Google Scholar does not curate content as rigorously as databases like Web of Science, meaning that the quality of indexed materials can vary widely.
2. **Limited Advanced Search Options**: While it offers some advanced search features, these are not as sophisticated as those found in paid databases.

Example Use Case

An engineering student preparing a literature review on artificial intelligence in robotics could use Google Scholar to find a wide range of academic papers, including recent preprints that might still need to be available in other databases. The student could also track citations to see how influential certain papers have been within the field.

3.7. EFFECTIVE SEARCH TECHNIQUES

In the digital age, where vast amounts of information are readily accessible online, the ability to conduct effective searches is an essential skill for engineering students and researchers. Whether conducting a literature review, gathering data for a project, or staying updated with the latest technological advancements, mastering search techniques can significantly enhance the efficiency and accuracy of information retrieval.

The Importance of Effective Search Techniques

Effective search techniques are fundamental to academic research for several reasons:

1. **Efficiency**: Proper search techniques save time by quickly narrowing down vast amounts of information to the most relevant sources.
2. **Accuracy**: They ensure that the information retrieved is accurate, credible, and directly relevant to the research question or topic.
3. **Comprehensiveness**: Using advanced search techniques helps in conducting comprehensive searches, ensuring that important literature or data is not overlooked.
4. **Reproducibility**: Well-documented search strategies allow other researchers to replicate the search process, which is crucial in systematic reviews and meta-analyses.

Basic Search Techniques

1. **Formulating a Clear Research Question:** The first step in conducting an effective search is to formulate a clear and focused research question or query. A well-defined question helps to determine the key concepts and keywords that will be used in the search process.
   Example: If researching the impact of nanotechnology on battery performance, the research question might be, "How does the application of nanotechnology improve the efficiency and lifespan of lithium-ion batteries?"
2. **Identifying Keywords and Synonyms:** Once the research question is established, the next step is to identify the main keywords and their synonyms or related terms. This helps to capture the full range of relevant literature.
   Example: For the research question above, the keywords might include "nanotechnology," "battery performance," "lithium-ion batteries," and "efficiency." Synonyms might include "nanotech," "energy storage," and "battery lifespan."
3. **Using Boolean Operators:** Boolean operators (AND, OR, NOT) are essential tools in search queries that help refine and expand search results.
   - **AND**: Narrows the search by combining keywords, ensuring that all search terms appear in the results. **Example**: "nanotechnology AND lithium-ion batteries" will retrieve documents that contain both terms.
   - **OR**: Expands the search by including synonyms or related terms. **Example**: "nanotechnology OR nanotech" will retrieve documents that contain either term.
   - **NOT**: Excludes certain terms from the search. **Example**: "nanotechnology NOT solar cells" will exclude documents that focus on solar cells.
4. **Phrase Searching:** Enclosing a phrase in quotation marks ensures that the search engine or database retrieves documents where the words appear together in the specified order. **Example**: Searching for "lithium-ion battery performance" will only retrieve documents where this exact phrase is mentioned.

3.8. INTRODUCTION TO TECHNICAL READING

Technical reading involves the process of comprehensively understanding and interpreting specialized documents, such as research papers, technical reports, standards, and patents. Unlike general reading, technical reading requires a higher level of engagement, critical thinking, and familiarity with domain-specific terminology.

Key Aspects of Technical Reading

i. **Understanding the Structure**: Technical documents often follow a specific structure, including sections like the abstract, introduction, methodology, results, discussion, and conclusion. Familiarity with this structure helps in navigating the document effectively.

   Example: In a research paper on material science, the methodology section might detail the experimental setup, while the results section presents data and observations.

ii. **Interpreting Data and Figures**: Technical reading often involves interpreting complex data presented in tables, graphs, and diagrams. Understanding how to read and analyze these visual elements is crucial.

   Example: A paper on thermal properties of materials may include graphs showing temperature vs. thermal conductivity. The ability to interpret these graphs is essential for understanding the study's findings.

iii. **Familiarity with Technical Vocabulary**: Technical documents use specialized vocabulary that may be unfamiliar to general readers. Building a strong technical vocabulary is essential for effective reading.

   Example: Terms like "Young's modulus," "shear stress," or "finite element analysis" are common in mechanical engineering literature.

iv. **Active Engagement**: Technical reading requires active engagement with the text, including asking questions, making annotations, and reflecting on the content.

   Example: While reading a technical report on renewable energy systems, students should actively consider how the findings could be applied to real-world engineering problems.

3.9. CONCEPTUALIZING RESEARCH

Conceptualizing research involves the process of forming a clear and structured understanding of a research problem or question. It includes defining the scope of the study, identifying key concepts, and formulating hypotheses or research objectives.

Steps in Conceptualizing Research

1. **Identifying the Research Problem**: The first step in any research project is to identify a specific problem or question that needs to be addressed. This problem should be relevant, original, and feasible within the constraints of the study.

   Example: In civil engineering, a research problem might focus on improving the durability of concrete in coastal environments.

2. **Literature Review**: Conducting a thorough literature review helps to understand what has already been studied, identify gaps in knowledge, and refine the research problem.

   Example: A literature review on smart grid technologies might reveal that while much research has been done on energy efficiency, there is a gap in studies addressing cybersecurity challenges.

3. **Defining Key Concepts and Variables**: Clearly defining the key concepts and variables involved in the research is essential for developing a structured approach to the study.

   Example: In a study on fluid dynamics, key concepts might include flow velocity, viscosity, and turbulence.

4. **Formulating Hypotheses or Objectives**: Based on the research problem and literature review, formulate hypotheses or research objectives that guide the study.

   Example: A hypothesis in an environmental engineering study might be, "The introduction of biochar in soil will significantly reduce heavy metal contamination."

5. **Developing a Research Plan**: Finally, outline a research plan that includes the methodology, data collection, analysis techniques, and timeline for the study.

   Example: A research plan for a mechanical engineering project might involve experimental testing of materials, computational modeling, and data analysis using statistical software.

3.10. CRITICAL AND CREATIVE READING

Critical and creative reading involves not only understanding the content of a text but also evaluating its validity, significance, and implications, while simultaneously considering alternative perspectives and possibilities.

3.10.1. CRITICAL READING

Critical reading requires analyzing and questioning the information presented in a text. It involves assessing the credibility of sources, evaluating the strength of arguments, and identifying any biases or assumptions.

1. **Questioning the Text**: Critical readers ask questions about the author's assumptions, the validity of the evidence, and the logic of the arguments presented.

    Example: In a paper on the environmental impact of construction materials, a critical reader might question the scope of the study or the generalizability of the findings.

2. **Evaluating Evidence**: Critical reading involves evaluating the quality and relevance of the evidence presented. This includes assessing the methodology used in studies and the reliability of the data.

    Example: When reading a study on the efficiency of solar panels, a critical reader would consider the sample size, experimental conditions, and potential biases in the data collection process.

3. **Identifying Biases and Assumptions**: Recognizing biases and assumptions in a text is essential for critical reading. This includes understanding the context in which the research was conducted and any potential conflicts of interest.

    Example: A critical reader might note that a study on fossil fuels funded by an oil company could be biased in its findings.

3.10.2. CREATIVE READING

Creative reading involves looking beyond the text to explore new ideas, connections, and possibilities. It encourages readers to think innovatively and apply the information in novel ways.

1. **Connecting Ideas**: Creative readers make connections between the ideas presented in different texts and disciplines, leading to new insights and perspectives.

    Example: A creative reader might link concepts from materials science and biomedical engineering to explore new applications for biocompatible materials in medical devices.

2. **Generating New Ideas**: Creative reading can inspire new research questions, hypotheses, or design ideas that push the boundaries of current knowledge.

    Example: After reading about advancements in nanotechnology, a creative reader might conceive a new application for nano-coatings in aerospace engineering.

3. **Exploring Alternative Perspectives**: Creative readers consider alternative interpretations and solutions, challenging the conventional understanding of a topic.

    Example: A creative reader might propose alternative materials or design approaches after critically evaluating the limitations of existing solutions in a technical document.

3.11. TAKING NOTES WHILE READING

Taking notes while reading is a crucial skill for effective learning and research. It involves summarizing key points, recording insights, and organizing information for future reference.

Techniques for Taking Effective Notes

1. **Summarization**: Summarizing the main ideas of a text in your own words helps reinforce understanding and retention.

    Example: While reading a chapter on renewable energy technologies, a student might summarize the key advantages and challenges of different types of solar cells.

2. **Annotation**: Annotating involves writing comments, questions, and reflections in the margins of the text or in a separate notebook. This technique encourages active engagement with the material.

    Example: Annotating a research paper on sustainable construction might include notes on potential applications of the findings to local projects or questions about the methodology used.

3. **Mind Mapping**: Creating mind maps is a visual way to organize information, showing relationships between concepts and ideas. This is particularly useful for complex subjects.

       Example: A mind map for a research project on smart grids might include branches for key concepts like energy efficiency, demand response, and cybersecurity.

4. **Highlighting and Underlining**: Selectively highlighting or underlining key phrases or concepts in a text can help to quickly locate important information when reviewing notes.

       Example: Highlighting definitions, important statistics, or significant findings in a technical report on material properties.

5. **Recording Questions and Insights**: Writing down questions that arise while reading, as well as any new ideas or insights, is important for deepening understanding and guiding further research.

       Example: After reading a paper on autonomous vehicles, a student might note down questions about the ethical implications of AI decision-making in emergency situations.

Organizing Notes

1. **Digital Tools**: Using digital tools like Evernote, OneNote, or Mendeley allows for easy organization, searchability, and sharing of notes.

       Example: Mendeley can be used to organize and annotate PDFs of research papers, making it easier to reference them later.

2. **Indexing and Categorization**: Indexing and categorizing notes by topic, author, or project helps in quick retrieval and organization.

       Example: Creating folders or tags for different courses or research projects in a digital note-taking app.

3. **Reviewing and Revising Notes**: Regularly reviewing and revising notes reinforces learning and ensures that the information is well understood.

       Example: Revising notes before an exam to ensure all key concepts are clear.

3.12. READING, READING MATHEMATICS AND ALGORITHMS

Reading mathematics and algorithms is a critical skill for engineering students, as these fields form the foundation of much of the work done in computer science, electrical engineering, mechanical engineering, and more. Unlike reading general texts, understanding mathematical and algorithmic content requires a structured approach, close attention to detail, and a solid grasp of the underlying concepts. Developing strategies for reading and comprehending mathematical equations, proofs, and algorithms will enhance the ability to apply these concepts in academic and professional work.

3.12.1. THE NATURE OF MATHEMATICAL READING

Reading mathematics differs significantly from reading prose or even technical reports. Mathematical texts are highly condensed, with every symbol and term carrying specific meaning that contributes to the overall logic of the argument. As a result, mathematical reading is often slow, methodical, and recursive.

Key Challenges in Reading Mathematics

1. **Symbolism and Notation**: Mathematical texts rely heavily on symbols and notation, which can be dense and unfamiliar to students. Each symbol often represents a complex concept that requires careful interpretation.

       Example: The summation symbol $\sum$ represents the sum of a series of terms, and its use may involve intricate limits and variable manipulations.

2. **Logical Structure**: Mathematics is built on a logical structure where each statement is supported by previous results, theorems, or axioms. Understanding this logical flow is essential for following the reasoning presented in mathematical texts.

Example: A proof might start with an assumption, proceed through logical deductions, and end with a conclusion that verifies the original hypothesis.

3. **Abstract Concepts**: Many mathematical texts deal with abstract concepts that lack physical representations, making them more difficult to conceptualize.

   Example: Concepts like vector spaces or complex numbers can be challenging for students who are accustomed to dealing with more concrete entities.

Strategies for Reading Mathematics

1. **Start with Definitions and Theorems**: Definitions and theorems are the building blocks of mathematical texts. When reading, start by carefully understanding the definitions of terms and symbols, followed by the statements of theorems and lemmas.

   Example: In calculus, understanding the definition of a limit is crucial before tackling theorems related to continuity or differentiability.

2. **Work Through Examples**: Mathematical texts often include worked examples to illustrate key concepts or theorems. Working through these examples step-by-step is an effective way to solidify understanding.

   Example: When reading about matrix transformations, students might find it helpful to work through examples of 2x2 matrices to understand how transformations apply in linear algebra.

3. **Break Down Equations**: Complex equations should be broken down into smaller parts to understand their components. Analyzing each term separately helps in grasping the overall structure and purpose of the equation.

   Example: A partial differential equation (PDE) might involve multiple terms representing different physical processes (e.g., heat transfer and diffusion). Breaking it down helps in understanding each process.

4. **Practice Proofs**: Proofs are central to many mathematical texts. When encountering a proof, students should try to understand each step logically and, if possible, attempt to reconstruct the proof on their own to ensure understanding.

   Example: Proving that the derivative of a function is continuous might involve applying the definition of limits and derivatives. Reconstructing this proof helps internalize the logic.

5. **Annotate and Take Notes**: Taking detailed notes, including re-writing definitions, drawing diagrams, and summarizing proofs in your own words, helps reinforce learning. It also provides a valuable reference for future study.

   Example: When reading about Fourier transforms, students might annotate key steps in the derivation and note down any assumptions or conditions involved.

3.12.2. THE NATURE OF ALGORITHMIC READING

Reading algorithms requires a combination of logical thinking and problem-solving skills. Algorithms are essentially step-by-step instructions for solving a problem or performing a computation. When reading an algorithm, it is essential to understand its purpose, structure, and efficiency.

Key Challenges in Reading Algorithms

1. **Understanding Pseudocode**: Many algorithms are presented in pseudocode, a notation that describes the algorithm in a structured but informal manner. While pseudocode is not tied to any specific programming language, it must be interpreted correctly to understand the algorithm.

   Example: An algorithm for sorting a list might be presented in pseudocode using terms like "for loop" and "swap," which require understanding of basic programming constructs.

2. **Complexity and Efficiency**: Algorithms are often evaluated based on their time complexity (how fast they run) and space complexity (how much memory they use). Understanding these aspects is critical for assessing an algorithm's practicality.

Example: Analyzing the time complexity of an algorithm for searching through a list might involve counting the number of operations performed as the size of the list increases (e.g., O(n) for linear search).

3. **Recursive and Iterative Constructs**: Many algorithms rely on recursion or iteration, which can be difficult to follow without careful attention to the flow of control and the base or termination conditions.
   Example: A recursive algorithm for calculating factorials calls itself repeatedly, so understanding how the recursion unwinds is key to grasping how the algorithm works.

Strategies for Reading Algorithms

1. **Understand the Problem**: Before diving into the algorithm, ensure that you have a clear understanding of the problem the algorithm is designed to solve. This often involves identifying the input, output, and constraints of the problem.
   Example: When studying the Dijkstra algorithm for finding the shortest path in a graph, first ensure you understand the graph's structure (nodes, edges, and weights) and the goal (minimizing total distance).

2. **Analyze Each Step**: Break the algorithm down into individual steps and understand the logic behind each one. Ask questions such as: What does this step do? Why is it necessary?
   Example: In the Merge Sort algorithm, breaking it down into the "divide" and "merge" steps helps clarify how the algorithm recursively divides a list and then recombines it in sorted order.

3. **Trace the Algorithm with Examples**: One of the most effective ways to understand an algorithm is to trace it through a simple example. Use small datasets to manually execute the algorithm step-by-step.
   Example: For a sorting algorithm like QuickSort, trace the algorithm using a small list of numbers (e.g., $\{4, 2, 7, 1\}$) and manually go through the partitioning and sorting steps.

4. **Understand Complexity Analysis**: Evaluate the time and space complexity of the algorithm using Big O notation. This helps in comparing algorithms and choosing the most efficient one for a given problem.
   Example: When comparing the efficiency of Bubble Sort ($O(n^2)$) and Merge Sort ($O(n \log n)$), it becomes clear that Merge Sort is more efficient for larger datasets.

5. **Relate to Real-World Applications**: Understanding how an algorithm applies to real-world problems can help make its purpose more concrete and meaningful.
   Example: The A* algorithm is used in pathfinding for robotics and game development, so understanding its heuristic-based approach to optimizing paths makes it easier to see why it's efficient.

3.12.3. COMBINING MATHEMATICS AND ALGORITHMS

In engineering, mathematics and algorithms often work hand-in-hand. Many algorithms are based on mathematical principles, such as graph theory, calculus, or linear algebra. Understanding the underlying mathematics behind an algorithm can enhance comprehension and implementation.

Example: The Fast Fourier Transform (FFT) algorithm is based on principles from signal processing and complex number theory. Understanding the mathematical basis of Fourier transforms helps in grasping why the FFT algorithm is used to efficiently compute discrete Fourier transforms in digital signal processing.

3.13. READING A DATASHEET

In the context of engineering research and technical reading, understanding how to read and interpret datasheets effectively is a critical skill. Datasheets provide essential technical specifications, performance characteristics, and operational guidelines for various components, materials, or systems. Whether dealing with electronic components, mechanical parts, or chemical substances, the ability to extract relevant information from a datasheet can significantly impact the success of a research project or product development process. This will provide a detailed guide on reading and understanding datasheets, emphasizing their importance in technical reading within engineering research.

Structure of a Datasheet

Datasheets typically follow a standardized format, though the exact structure may vary depending on the manufacturer or industry. However, most datasheets include the following key sections:

1. **Title and Product Overview**: The title section usually contains the name of the product, part number, and a brief description or overview. This section provides a high-level summary of what the product is and its intended application.

2. **Features and Benefits**: This section highlights the key features of the product and the advantages it offers. It may include information about unique selling points, performance metrics, and any special characteristics that differentiate the product from similar ones in the market.

3. **Technical Specifications**: The technical specifications are the core of the datasheet. They provide detailed information about the product's operational parameters, such as voltage ratings, temperature ranges, mechanical dimensions, and tolerances. For electronic components, this might include electrical characteristics like input/output voltages, currents, power consumption, and frequency response.

4. **Electrical Characteristics and Pin Configuration (for electronic components)**: For electronic components, the datasheet often includes a detailed breakdown of the electrical characteristics, such as maximum ratings, typical operating conditions, and pin configuration. This section is critical for understanding how the component behaves under different conditions and how it should be integrated into a circuit.

5. **Mechanical and Physical Dimensions**: Mechanical components or systems often include detailed diagrams and measurements. These diagrams provide the necessary information for integrating the component into larger systems, ensuring compatibility with other parts, and understanding the space requirements.

6. **Application Information**: Some datasheets provide specific application guidelines, including typical use cases, recommended operating conditions, and design considerations. This section can be particularly valuable for understanding how to effectively implement the component in a real-world scenario.

7. **Graphs, Tables, and Charts**: Datasheets often include graphical representations of performance metrics, such as efficiency curves, load vs. temperature graphs, or frequency response plots. These visual aids help engineers and researchers quickly interpret complex data and compare performance under various conditions.

8. **Compliance and Standards**: This section lists the standards and certifications that the product complies with, such as ISO, CE, RoHS, or UL. Compliance information is essential for ensuring that the product meets regulatory requirements and industry standards.

9. **Packaging and Handling Information**: Information on packaging, handling, and storage is often included, particularly for components sensitive to environmental conditions. This section may also provide guidelines on safe handling practices to prevent damage or degradation of the product.

10. **Revision History**: Some datasheets include a revision history that tracks changes made to the document over time. This section is useful for understanding updates, corrections, or improvements made to the product or its documentation.

Importance of Datasheets in Engineering Research

Datasheets are indispensable resources in engineering research for several reasons:

1. **Component Selection**: Engineers rely on datasheets to select the appropriate components for their designs. By comparing the specifications of different products, researchers can identify the component that best meets the performance requirements of their project.

2. **Design Verification**: Datasheets provide the necessary parameters for verifying that a design will function as intended. This includes ensuring that components will operate within safe limits and that they will interact correctly within a system.

3. **Troubleshooting**: When issues arise during the development or testing phases, datasheets serve as a reference to diagnose and resolve problems. By understanding the component's limitations and operating characteristics, engineers can pinpoint the root cause of failures or malfunctions.

4. **Regulatory Compliance**: Compliance with industry standards and regulations is often a critical aspect of engineering projects. Datasheets provide the necessary certification information to ensure that the selected components meet all regulatory requirements.

Questions

1. What are the primary goals of conducting a literature review in academic research?

2. How does the new and existing knowledge can contribute to the research process? Explain with relevant points.

3. What are datasheets and write their contents?

4. Explain the various steps involved in the critical and creative reading process.

5. How does the existing knowledge can contribute to the research process? Explain with relevant points.

6. What are the key features of the bibliographic database of the Web of Science (WoS), and how is it commonly used in research?

7. List and explain the Importance of Note-taking while reading research papers.

8. How do researchers distinguish between new and existing knowledge during a literature review?

9. How can researchers effectively use search engines to find relevant literature in their fields?

10. What challenges do researchers commonly face when reading mathematical content or algorithm?

"Your manuscript is both good and original; but the part that is good is not original, and the part that is original is not good."

: Samuel Johnson

Module - 2

Chapter 4:
ATTRIBUTIONS AND CITATIONS

INTRODUCTION

In research world, giving proper credit is not just a matter of ethics but a fundamental aspect of scholarship. This chapter delves into the essentials of **Attributions and Citations**. We will explore why it is crucial to give credit wherever it is due, understand the functions and attributes of citations, and how the right choice of title and keywords can impact the research's visibility. We will also discuss the flow of knowledge through citations, the importance of citing datasets, and the various citation styles used across disciplines. Additionally, this chapter will guide what should be acknowledged in work, including in books, dissertations, and the significance of dedications and acknowledgments. Through this, we will learn to uphold academic integrity and contribute responsibly to the body of knowledge.

Attributions[10]: Attribution refers to the act of acknowledging the original source of information, ideas, data, or images used in your work. It's an ethical practice that respects the intellectual property rights of the creators. Attributions can be included in the text, in footnotes, or as part of a bibliography or reference list.

Citations[11]: Citations are formal references to sources from which you have borrowed information or ideas. They provide readers with the details needed to find the original source. Different citation styles have different formats for citations, but they typically include the author's name, publication date, title of the work, and publication details.

4.1. GIVING CREDIT WHEREVER DUE

In academic research and professional work, giving credit wherever it is due is not merely a matter of courtesy but a fundamental ethical responsibility. This practice ensures that original ideas, contributions, and efforts are properly acknowledged, fostering a culture of integrity and respect within the academic community. Understanding the significance of giving credit is crucial as it not only upholds ethical standards but also enhances the credibility and reliability of their work.

4.1.1. IMPORTANCE OF GIVING CREDIT

1. **Ethical Responsibility**: Giving credit is deeply rooted in the ethical principles that govern academic and professional conduct. According to the Committee on Publication Ethics (COPE), failing to acknowledge the work of others constitutes plagiarism, which is a serious form of academic

---

[10] *Attribution: To believe that something done by somebody*
[11] *Citations: A word or piece of writing taken from a written work*

misconduct[3]. By giving credit, students and researchers demonstrate honesty, transparency, and respect for the intellectual property of others.

2. **Recognition of Original Work**: Acknowledging the contributions of others recognizes the originality of their work. This is particularly important in fields like engineering, where innovation and new discoveries are highly valued. Proper attribution ensures that the rightful creators receive recognition for their efforts, thereby encouraging innovation and creativity.

3. **Building Trust and Credibility**: Credibility is a cornerstone of academic research. When credit is appropriately given, it builds trust among peers, educators, and the wider academic community. It signals that the work presented is based on a thorough understanding of existing knowledge and that all sources have been duly acknowledged. This trust is essential for the dissemination and acceptance of new ideas and research findings.

4. **Preventing Plagiarism**: Plagiarism, defined as the appropriation of another person's ideas, processes, results, or words without giving appropriate credit, is a serious offense in academia [4]. By properly citing sources and giving credit, students can avoid plagiarism, thereby upholding the integrity of their work and protecting themselves from potential academic consequences.

4.1.2. METHODS OF GIVING CREDIT

1. **Citations and References**: The most common method of giving credit is through citations and references. Citations are brief mentions within the text that indicate where a particular idea, data, or quote was sourced from, while references provide detailed information about the source at the end of the document. Various citation styles, such as APA, MLA, and IEEE, provide guidelines on how to properly format citations and references [5]. **Example**: If a student uses data from a study by Smith et al. (2020), they should cite the source within their text as follows: (Smith et al., 2020). The full reference would then appear in the reference list at the end of the document.

2. **Acknowledgments**: In addition to citations, acknowledgments are another way to give credit. This section of a research paper or project report is used to recognize individuals or organizations that contributed to the work but are not included as authors. This may include mentors, funding bodies, or institutions that provided resources or support. **Example**: "The authors would like to acknowledge the support of the XYZ Research Institute for providing the necessary equipment for this study."

3. **Attribution in Collaborative Work**: In collaborative projects, it is essential to clearly define and attribute the contributions of each team member. This not only ensures that everyone receives appropriate credit but also clarifies the division of labor, it is important for evaluating individual contributions. **Example**: In a group project report, the contributions of each member can be described in a section titled "Contributions of Authors," detailing who was responsible for each part of the work.

4.2. CITATIONS: FUNCTIONS AND ATTRIBUTES

Citations are a cornerstone of academic writing and research. They serve as a bridge between the existing body of knowledge and new research contributions. Citations acknowledge the intellectual property of others and enhance the credibility, reliability, and scholarly value of a research work. Understanding the functions and attributes of citations is crucial, as it lays the foundation for ethical and effective research practices.

4.2.1. FUNCTIONS OF CITATIONS

Citations fulfill several essential functions in academic research

1. **Acknowledgment of Sources**: The primary function of a citation is to acknowledge the original sources of ideas, data, theories, or methodologies that have been used in a research work. By citing sources, researchers show respect for the intellectual property of others and avoid plagiarism, which is considered a serious academic offense.

2. **Supporting Evidence**: Citations provide the necessary evidence to support claims, arguments, and hypotheses made in a research paper. For example, if a student states that "the tensile strength of aluminum alloys is significantly improved by heat treatment," they should back this claim with relevant studies or data from credible sources.

3. **Enabling Verification**: Citations allow readers to verify the information presented in a research work. This transparency enables other researchers to trace the origins of the data, methods, or ideas, which is critical for replicability and further exploration. For instance, if a paper mentions a specific experimental procedure, the citation enables others to follow the same procedure and test the results independently.

4. **Building on Existing Knowledge**: Citations illustrate how a new research work is connected to the existing body of knowledge. They show that the researcher is aware of previous studies and is contributing to an ongoing academic conversation. This is particularly important in engineering, where innovation often builds upon earlier discoveries and developments.

5. **Demonstrating Rigor and Scholarly Engagement**: The use of citations demonstrates that the researcher has engaged thoroughly with existing literature. It indicates that the researcher has conducted a comprehensive literature review and is well-informed about the current state of research in their field. For example, a review of the literature on topological optimization techniques in mechanical engineering would include citations to seminal papers and recent advancements to show the depth of the research.

6. **Establishing the Context of Research**: Citations help to situate new research within the broader academic context. They provide background information and set the stage for the new research question or problem. For example, when researching the transition from steel to aluminum in automotive components, citations to previous studies on material properties and manufacturing processes establish the relevance and significance of the new research.

4.2.2. ATTRIBUTES OF CITATIONS

Citations possess specific attributes that ensure their effectiveness and reliability:

1. **Accuracy**: A citation must accurately reflect the source material. This includes correct author names, publication dates, titles, and page numbers. Inaccurate citations can lead to misinformation and undermine the credibility of the research. For instance, if citing a standard reference book in mechanical engineering, all details must be meticulously checked to avoid errors.

2. **Relevance**: The cited sources should be directly relevant to the topic. Irrelevant citations can confuse readers and dilute the focus of the research. Example: When discussing stress-strain behavior in materials, citations should come from studies related to material science rather than unrelated fields.

3. **Completeness**: A citation should include all necessary information to enable readers to locate the source. This typically includes the author's name, title of the work, journal or book title, volume and issue numbers, page numbers, and publication year. Omitting any of these details can make it difficult for readers to verify the source.

4. **Consistency**: Citations should follow a consistent format throughout the research work. This consistency aids in readability and ensures that the research adheres to academic standards. Common citation styles include APA, MLA, Chicago, and IEEE. In engineering, IEEE is often preferred due to its alignment with technical fields.

5. **Ethical Attribution**: Citations should be used ethically, giving credit to the original authors for their contributions. This ethical practice is crucial in maintaining the integrity of academic research. Example: Researcher paraphrases a concept, they must still provide a citation to avoid plagiarism.

6. **Accessibility**: The sources cited should be accessible to readers. If the cited material is behind a paywall or not widely available, it is helpful to provide alternative references or supplementary explanations. For instance, citing widely recognized textbooks or open-access journals can increase the accessibility of the cited information.

4.3. IMPACT OF TITLE AND KEYWORDS ON CITATIONS

The title and keywords of a research paper are critical components that influence its visibility, accessibility, and, ultimately, its citation count. Understanding the impact of these elements is essential for optimizing the reach and influence of their research work. A well-crafted title and strategically chosen keywords can significantly enhance the discoverability of a paper in academic databases, search engines, and other research platforms.

4.3.1. THE ROLE OF THE TITLE IN CITATIONS

1. **First Impression and Relevance**: The title of a research paper is the first element that readers and researchers encounter. It provides a snapshot of the study's content, scope, and focus. A clear, concise, and descriptive title helps potential readers quickly determine the paper's relevance to their own research. Example: a title like "Optimization of Composite Materials for Automotive Applications" immediately signals the paper's focus on material optimization in the automotive industry, attracting researchers in this area.

2. **Search Engine Optimization (SEO)**: Titles play a crucial role in search engine optimization (SEO), which determines how easily a paper can be found in search results. A title that includes relevant keywords and accurately reflects the content of the paper is more likely to rank higher in search engine results.Example: Title "Finite Element Analysis of Stress Distribution in Mechanical Joints" is more likely to be discovered by researchers looking for finite element analysis in mechanical engineering.

3. **Attracting a Broader Audience**: A well-chosen title can attract a broader audience beyond the immediate field of study. Too technical or jargon-laden[12] titles deter readers from other disciplines who could benefit from the research. Conversely, a title that is too general may not convey the specific focus of the study, reducing its appeal to specialized audiences. Striking a balance between specificity and accessibility is key to maximizing the paper's reach and, consequently, its citations.

4. **Influence on Citation Count**: Studies have shown that papers with well-crafted titles tend to receive more citations. According to a study by Jamali and Nikzad (2011), articles with concise, descriptive titles are more likely to be cited than those with lengthy titles[6]. This is because a clear title improves the visibility and perceived relevance of the paper, leading to more researchers reading and citing it.

4.3.2. THE ROLE OF KEYWORDS IN CITATIONS

1. **Enhancing Discoverability**: Keywords are vital for enhancing the discoverability of a research paper in academic databases, repositories, and search engines. They act as the primary search terms that researchers use to find relevant literature. Selecting appropriate keywords ensures that the paper appears in search results when other researchers query topics related to the study. For example, for a paper on "Topology Optimization of Aerospace Structures," keywords like "topology optimization," "aerospace engineering," and "structural analysis" would help target the right audience.

2. **Indexing in Academic Databases**: Keywords play a significant role in how a paper is indexed in academic databases such as Google Scholar, IEEE Xplore, and Scopus. These databases rely on keywords to categorize and tag papers, making them easier to retrieve during searches. The more accurate and representative the keywords, the more likely it is that the paper will be indexed under the correct categories, increasing its chances of being cited.

3. **Reflecting the Paper's Content**: Keywords should accurately reflect the content and focus of the paper. They should include key terms related to the study's methodology, scope, and findings. For instance, in a study on "Additive Manufacturing of Titanium Alloys," keywords such as "3D printing," "titanium alloys," "material properties," and "manufacturing processes" would effectively capture the essence of the research, guiding interested readers to the paper.

---

[12] *Jargon-laden: Words that are used by a certain profession or group and are difficult for others to understand.*

4. **Avoiding Overly Specific or Broad Keywords**: While it is essential for keywords to be specific, overly specific terms can limit the paper's visibility. Conversely, overly broad keywords may increase visibility but reduce the relevance of search results. For instance, using "mechanical engineering" as a keyword is broad, whereas "finite element analysis of hyperelastic materials" might be overly specific. A balanced approach ensures that the paper is neither lost in a sea of results nor excluded from relevant searches.

5. **Impact on Citation Metrics**: Research has indicated that papers with well-chosen keywords tend to have higher citation counts. A study by Li, Rollins, and Yan (2018) suggests that the strategic use of keywords directly correlates with higher visibility in searches, leading to more frequent citations[7]. As a result, keywords should be selected with careful consideration of their potential to enhance the paper's reach within the academic community.

4.4. KNOWLEDGE FLOW THROUGH CITATION

Citations are more than just references or acknowledgments; they are the lifeblood of academic discourse, enabling the flow of knowledge across disciplines, time, and geographical boundaries. Understanding the concept of knowledge flow through citation is crucial as it provides insight into how ideas evolve, how research is interconnected, and how individual contributions fit into the broader academic ecosystem.

1. **The Concept of Knowledge Flow:** Knowledge flow refers to the movement and exchange of information, ideas, and research findings within and across academic disciplines. Citations are pivotal in linking research works, allowing new ideas to build upon existing knowledge. This connection facilitates the development of new theories, technologies, and innovations. Knowledge flow through citation can be seen as a continuous dialogue between past, present, and future research[1].

2. **Role of Citations in Knowledge Flow:** Citations are crucial for the transmission of knowledge from previous work to new innovations. They create a network through which knowledge flows among researchers, papers, journals, and institutions. This network facilitates the development of new ideas by building on existing research.

3. **Collaboration and Citation Impact:** Research collaboration enhances the flow of knowledge. Co-authored publications tend to receive more citations than those authored by a single individual. This suggests a positive correlation between the number of authors and citation counts, indicating that collaboration can significantly impact the visibility and influence of research.

4. **Citation Networks:** Knowledge flow occurs not only between co-authors but also among different institutions, departments, and research fields. When a paper cites another, it creates a link in the citation network, allowing knowledge to traverse across various academic and research boundaries.

5. **Self-Citation and Co-Author Networks:** Within citation networks, self-citations and co-author citations play distinct roles. Self-citations refer to instances where authors cite their own previous work, while co-author citations involve citing work by collaborators. These practices contribute to the complexity and richness of the citation network.

6. **Interdisciplinary Nature of Research:** The interdisciplinary nature of modern research encourages collaboration, which in turn enhances the flow of knowledge. By working together, researchers from different fields can combine their expertise, leading to more comprehensive and innovative outcomes.

4.4.1. CITATION-BASED KNOWLEDGE FLOW NETWORK

The fig. 4.1 represents a "Citation-based Knowledge Flow Network," which visually represents how knowledge is shared and disseminated through citations in academic research.

Components of the Flowchart

1. **Institutions (Square Boxes)**: These represent academic or research institutions where the authors work. The diagram shows two institutions, Institution I_1 and Institution I_2.

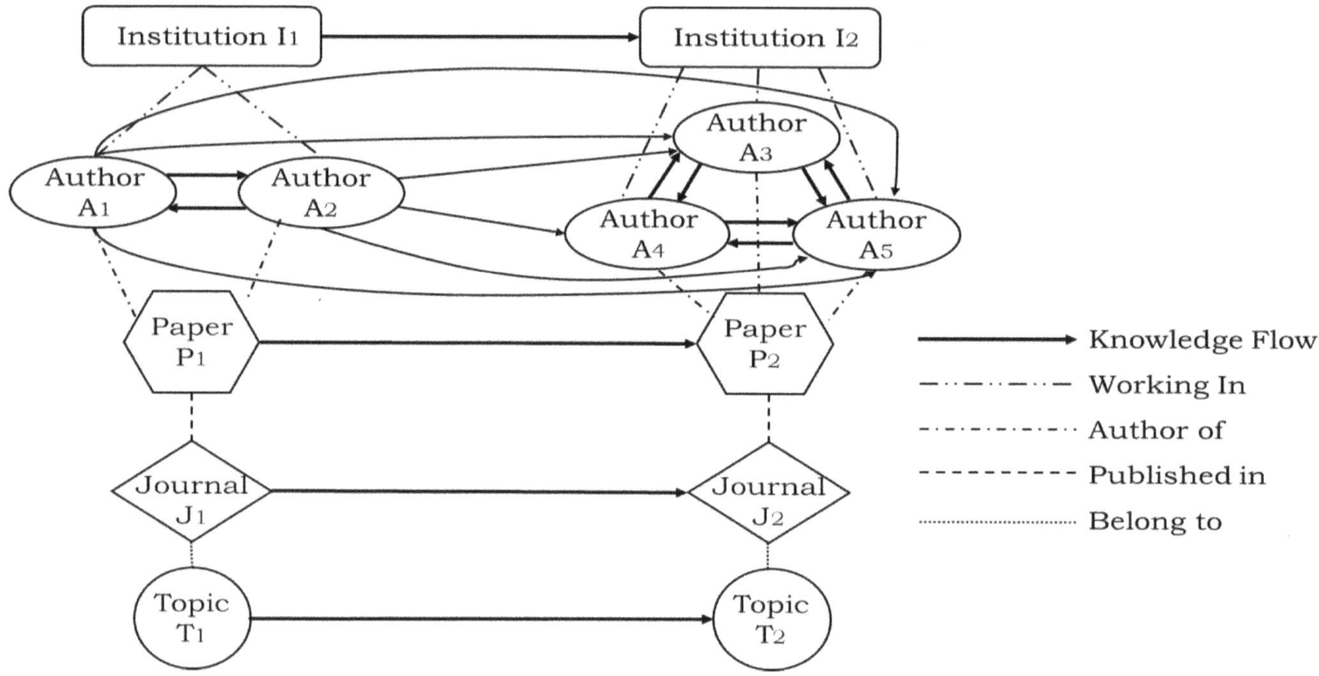

Fig. 4.1 Citation-based Knowledge Flow Network[8]

2. **Authors (Ellipses)**: The ellipses labeled Author A_1 to Author A_5 represent different researchers or authors who contribute to academic papers. Each author is associated with an institution, and they collaborate with each other to produce research papers.

3. **Papers (Hexagonal Boxes)**: Paper P_1 and Paper P_2 boxes represent academic papers or publications authored by the researchers. These papers are the medium through which knowledge is shared.

4. **Journals (Diamond Boxes)**: These represent academic journals where the papers are published. Journal J_1 and Journal J_2 are the platforms that distribute the research to a broader audience.

5. **Topics (Oval Shape)**: Topics T_1 and T_2 represent the specific research areas or fields that the papers address. Each paper belongs to a specific topic or field of study.

6. **Legend**: The legend on the right-hand side explains the different types of relationships or flows represented by the arrows in the diagram.

Explanation of the Arrows and Flows

1. **Knowledge Flow (Black Arrows)**: This represents the flow of knowledge between authors, papers, journals, and topics. For example, if Author 1's work is cited by Author 2, this creates a knowledge flow from Author A_1 to Author A_2.

2. **Work In**: These arrows show the relationship between authors and their respective institutions. For example, Author A_1 and Author A_2 work in Institution I_1, while Author A_3, A_4 and Author A_5 work in Institution I_2.

3. **Author Of**: These arrows indicate the relationship between authors and the papers they have authored. For instance, Author A_3, A_4 and Author A_5 have co-authored Paper P_1.

4. **Published In**: This shows the relationship between papers and the journals in which they are published. For example, Paper P_1 is published in Journal J_1.

5. **Belong To**: These arrows indicate the connection between journals and the specific topics they cover. For example, Journal J_2 publishes papers related to Topic T_2.

Understanding the Flow

➢ **Collaboration and Knowledge Sharing**: The flowchart illustrates how authors from different institutions collaborate to produce research papers. These papers are then published in journals, contributing to specific research topics.

- ➢ **Citation and Knowledge Dissemination**: Knowledge is disseminated when one paper cites another, creating a citation-based link between authors and their work. This process facilitates the spread of ideas and innovations across different research communities.
- ➢ **Interdisciplinary Connections**: The flowchart also highlights how knowledge can flow between different institutions and topics, reflecting the interdisciplinary nature of modern research.

4.4.2. UNDERSTANDING CO-AUTHORSHIP AND CITATIONS

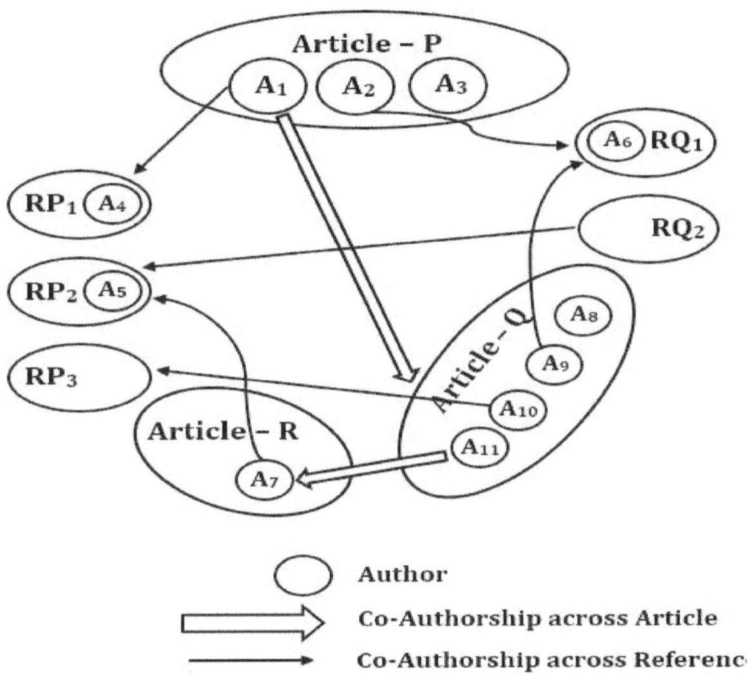

Fig. 4.2 Co-authorship network[1]

Introduction to Co-Authorship and Citations:
- ➢ **Co-Authorship:** This means when two or more people work together to write a paper or article. For example, if you and your friend write a story together, you are co-authors.
- ➢ **Citations:** When one article mentions or refers to another article, it is called a citation. It's like saying, "I got this information from this other book or paper."

Understanding the Example with Articles and Authors:
- ➢ **Articles and Authors:** We have three articles named P, Q, and R. Article P is written by authors A_1, A_2, and A_3. Article Q is written by authors A_8, A_9, A_{10}, A_{11}, and also A_1. Article R is written by authors A_7 and A_{11}.
- ➢ **References:** These are like the sources or other articles that the main articles (P and Q) mention. Article P has references RP_1, RP_2, and RP_3. Article Y has references RQ_1 and RQ_2.

Who Wrote the References?
- ➢ Reference RP_1: Written by authors A_1 and A_4.
- ➢ Reference RP_2: Written by authors A_5 and A_7.
- ➢ Reference RP_3: Written by author A_{10}.
- ➢ Reference RQ_1: Written by authors A_2, A_6 and A_9.
- ➢ Reference RQ_2: Written by author R.

Types of Citations Explained:
- ➢ **Self-Citation:** This happens when an author cites their own previous work. **Example:** references RP_1 and RQ_1 are self-citations. This means the authors of the main articles are citing their own past work.

> **Level-1 Co-Author Citation:** This is when an author cites a paper written by someone they have directly worked with. For example, reference RP_3 is a level-1 co-author citation because the author of article Q (who is a direct collaborator of author A_1) is involved.

> **Level-1 Co-Author Network:** This is a bit more complex. It means citing a paper written by someone who has worked with someone you have worked with. Reference RP_2 is an example of this because author A_1 has worked with A_{11}, who has worked with A_7.

Conclusion on Citation Patterns:

> **Collaborator Citations:** The text concludes that if authors often cite their collaborators, they are also likely to cite the collaborators of their collaborators. This means if you work with someone, you might cite their work, and also the work of people they have worked with.

> **Impact on Citation Counts:** Collaborations can increase the number of times a paper is cited. This is because when people work together, they are more likely to refer to each other's work.

4.5. CITING DATASETS

In the current landscape of academic research, datasets have become crucial resources, often holding as much value as traditional scholarly articles and books. Properly citing datasets is essential to give credit to the creators and ensure transparency, reproducibility, and research integrity.

The Role of Data in Engineering Research

> **Data is Essential:** In engineering research, data is very important. Researchers use data to support their ideas and show proof of their experiments. This means that data is like evidence in a court case; it helps prove what the researchers say is true.

> **Data Citations:** Just like when you write a paper and mention other people's work, you need to give credit to the people who created the data you use. This is called a data citation. It's like saying, "I got this information from this person."

Giving Credit and Legal Rights

> **Proper Credit:** When you cite data, you must give proper credit to the person or team who made the data. This is important because it acknowledges their hard work and contribution, just like how you would credit an author of a book or article.

> **Legal Attribution:** Legal attribution means recognizing the legal rights of the data creators. This is important because it respects the ownership and intellectual property of the data.

Challenges with Data Ownership

> **Complicated Ownership:** Figuring out who owns the data is tricky, especially with big datasets. Imagine a big puzzle where many people have added pieces; it is hard to say who owns the whole puzzle.

> **Funding Issues:** Sometimes, the money used to create the data can complicate ownership. If a company or government paid for the data, they might have a say in who can use it.

Permissions and Access

> **Getting Permission:** Before using someone else's data, a researcher should ask for permission. This is like asking to borrow a book from a library; you need to make sure it's okay to use it.

> **Finding Data Again:** When you cite data, you should include enough details so that someone else can find the same data later. This is important because links can break or change.

Including Detailed Information

> **General and Specific Information:** A good data citation includes both general and specific details. General information might be the name of the dataset, while specific information could be the version or date it was created. This helps others be sure they have found the exact data you used.

> **Example:** Imagine you are citing a dataset about weather patterns. You would include the name of the dataset, the organization that collected it, the date it was published, and maybe even a unique identifier like a DOI (Digital Object Identifier).

Conclusion

- ➢ **Importance of Data Citations:** Data citations are crucial in research because they ensure that data creators get the recognition they deserve. They also help maintain the integrity of research by allowing others to verify and build upon existing work.
- ➢ **Ensuring Accessibility:** By providing detailed citations, researchers ensure that data remains accessible and usable for future studies, even if the original source changes, like leaving a map for others to follow.

4.6. STYLES FOR CITATIONS

Citations are essential to academic writing, ensuring that credit is given to the original sources of ideas, theories, and data. Citation styles provide a structured format for referencing sources in academic work. These styles ensure consistency, clarity, and transparency in scholarly communication.

1. APA (American Psychological Association) Style

The APA style is widely used in the social sciences but is also commonly adopted in engineering research. APA focuses on clarity and conciseness, making it ideal for technical writing. The key elements of APA style include the author-date citation method, in which in-text citations consist of the author's last name and the publication year, with full details in the reference list at the end.

Example (In-text citation):
- ➢ "The aerodynamic efficiency of the design was optimized **(Smith, 2020)**."

Example (Reference List):
- ➢ Smith, J. (2020). Advanced Computational Fluid Dynamics. Springer.

APA style is often used when writing reports, proposals, and academic papers, mainly when focusing on recent developments or experiments.

2. MLA (Modern Language Association) Style

MLA is typically used in the humanities but can be applied in interdisciplinary research that intersects with engineering. MLA style uses parenthetical citations within the text, including the author's last name and page number, which directs the reader to the full citation in the works cited section. It emphasizes the authorship of ideas, often used when analyzing technical documents.

Example (In-text citation):
- ➢ "The tensile strength of aluminum alloys can be significantly increased (Johnson 45)."

Example (Works Cited):
- ➢ Johnson, Mark. Material Science in Engineering. Oxford University Press, 2018.

While less common in purely technical fields, MLA helps cite sources in research involving historical analysis or theoretical reviews.

3. Chicago Style

Chicago style is versatile and used across various disciplines, including engineering. It offers two systems: the **notes and bibliography** system and the **author-date** system. The **notes and bibliography** system use footnotes or endnotes to cite sources, while the **author-date** system is more similar to APA style.

Example (Notes and Bibliography System):
- ➢ Footnote: [1]John R. Anderson, Introduction to Robotics (Cambridge University Press, 2019), 57.
- ➢ Bibliography: Anderson, John R. Introduction to Robotics. Cambridge University Press, 2019.

Example (Author-Date System):
- ➢ "Robotic arms have evolved significantly in manufacturing processes (Anderson 2019, 57)."

The **Chicago style** is often preferred for its flexibility, making it useful in technical writing that requires detailed explanations and in fields where interdisciplinary research is conducted.

4. IEEE (Institute of Electrical and Electronics Engineers) Style

The IEEE style is widely used in technical fields, especially in engineering and computer science. It employs a numerical citation system, with in-text citations corresponding to numbered entries in the reference list.

This style is efficient for long, complex texts with multiple sources, as it simplifies in-text citation.

Example (In-text citation):

➢ "Signal processing techniques are essential for modern communication systems [3]."

Example (Reference List):

➢ [3] S. M. Kay, Fundamentals of Statistical Signal Processing, Prentice-Hall, 1998.

The IEEE format is widely adopted in engineering journals and conference papers, making it a crucial citation style for students in the field.

5. Harvard Style

The Harvard citation style is another author-date system, similar to APA but with more flexible rules. It is common in technical and scientific writing. Harvard style requires in-text citations with the author's last name and the publication year, accompanied by a detailed reference list.

Example (In-text citation):

➢ "Control systems are essential in automation (Miller, 2015)."

Example (Reference List):

➢ Miller, A., 2015. Control Systems Engineering. Wiley.

Harvard style is straightforward and allows for quick referencing, making it suitable for technical reports and academic research.

6. Vancouver Style

Primarily used in medical and biological sciences, the Vancouver style is also applicable in certain engineering contexts, especially when referencing experimental data and studies. Like IEEE, Vancouver uses a numerical system, with references listed in the order of appearance.

Example (In-text citation):

➢ "The new material exhibited improved thermal conductivity [4]."

Example (Reference List):

➢ [4] Brown, P. et al. Thermal Properties of Composite Materials. Journal of Materials Science, 2020.

The Vancouver style is efficient for research with heavy reliance on experimental data and empirical studies, aligning well with engineering research methodologies.

Importance of Consistency in Citation

One of the key elements of citation styles is **consistency**. Once a citation style is chosen, it must be followed consistently throughout the paper or report. Inconsistencies in citation can confuse readers and weaken the credibility of the work.

Selection of Citation Style

The choice of citation style often depends on:

➢ **The discipline**: IEEE is preferred in technical fields, APA in social sciences, and MLA in humanities.

➢ **Journal or institutional requirements**: Many journals and universities specify the citation style to be used in research papers.

➢ **Type of source**: Different styles have specific rules for citing books, journal articles, websites, patents, and technical reports.

4.7. ACKNOWLEDGMENTS AND ATTRIBUTIONS

1. What Are Acknowledgments?

➢ **Definition**: Acknowledgments are a way to say "thank you" to people or organizations that helped with a research project. This could be anyone who contributed in some way, like providing money, equipment, or advice.

➢ **Placement**: If there are no specific rules about where to put acknowledgments in a paper, they can be added at the end of the text or as a footnote. A footnote is a small note at the bottom of a page.

➢ **Purpose**: The main goal of acknowledgments is to show appreciation and recognize the help received. It highlights the connections between the researcher and others who supported the work.

2. **Who Gets Acknowledged?**
   ➢ **Non-Authors:** Sometimes, people help with research but don't qualify to be listed as authors. For example, someone might give advice or lend equipment. These contributions should still be acknowledged as a sign of gratitude.
   ➢ **Categories of Support:** Acknowledgments can be divided into different types, such as:
      ❖ **Moral Support:** Encouragement or motivation.
      ❖ **Financial Support:** Money or funding.
      ❖ **Editorial Support:** Help with writing or editing.
      ❖ **Institutional Support:** Resources or facilities from an organization.
      ❖ **Technical Support:** Assistance with technical aspects or equipment.
      ❖ **Conceptual Support:** Ideas or intellectual input.

3. **Importance of Acknowledgments and Attributions**
   ➢ **Credit Where It's Due**: It's important to give credit to everyone who contributed, even if their role was small. This shows respect for their work and contributions.
   ➢ **Proprietary Interest**: Researchers should recognize the ownership or rights of others. For example, if someone invented a tool used in the research, they should be acknowledged.
   ➢ **Naming Contributors**: Whenever possible, the names of people who contributed should be mentioned. This includes those responsible for designs, inventions, or writings.

4. **Authorship and Acknowledgments**
   ➢ **Authorship Importance**: Being listed as an author is a big deal because it shows who was responsible for the main parts of the research. Acknowledgments are for those who helped but aren't authors.
   ➢ **Reward Triangle Theory**: This theory explains the relationship between citations (when other researchers mention your work), acknowledgments, and authorship. It shows how these elements are interconnected in recognizing contributions.

5. **Specifics in Engineering Research**
   ➢ **Who to Acknowledge**: In engineering, acknowledgments often include technicians, students, funding agencies, grant numbers, institutions, or anyone who provided scientific input, shared unpublished results, provided equipment, or participated in discussions.
   ➢ **Examples**: If a student helped with data collection, they should be acknowledged. If a company provided a special machine for experiments, they should be mentioned too. By understanding these points, researchers can properly acknowledge all the help they received, ensuring everyone gets the credit they deserve. This practice not only shows gratitude but also maintains integrity and transparency in research.

6. **Understanding Attributions:**

Attributions, on the other hand, are specific references made to the original sources of ideas, data, or text that are incorporated into a researcher's work. This practice is fundamental to academic integrity, as it ensures that credit is given to the rightful creators of the content used. Attribution is typically achieved through citations, which allow readers to trace the origin of the information and verify its authenticity.

Attributions are essential for several reasons:
   ➢ **Avoiding Plagiarism:** Proper attribution prevents the researcher from unintentionally presenting someone else's work as their own.
   ➢ **Enhancing Credibility:** Attributing sources accurately adds to the credibility of the research, as it demonstrates a thorough engagement with existing literature.
   ➢ **Facilitating Further Research:** Accurate citations allow others to follow the research trail, enabling them to explore the sources for further study or verification.

4.8. WHAT SHOULD BE ACKNOWLEDGED

1. **Quotations and Ideas:** Authors should acknowledge any quotations, ideas, or facts that are not their own. This includes paraphrasing and any intellectual contributions from others.
2. **Personal and Emotional Support:** While not always mandatory, many researchers choose to acknowledge family, friends, and colleagues who provided moral or emotional support during the research. This recognition emphasizes the personal challenges often associated with long-term research projects.
3. **Intellectual Contributions:** Acknowledgments should include individuals who have contributed to the research but may not meet the criteria for authorship. This includes those who have provided significant advice, critical feedback, or mentorship. **Example:** a senior researcher who provided insight into the methodology but did not actively participate in the research process should be acknowledged.
4. **Funding and Grants:** If the research received financial support from a funding agency, it is crucial to acknowledge this support. Authors should provide full details of the funding program and grant number in the acknowledgment section.
5. **Contributors and Collaborators:** Acknowledge individuals who contributed scientifically or technically, such as assistants, students, or technicians who helped experimentally or theoretically during the research.
6. **Institutional and Organizational Support:** Institutions and organizations that have provided resources, such as access to libraries, laboratories, or research facilities, should be acknowledged. This also includes any administrative support that facilitated the research process.
7. **Presentation of Results:** If the results have been presented elsewhere, such as in a journal abstract or at a scientific meeting, this should be cited appropriately, including details like the name of the gathering and the year.
8. **Integrity and Professional Impact:** Acknowledging contributions demonstrates integrity and can bolster colleagues' careers, as being credited in an acknowledgment section is increasingly recognized as a measure of professional impact.
9. **Avoiding Reviewer Acknowledgment:** Many technical journals discourage thanking reviewers in submissions to avoid perceptions of favoritism or attempts to influence the review process.
10. **Common Knowledge and Attribution:** Proper attribution is required for ideas, algorithms, or methodologies unless the information is considered common knowledge, even in double-blind review settings.

Acknowledging these elements not only fulfills ethical obligations but also fosters a collaborative research environment by recognizing the contributions of others.

4.9. ACKNOWLEDGMENTS IN BOOKS AND DISSERTATIONS

Acknowledgments in books and dissertations provide authors an opportunity to express their gratitude to individuals and institutions that have supported their research or writing process. This section typically appears at the beginning of the work. The purpose of acknowledgments is to recognize those whose contributions were pivotal to the project's success, including academic mentors, funding agencies, family members, and colleagues.

1. **Purpose of Acknowledgments:**
    - **Expressing Gratitude:** The main purpose of the acknowledgments section is to say **"thank you"** to everyone who helped you with your research. This is more detailed than the short thank-you notes you might see in journal articles or conference papers.
    - **Detailed Thanks:** Unlike short acknowledgments in articles, this section in a thesis is longer. It allows the researcher to thank many people who contributed to the research work.
2. **Who to Thank or Key Components of Acknowledgments:**
    i.   **Main Supervisor:** This is the person who guided you the most during your research. They are usually thanked first because of their significant role.

Example: *"I wish to express my sincere appreciation to my supervisor Prof. BKK for the useful comments, remarks, and encouragement throughout this thesis work."*

ii.   **Second Supervisor:** If you had another supervisor, they are also important to mention. They might have provided additional guidance or support.

Example: *"Furthermore, I wish to express my thanks to Prof. SDI for introducing me to the topic and for the support along the way."*

iii.   **Peers in the Lab:** These are your fellow researchers or students who worked with you. They might have helped with experiments or shared ideas.

Example: *"Also, I like to thank my peers in the Adaptive Control Lab such as Mr. SJA and Mr. PM, who have shared their precious time during many lively technical discussions."*

iv.   **Academic Staff:** Other teachers or professors in your department who might have helped in work.

v.   **Technical or Support Staff:** These are people who help with equipment or administrative tasks. They make sure everything runs smoothly.

vi.   **Colleagues from Other Departments or Institutions:** Sometimes, people from other places might have helped with your research. It's good to acknowledge their support.

vii.   **Former Students:** If past students helped you, maybe by sharing their experiences or notes.

viii.   **Family and Friends:** These are the people who supported you emotionally or in other ways during your research journey.

Example: *"I would like to thank my family members who have supported me throughout this journey in many different ways."*

3. **How to Write Acknowledgments:**

➢ **Order of Thanks:** Think carefully about who to thank first. Usually, the most important contributors are mentioned first.

➢ **Concise and Clear:** Keep you thank-you notes short and to the point. Avoid using too much emotional language. It's more about being professional and respectful.

4. **Why Acknowledgments Matter:**

➢ **Showing Appreciation:** Acknowledgments show that you appreciate the help and support you received. It's a way to recognize the contributions of others.

➢ **Building Relationships:** By thanking people, you maintain good relationships with them. This can be important for future collaborations or support.

➢ **Professional Courtesy:** It's a professional way to acknowledge the teamwork and support that goes into completing a research project.

The acknowledgments section is a crucial part of a thesis or dissertation. It allows you to express gratitude to everyone who helped you along the way, from supervisors to family members.

4.10. DEDICATION OR ACKNOWLEDGMENTS

While acknowledgments are a standard feature in academic dissertations and books, the concept of **dedication** adds a more personal layer to the work, often reflecting emotional or moral support from specific individuals. Unlike acknowledgments, which focus on academic, technical, and financial contributions, dedications are more symbolic and may recognize individuals who inspired or motivated the author, often without having a direct impact on the research or writing process.

4.10.1. Difference Between Dedication and Acknowledgments:

1. **Purpose:**

➢ **Acknowledgments** are meant to recognize people or organizations that have directly contributed to the research or project, whether academically, technically, or financially.

> **Dedications** are personal tributes to someone important in the author's life, often reflecting gratitude for emotional support, inspiration, or personal significance. For example, an author may dedicate their book to a parent, spouse, or teacher as a form of personal respect or gratitude.

2. **Placement:**
   > **Dedications** usually appear before the acknowledgments, often on a separate page, and consist of a single sentence or paragraph.
   > **Acknowledgments** can be lengthier, covering several paragraphs or even pages, depending on the extent of contributions.

3. **Tone:**
   > **Dedications** are typically shorter and may include personal or emotive language. example: This book is dedicated to my parents; whose unwavering support made this journey possible."
   > **Acknowledgments**, in contrast, are more formal, acknowledging concrete contributions and often using more specific language regarding professional support.

4. **Examples:**

Dedication
   > "To my wife, for her love and patience."
   > "In memory of Professor XYZ, whose teachings inspired this work."

Acknowledgments:
   > An author might write, "I would like to thank my spouse for their unwavering support and patience during the stressful times of writing this book." This shows appreciation for the spouse's support.

5. **Usage in Academic Contexts:**
   > Dedications are more common in books. They may also appear in personal dissertations but are less frequent in strictly academic publications such as journal articles.
   > For students, including a dedication in a dissertation is optional and is usually seen as a personal touch rather than an academic necessity. However, the acknowledgment section is generally required to ensure proper recognition of contributions.

6. **Combining Dedications and Acknowledgments:**
   > **Can You Use Both?**
   Yes, an author can both dedicate their work to someone and also mention them in the acknowledgments. **Example:** An author might dedicate their book to their spouse and also thank them in the acknowledgments for their support and patience.
   > **Example of Using Both:**
   An author might write, "Dedicated to my spouse, ABC, for being my rock," and in the acknowledgments, they might add, "Thank you, ABC, for your endless support and understanding."

Questions

1. Define the term Citation. Describe the three functions of Citation.

2. Explain how knowledge flows through a citation network using a flow diagram.

3. Illustrate using a flowchart, how collaboration in a Co-authorship network can improve the flow of knowledge in the research.

4. Explain the most common styles for citation used by engineers during research, and provide an example.

5. What types of citations fail to achieve their goal and do not benefit the reader? Explain.

6. What is impact of Title and Keywords on Citations? Explain Citation based knowledge flow.

7. Identify acknowledgement and attributions in research process and briefly explain.

"Intellectual property has the shelf life of a banana."

: Bill Gates

Module - 3

Chapter 5:
INTRODUCTION TO INTELLECTUAL PROPERTY

INTRODUCTION

Intellectual Property (IP) plays a crucial role in shaping the economic and cultural development of society by protecting the innovations and creations of individuals and organizations. It serves as a key global indicator of innovation, influencing various industries and economies worldwide. The concept of IP has a long history, and its governance has evolved to support creators and businesses. In India, IP laws have seen significant amendments, reflecting the country's growing emphasis on innovation and legal protection. This chapter explores the origin of IP, its governance, and its impact on global and national development.

5.1. INTRODUCTION TO INTELLECTUAL PROPERTY (IP)

Intellectual Property (IP) refers to the legal rights that arise from intellectual activity in the industrial, scientific, literary, and artistic fields. It encompasses the ownership of creations of the mind, such as inventions, designs, brands, artistic works, and technologies. The fundamental aim of IP laws is to protect and promote innovation, thereby fostering economic growth and cultural development. In the modern knowledge-based economy, IP is a critical asset for individuals, businesses, and nations.

Definition of Intellectual Property: The World Intellectual Property Organization (WIPO) defines IP as *"creations of the mind, such as inventions, literary and artistic works, designs, symbols, names, and images used in commerce"*[9]. It grants exclusive rights to creators and inventors over the use of their innovations for a limited time, encouraging innovation while balancing the interests of creators and the public.

The concept of IP revolves around the protection of the intangible creations of the human intellect. The purpose of IP laws is to encourage innovation and creativity by granting exclusive rights to creators or inventors to exploit their works or inventions for a certain period, after which they enter the public domain.

The scope of IP covers a range of categories, including:

1. **Patents:** Protect inventions and technological advancements.
2. **Copyrights:** Protect literary, artistic, and musical works.
3. **Trademarks:** Protect symbols, names, and slogans used to distinguish goods or services.
4. **Industrial Designs:** Protect the aesthetic appearance of objects.
5. **Geographical Indications:** Indicate the origin of products based on geographic locations that confer certain quality or characteristics.
6. **Trade Secrets:** Protect confidential business information.

5.2. ROLE OF IP IN THE ECONOMIC AND CULTURAL DEVELOPMENT OF THE SOCIETY

5.2.1. ECONOMIC DEVELOPMENT THROUGH IP

Intellectual Property rights play a pivotal role in enhancing economic growth by enabling innovators and creators to capitalize on their inventions. Here are some key ways in which IP contributes to economic development:

1. **Encouragement of Innovation and Investment:** IP provides a legal framework that protects inventors' and creators' rights, encouraging further research and innovation. With secure IP rights, businesses are more likely to invest in research and development (R&D), knowing that they can reap the financial benefits of their innovations. For example, pharmaceutical companies heavily rely on patents to protect their new drugs, ensuring a return on the large investments they make in R&D[10].

2. **Economic Competitiveness:** Nations that have strong IP systems tend to be more competitive in the global market. The ability to protect innovations leads to an increase in high-tech industries, boosting economic productivity and exports. For instance, countries like the United States and Japan, known for robust IP regimes, lead in sectors such as technology, pharmaceuticals, and manufacturing.

3. **Job Creation:** IP-intensive industries contribute significantly to job creation. According to a World Intellectual Property Organization (WIPO) report, industries that heavily rely on IP rights create millions of jobs globally, offering skilled employment opportunities in areas like technology, entertainment, and pharmaceuticals[9].

4. **Small and Medium Enterprises (SMEs) Growth:** IP is essential for SMEs as it helps them grow and compete with larger enterprises. By securing patents, trademarks, or copyrights, SMEs can differentiate themselves from competitors and create unique market positions. In India, for example, startups in sectors like biotechnology and IT have benefited from patent protections, enabling them to attract investment and scale their businesses[11].

5. **Increased Productivity and Technology Transfer:** Academic-industry collaborations, facilitated by IP protections, have led to increased productivity. Industry-supported university research has produced four times more patents per dollar than industry research alone, accelerating the transfer of technology from laboratories to useful products.

6. **Protection of Financial Interests and Risk Justification:** IP laws protect the financial interests of businesses, encouraging them to invest in R&D. Businesses view R&D funding as a risk that can be justified only if there is an expectation of a reasonable return on investment. IP laws enable businesses to control the products of their R&D investments.

7. **Balancing Private Gains and Public Benefits:** Patent and copyright protections strike a balance between private gains and public benefits. They give researchers, nonprofit organizations, and companies the right to profit from new ideas while requiring them to make these ideas public[10].

8. **Facilitation of International Cooperation**: International IP treaties, such as the Paris Convention and the Agreement on Trade-Related Aspects of IP Rights (TRIPS), facilitate international cooperation by ensuring that nations honor each other's IP laws. This cooperation helps prevent the importation of pirated software and unauthorized generic drugs, promoting global economic stability.

5.2.2. CULTURAL DEVELOPMENT THROUGH IP

Beyond its economic benefits, IP also plays a crucial role in promoting cultural growth and preserving heritage. By recognizing and protecting creative works, IP supports the creation of a vibrant cultural environment.

1. **Promotion of Cultural Expression:** IP protects the rights of creators, such as writers, artists, and musicians, allowing them to be fairly compensated for their work. This creates an environment that encourages the production of cultural goods, enriching society's cultural landscape. Copyright laws, for example, protect the works of authors and artists, thereby promoting a continuous flow of literature, music, films, and other cultural artifacts.

2. **Preservation of Traditional Knowledge and Cultural Heritage:** IP also helps safeguard traditional knowledge (TK) and cultural expressions from unauthorized use. Many indigenous communities rely on collective IP systems to protect their traditional crafts, medicines, and agricultural practices. India's Traditional Knowledge Digital Library (TKDL) is a prime example, where ancient knowledge about medicinal plants and practices is documented and protected from being patented by others[12].

3. **Boost to Creative Industries:** Creative industries, such as film, music, and fashion, heavily rely on copyright and design rights to protect their creations. In countries like India, Bollywood and the music industry have seen significant growth due to copyright protections that allow artists and producers to earn from their creations. Similarly, the global fashion industry thrives due to the protection of unique designs through design rights.

4. **Cultural Diversity:** IP facilitates cultural exchange by ensuring that creators from different regions and backgrounds are recognized and rewarded for their contributions. This helps promote cultural diversity and the sharing of different artistic and intellectual traditions across the globe. For instance, geographical indications (GIs) protect the unique cultural products of specific regions, such as Darjeeling tea and Kancheepuram silk in India, ensuring that these products retain their cultural and economic value[13].

5.2.3. BALANCING IP AND PUBLIC INTEREST

While IP plays a crucial role in promoting economic and cultural development, it is essential to balance the protection of IP rights with the broader public interest. Excessive protection of IP may lead to monopolies, limiting access to essential goods like medicines and technology. Therefore, international frameworks like the Trade-Related Aspects of Intellectual Property Rights (TRIPS) agreement allow for flexibilities, such as compulsory licensing, to ensure that essential goods remain accessible while still protecting IP[10].

5.3. IP GOVERNANCE

Intellectual Property (IP) Governance refers to the frameworks, policies, and institutions that regulate the creation, protection, and enforcement of intellectual property rights (IPR). It encompasses both national and international mechanisms to ensure that IP rights are managed to fosters innovation, economic growth, and social welfare while balancing the rights of creators with the public interest. IP governance is essential for promoting creativity, protecting cultural heritage, ensuring economic development, and encouraging fair competition.

5.3.1. COMPONENTS OF IP GOVERNANCE

IP governance involves a variety of key components that work together to create a coherent and functional IP system. These components include legal frameworks, regulatory bodies, international treaties, enforcement mechanisms, and policy development processes.

1. **Legal Frameworks:** IP governance is underpinned by legal frameworks that define the scope and nature of IPR. National laws such as patents, copyrights, trademarks, and industrial designs outline the rights granted to creators and innovators. These laws define the duration of protection, the requirements for obtaining rights, and the exceptions and limitations to those rights. For example, in India, the Patent Act of 1970 governs patent protection, while the Copyright Act of 1957 regulates copyrights. These laws are regularly updated to align with international standards and technological advancements.

2. **Regulatory Bodies and Institutions:** IP governance involves various regulatory bodies and institutions responsible for administering and enforcing IPR. In India, these institutions include the Controller General of Patents, Designs, and Trademarks (CGPDTM) and the Copyright Office. These bodies are tasked with examining applications, granting rights, and resolving disputes related to IP. Internationally, the World Intellectual Property Organization (WIPO) plays a central role in coordinating IP governance by providing a platform for international cooperation on IP issues and administering global IP treaties.

3. **International Treaties and Agreements:** IP governance operates not only at the national level but also at the international level through treaties and agreements that harmonize IP laws across countries. The most significant of these treaties is the Agreement on Trade-Related Aspects of Intellectual Property Rights (TRIPS), administered by the World Trade Organization (WTO). TRIPS set minimum standards for IP protection and enforcement that all WTO member countries must comply with. Other important treaties include the Paris Convention for the Protection of Industrial Property (1883), the Berne Convention for the Protection of Literary and Artistic Works (1886), and the Patent Cooperation Treaty (PCT) of 1970.

4. **IP Enforcement Mechanisms:** Enforcement is a critical aspect of IP governance, as it ensures that IP rights are respected and protected. Effective enforcement mechanisms help prevent the infringement of IP rights and provide remedies for rights holders. Enforcement involves both civil and criminal actions, as well as administrative measures such as border control to prevent the import and export of counterfeit goods. In India, specialized IP courts and tribunals have been established to handle IP-related cases, ensuring that disputes are resolved efficiently.

5. **Policy Development and IP Governance**: Governments and international organizations play an essential role in developing policies that shape IP governance. These policies aim to strike a balance between protecting IP rights and promoting public interest. For example, policies that promote access to affordable medicines while maintaining patent protection for pharmaceutical innovations are critical for public health. India's compulsory licensing provisions under the Patent Act allow the government to issue licenses for essential drugs when public health is at stake.

5.3.2. CHALLENGES IN IP GOVERNANCE

Despite the benefits of a well-structured IP governance system, several challenges arise in its implementation, particularly in balancing the interests of rights holders with those of the public.

1. **Access to Knowledge and Public Goods** One of the key challenges in IP governance is ensuring that IP laws do not restrict access to essential knowledge and public goods, such as medicines, educational resources, and technology. Overly stringent IP laws can create monopolies that limit access to these resources, particularly in developing countries. For instance, the high cost of patented drugs has raised concerns about the affordability of healthcare in many countries. To address this, international frameworks like TRIPS include provisions for compulsory licensing, which allows governments to authorize the use of a patented invention without the patent holder's consent under certain conditions.

2. **Technological Advancements and IP Governance** Rapid advancements in technology present challenges for IP governance, as traditional IP systems may struggle to keep pace with new forms of innovation. For example, digital technologies have revolutionized the way creative works are produced, distributed, and consumed, leading to new issues related to copyright protection. Similarly, emerging technologies such as artificial intelligence (AI) and biotechnology raise questions about how to grant and enforce IP rights for inventions that involve non-human creators.

3. **Piracy and Counterfeiting** The rise of digital piracy and counterfeiting of physical goods poses a significant challenge to IP governance. Counterfeit products not only harm legitimate businesses but also pose risks to consumers, particularly in the case of fake medicines and safety-critical products. Governments around the world have implemented measures to combat piracy and counterfeiting, including international cooperation and the use of technology such as blockchain for supply chain transparency.

4. **Equitable Access and Fair Use** Balancing IP protection with the need for equitable access to information is a crucial aspect of IP governance. This challenge is often addressed through exceptions and limitations to IP rights, such as the concept of fair use in copyright law. Fair use allows individuals to use copyrighted material without permission for purposes such as research, education, and commentary. However, determining what constitutes fair use can be complex, leading to ongoing debates in the legal and academic communities.

IP governance is a complex and dynamic system that involves a range of legal, institutional, and policy frameworks designed to protect intellectual property rights while promoting innovation, economic growth, and social welfare. As the global economy evolves and new technologies emerge, IP governance must adapt to ensure that it continues to serve the interests of both creators and the public. By striking a balance between protection and access, effective IP governance can contribute to sustainable development and the well-being of societies worldwide.

5.4. IP AS A GLOBAL INDICATOR OF INNOVATION

Intellectual Property (IP) has become a key global indicator of a country's innovation capacity and technological advancement. The protection of intellectual assets, such as patents, trademarks, copyrights, and industrial designs, reflects the level of innovation in various sectors of the economy, such as science, technology, engineering, and culture. By examining IP metrics, such as the number of patents filed, IP-intensive industries, and the contribution of IP to economic growth, policymakers and researchers can assess a nation's competitiveness in the global innovation landscape.

5.4.1. IP AND INNOVATION: THE LINKAGE

The relationship between IP and innovation is well-established in economic theory and practice. IP rights incentivize innovation by granting inventors and creators exclusive rights to their creations, which allows them to monetize their innovations and recover the investments made in research and development (R&D). This, in turn, fosters further innovation, as individuals and companies are motivated to engage in creative and technological advancements.

1. **Patents as a Measure of Technological Innovation:** Patents are one of the most widely used indicators of innovation at the global level. A patent is granted to an inventor for a novel, useful, and non-obvious invention, giving them exclusive rights to their innovation for a limited period. The number of patent applications filed and granted is often used as a proxy for a country's innovation capacity. Countries that file large numbers of patents, such as the United States, Japan, and South Korea, are considered global leaders in technological innovation.

   Example: The World Intellectual Property Organization (WIPO) reported that in 2022, China led the world in patent filings, with over 1.5 million patent applications, followed by the United States and Japan. The rise in Chinese patent filings reflects the country's significant investment in R&D and its emergence as a global innovation hub in areas like telecommunications, AI, and renewable energy[14].

2. **Trademarks and Brand Innovation** Trademarks, which protect brand names, logos, and symbols, serve as an indicator of innovation in business and marketing. Trademarks allow companies to differentiate their products and services in the marketplace, fostering competition and encouraging firms to innovate in their branding strategies. The registration of trademarks is often correlated with a country's business innovation environment, with higher trademark filings indicating a more vibrant entrepreneurial ecosystem.

   Example: The United States and the European Union are known for having high rates of trademark registrations, which reflect their strong market innovation and the development of new consumer products. India has also seen a rise in trademark applications in recent years, indicating growth in its entrepreneurial sector, particularly in areas such as e-commerce and consumer goods.

3. **Copyright and Creative Innovation** Copyright is another form of IP protection that serves as a measure of innovation in the creative industries. Copyright protects the rights of creators in literary, artistic, and musical works, encouraging further creative output. The number of copyright applications and the performance of copyright-intensive industries, such as film, music, and publishing, can serve as indicators of cultural innovation.

   Example: In countries like the United States, the entertainment industry is a major contributor to the economy, supported by strong copyright protections. India's film industry, particularly Bollywood, is one of the largest in the world, reflecting its vibrant creative sector driven by copyright-protected works.

5.4.2.   IP AS A GLOBAL INDICATOR

Global IP filings and IP-based metrics have become a standard tool for measuring a country's innovation performance. International organizations such as WIPO, the World Bank, and the Global Innovation Index (GII) use IP data to assess innovation output and rank countries based on their innovation ecosystems.

1. **Global Innovation Index (GII):** The Global Innovation Index (GII) is one of the most widely recognized tools for assessing innovation at the global level. It ranks countries based on a combination of input and output indicators, including IP filings, R&D investments, and knowledge creation. Patent applications, trademarks, and industrial designs are key indicators used in the GII to measure the innovation output of a country. **Example:** In the 2023 GII report, Switzerland, the United States, and Sweden ranked as the top three most innovative countries, with high patent filings and R&D spending being major factors. Countries that perform well in the GII often have strong IP frameworks, indicating that the protection and management of intellectual property are central to their innovation policies[15].

2. **WIPO's World Intellectual Property Indicators Report:** WIPO's annual World Intellectual Property Indicators Report tracks global trends in IP filings and registrations, providing a snapshot of innovation activity worldwide. The report highlights trends in patent, trademark, copyright, and industrial design filings, allowing policymakers to understand which sectors and regions are driving global innovation. **Example:** The 2022 report showed significant growth in IP filings in Asia, with China, South Korea, and Japan leading in patent applications. This indicates that Asia is emerging as a global hub for technological innovation. The report also pointed to the increasing importance of IP in sectors such as clean energy, biotechnology, and digital technologies[14].

3. **Patent Cooperation Treaty (PCT) Applications:** The Patent Cooperation Treaty (PCT) allows inventors to file a single international patent application, which can then be used to seek patent protection in multiple countries. The number of PCT applications filed is another indicator of a country's innovation capacity and its integration into the global innovation system. Countries with high PCT filings are generally those that invest heavily in R&D and have a strong export-driven economy based on high-tech industries. **Example:** In 2021, the United States, China, and Germany were the top filers of PCT applications, reflecting their dominance in global innovation. India's PCT filings have also been increasing, particularly in sectors such as information technology and pharmaceuticals, indicating the country's growing role in global innovation.

5.4.3.   THE ROLE OF IP IN FOSTERING A GLOBAL INNOVATION ECOSYSTEM

IP plays a critical role in fostering a global innovation ecosystem by facilitating the diffusion of knowledge and technology across borders. When inventors file patents or trademarks internationally, they help disseminate new technologies, products, and processes to other countries, promoting global economic development.

1. **Technology Transfer and Collaboration:** IP rights facilitate international collaboration and technology transfer by providing legal certainty to both parties involved. For example, when a company licenses its patented technology to a foreign partner, the patent protection ensures that the company's innovation is safeguarded, while allowing the foreign partner to benefit from advanced technologies. This exchange of knowledge accelerates innovation globally. **Example:** India's pharmaceutical industry, known for its expertise in producing generic medicines, has benefited from technology transfer agreements with global pharmaceutical firms. Through patent licensing, Indian companies have gained access to cutting-edge drug formulations, allowing them to produce affordable medicines for both domestic and international markets.

2. **FDI and Innovation** Foreign direct investment (FDI) is another channel through which IP fosters global innovation. Countries with strong IP protection regimes are more likely to attract FDI, as investors are confident that their intellectual property will be protected. This investment brings new technologies, processes, and knowledge into the country, further enhancing its innovation capacity. **Example:** Countries in Southeast Asia, such as Singapore and Malaysia, have developed strong IP regimes to attract FDI in

high-tech sectors like electronics and biotechnology. As a result, these countries have become important players in the global innovation ecosystem.

Intellectual Property serves as a crucial global indicator of innovation, reflecting a country's capacity to produce and protect new knowledge, technologies, and creative works. By analyzing IP metrics such as patent filings, trademark registrations, and copyright protections, policymakers and researchers can gauge the strength of a nation's innovation ecosystem. Countries that prioritize IP protection and foster IP-intensive industries tend to perform well in global innovation rankings, driving economic growth and technological advancement.

5.5. ORIGIN OF IP

The origins of intellectual property can be traced back to ancient times when various forms of creativity and invention were recognized and protected. The earliest known attempt to protect innovation was in **ancient Greece**, where chefs were granted short-term monopolies[13] over their recipes. However, modern intellectual property laws evolved primarily in **Europe** during the **Renaissance**[14] and the subsequent rise of commercialism and industrialism.

The modern IP system began to take shape in the 18th century, particularly with the introduction of patents. In 1623, the **Statute of Monopolies** was passed in England, which laid the foundation for patent law by abolishing most royal monopolies but granting a form of protection to inventors of new products or processes. The **Statute of Anne** (1710) in England was another landmark, establishing the first copyright law that allowed authors to have exclusive rights over their written works.

As international trade expanded, there was a growing need for IP protection across borders. The **Paris Convention for the Protection of Industrial Property** (1883) and the **Berne Convention for the Protection of Literary and Artistic Works** (1886) were among the first international treaties to address the cross-border protection of patents and copyrights, respectively. These frameworks helped shape the IP systems that exist worldwide today.

5.6. HISTORY OF IP IN INDIA

Intellectual Property (IP) in India has a long and rich history, shaped by cultural, economic, and legislative developments over time. The concept of protecting intellectual creations has evolved from ancient practices to modern IP laws that meet global standards. Here's an overview of the history of IP in India, with a focus on the milestones that have contributed to its development:

5.6.1. PATENTS

1. **Introduction to Patents:**
   - ➤ **What is a Patent?**
     A patent is a special right given to an inventor. It means that only the inventor can make, use, or sell their invention for a certain number of years. This helps inventors protect their ideas and make money from them.
   - ➤ **Why are Patents Important?**
     Patents encourage people to invent new things because they know their ideas will be protected. This leads to more innovation and progress in society.
2. **Early Patent Legislation in India**
   - ➤ The Indian patent system dates back to British rule.
   - ➤ The first patent-related legislation was Act VI of 1856, adapted from the British Patent Law of 1852.
   - ➤ Objective: Encourage the invention of new and useful manufactures.
   - ➤ The rights conferred to inventors were termed "Exclusive Privileges."

---

[13] *Monopolies: exclusive ownership through legal privilege*
[14] *The Renaissance was a fervent period of European cultural, artistic, political and economic "rebirth" following the Middle Ages.*

3. **Amendments in 1859**
   - ➢ Exclusive privileges were granted for useful inventions.
   - ➢ Priority time was increased from 6 months to 12 months.
   - ➢ Importers were excluded from the definition of the inventor.

4. **Inclusion of Designs in Patent Legislation**
   - ➢ The term "Designs" was later included in the Patent Act.
   - ➢ The law was renamed "The Patterns and Designs Protection Act" (Act XIII of 1872).
   - ➢ The Act was amended in 1883 to include provisions for protecting "Novelty" in inventions.

5. **The Indian Patents and Designs Act, 1911**
   - ➢ Earlier Acts were replaced by the Indian Patents and Designs Act, 1911.
   - ➢ Governance of patents was placed under the Controller of Patents.
   - ➢ Several amendments were introduced, including:
     - ❖ Use of inventions by the government.
     - ❖ Patent of Addition.
     - ❖ Enhancement of the patent term from 14 to 16 years.
     - ❖ Provisional applications with the submission of complete specifications within 9 months.

6. **Post-Independence Review of the Patent System**
   - ➢ After India's independence in 1947, the Indian Patents and Designs Act, 1911 was reviewed.
   - ➢ The Bakshi Tek Chand Committee (1949) recommended several changes:
     - ❖ Prevention of patent misuse.
     - ❖ Ensuring food, medicine, and surgical devices are made affordable, with reasonable compensation to patent holders.
     - ❖ Amendments to Sections 22, 23, and 23A in line with the UK Patent Act.

7. **Key Amendments of the 1950s**
   - ➢ Act XXXII of 1950 introduced recommendations from the Bakshi Tek Chand Committee.
   - ➢ Act LXX of 1952 provided compulsory licensing for patents related to food, drugs, and chemicals.
   - ➢ A 1953 bill based on these amendments was rejected by the Parliament.

8. **The Rajagopala Ayyangar Committee (1957)**
   - ➢ Another committee was formed under Justice N. Rajagopala Ayyangar to further strengthen Indian patent law.
   - ➢ The committee's report (1959) led to the introduction of the Patents Act, 1970.

9. **The Patents Act, 1970**
   - ➢ The Patents Act, 1970, superseded previous laws related to patents.
   - ➢ The Indian Patents and Designs Act, 1911 remained applicable for designs until 1994.

10. **TRIPS Agreement and Amendments**
    - ➢ India signed the TRIPS Agreement in 1995, receiving a 10-year transition period (1995-2005) to align domestic laws.
    - ➢ The Patents (Amendment) Act, 1999 allowed for product patents in drugs, pharmaceuticals, and agrochemicals (previously, only processes were patented).
    - ➢ The Act also included provisions for Exclusive Market Rights (EMRs).

11. **The Patents (Amendment) Act, 2002**
    - ➢ Key changes in the 2002 amendment included:
      - ❖ 20-year protection term for all inventions.
      - ❖ Expanded non-patentable inventions, including traditional knowledge.
      - ❖ Mandatory disclosure of biological material's source and geographical origin.
      - ❖ Simplified procedures for convention countries.
      - ❖ Establishment of an Appellate Board and strengthening compulsory licensing provisions.

12. The Patents (Amendment) Act, 2005
- ➤ Key highlights of the 2005 amendment included:
  - ❖ Introduction of product patents across all fields of technology.
  - ❖ Exclusion of new forms of known substances to prevent "evergreening."
  - ❖ Rationalization of the opposition procedure.
  - ❖ Pre-grant and post-grant opposition procedures introduced.
  - ❖ Compulsory licensing provisions for export and manufacture.
  - ❖ Grace period for patent filing extended from 6 to 12 months for government exhibitions.

13. India's Participation in International Agreements
- ➤ India is a member of key international conventions and treaties for patent protection, including:
  - ❖ **TRIPS Agreement (1995)**
  - ❖ **Paris Convention (1883)**
  - ❖ **Patent Cooperation Treaty (PCT) (1970)**
  - ❖ **Budapest Treaty (1977)**

> ➤ World's first patent granted in 1790 to *Samuel Hopkins* (USA) for making *potash and pearl ash* by a new process.
> ➤ In India, the first patent (Exclusive Privileges) was awarded in 1856 to *George Alfred DePenning*, a civil engineer from Calcutta, for his invention, *"An Efficient Punkah Pulling Machine."*

5.6.2. COPYRIGHTS AND RELATED RIGHTS

1. What is Copyright?
- ➤ **Definition:** Copyright is a legal right that gives the creator of original work exclusive rights to its use and distribution. This means only the creator can decide how their work is used.
- ➤ **Purpose:** It protects the creator's work from being used without permission, ensuring they can benefit from their own creations.

2. Origins of Copyright Concept
- ➤ Copyright as a concept began in the 15th century.
- ➤ Before the invention of printers, writing was created manually, which was laborious and prone to errors due to manual copying by scribes.
- ➤ The invention of printing in the 15th and 16th centuries in Europe made copying easier, with the Bible being one of the first printed works.
- ➤ Initially, governments allowed unrestricted printing, leading to the widespread dissemination of governmental information.
- ➤ As a response, governments began issuing licenses for printing.

3. Phases of Copyright Evolution in India
- ➤ The evolution of copyright law in India occurred in three phases:

   i. First Phase: Introduction of Copyright (British Raj)
  - ❖ The concept of copyright was introduced in India in 1847 under the East India Company regime.
  - ❖ The term of copyright was **for the lifetime of the author plus seven years after their death.**
  - ❖ Unlike modern times, copyright protection was not automatic; registration of the work was mandatory for the enforcement of rights under this Act.
  - ❖ The government could grant a **compulsory license** for publication if the copyright owner refused to publish a work after the author's death.

   ii. Second Phase: The Copyright Act of 1914
  - ❖ The Indian legislature, under the British Raj, enacted the **Copyright Act of 1914.**
  - ❖ This Act was based on the **Imperial Copyright Act (1911) of the UK.**
  - ❖ The 1914 Act introduced criminal sanctions for copyright infringement.

    iii.   Third Phase: Post-Independence
- After independence, the **Copyright Act of 1957** was enacted, replacing the Copyright Act of 1914.
- The 1957 Act aligned with the provisions of the **Berne Convention (1886).**
- The Act has been amended **six times** to comply with international treaties: in **1983, 1984, 1992, 1994, 1999, and 2012.**
- These amendments made Indian copyright law compliant with:
    - **WIPO Copyright Treaty (WCT), 1996**
    - **WIPO Performances and Phonograms Treaty (WPPT), 1996**

4. Major Amendments in Copyright Law (Digital Environment)
- Amendments related to the digital environment include:
    - Penalties for **circumvention of technological protection measures.**
    - Rights management information provisions.
    - **Liability of internet service providers** (ISPs).
    - Introduction of **statutory licenses** for cover versions (re-recordings of original songs, also known as remakes or revival versions).
    - **Broadcasting organizations** received statutory licensing rights.
    - Introduction of **royalties for authors and music composers.**
    - Granting exclusive **economic and moral rights to performers.**
    - Equal membership rights in copyright societies for **authors and other rights owners.**
    - Copyright exceptions for **physically disabled individuals** to access works.

5. India's Participation in International Copyright Conventions
- India is an active member of major international copyright treaties and conventions:
    - **Berne Convention (as modified in Paris in 1971).**
    - **Universal Copyright Convention (1951).**
    - **Rome Convention (1961).**
    - **WIPO Copyright Treaty (WCT), 1996.**
    - **WIPO Performances and Phonograms Treaty (WPPT), 1996.**
    - **TRIPS Agreement (1995).**

5.6.3. TRADEMARKS

1. **Introduction to Trademarks (TM):** A trademark is a special symbol, word, or phrase that represents a company or product. It helps people recognize the brand and ensures that no one else can use the same symbol or name for their products.
2. **The First Trademark Law in India:** The first official law about trademarks in India was called the **Trade Marks Act, 1940**. This law was based on a similar law from the United Kingdom, known as the **Trade Marks Act, 1938**. This means India took the UK's law and made it fit for their own country.
3. **Incorporation with Other Laws:** After the Trade Marks Act, 1940 was introduced, some parts of it were also included in other important Indian laws. These were:
    - **Indian Penal Code:** This is a set of laws that define crimes and punishments in India.
    - **Criminal Procedure Code:** This law explains how criminal cases should be handled in courts.
    - **Sea Customs Act:** This law deals with the import and export of goods by sea.
4. **Renaming and Updating the Law:** In 1958, the original Trade Marks Act, 1940 was updated and given a new name: **Trade and Merchandise Marks Act, 1958**. This was done to make the law more comprehensive and cover more aspects of trademarks and merchandise.
5. **The Need for a New Law:** After almost 40 years, in 1999, the Trade and Merchandise Marks Act, 1958 was replaced by a new law called the **Trade Marks Act, 1999**. This change was necessary to align with international standards ie **TRIPS**.

6. **Understanding TRIPS:** The reason for the new law in 1999 was to comply with something called **TRIPS**. TRIPS stand for **Trade-Related Aspects of Intellectual Property Rights**. It is an international agreement that sets down minimum standards for many forms of intellectual property regulation, including trademarks, for all member countries of the World Trade Organization (WTO).

7. **Current Governing Law:** Today, the Trade Marks Act, 1999 is the main law that governs how trademarks are registered and protected in India. This law ensures that trademarks are used properly and that businesses can protect their brand identity.

8. **Why Trademarks Matter:** Trademarks are important because they help consumers identify the source of a product. For example, when you see the **golden arches**, you know it's **McDonald's**. This helps build trust and loyalty with customers.

5.6.4. GEOGRAPHICAL INDICATIONS

1. **What are Geographical Indications?**
   - Geographical Indications (GIs) are special names or signs used on products that have a specific geographical origin. These products have qualities, reputation, or characteristics that are essentially due to that place of origin. *For example, Darjeeling tea is famous worldwide, and its unique taste and quality are linked to the region of Darjeeling in India.*

2. **India's Role in Geographical Indications**
   - India is a member of the World Trade Organization (WTO). The WTO is an international organization that deals with the global rules of trade between nations. Being a member means India follows certain international trade agreements and rules.
   - To protect Geographical Indications, **India created a law called the Geographical Indications of Goods (Registration and Protection) Act in 1999.** This law helps protect the names of products that come from specific places in India.

3. **When Did the Law Start?**
   - The law officially started on 15th September 2003. This means from this date, India began to register and protect the names of products that have a special link to a particular place.

4. **Connection to WTO and TRIPS**
   - Article 22 (1) of the TRIPS agreement specifically talks about Geographical Indications. It defines what they are and how they should be protected. This means that India's law on Geographical Indications is aligned with international standards set by the WTO.

5. **Examples of Geographical Indications in India**
   - Apart from Darjeeling tea, other examples include Basmati rice, which is known for its unique aroma and long grains, and Mysore silk, famous for its quality and craftsmanship.

5.6.5. TRADE SECRETS

1. **What are Trade Secrets?**
   - Trade secrets are special kinds of information that businesses keep private. This information gives them an advantage over competitors. For example, a secret recipe for a popular drink or a unique way of making a product can be a trade secret.

2. **India's Approach to Trade Secrets**
   - In India, there is no specific law for trade secrets. Instead, India uses different existing laws to protect them like contract law, Copyright law, the principles of equity and the common law action of breach of confidence.

3. **Why Protect Trade Secrets?**
   - Protecting trade secrets is important because it helps businesses stay competitive. If a secret gets out, competitors might copy it, and the original business could lose its advantage.

5.6.6. SEMICONDUCTOR INTEGRATED CIRCUITS AND LAYOUT DESIGNS

1. Impact of Information Technology (IT) on Intellectual Property (IP)
- ➤ In the 21st century, Information Technology (IT) has significantly influenced global economic and societal growth.
- ➤ Rapid scientific advancements in IT led to the creation of a new class of Intellectual Property (IP) known as the **Layout-Design of Semiconductor Integrated Circuits**.
- ➤ **Semiconductor Integrated Circuits** are tiny electronic parts that make devices like computers and smartphones work. They are like the brains of electronic devices, helping them process information and perform tasks.
- ➤ Protecting these designs is important because they are valuable and take a lot of time and effort to create. If someone copies them without permission, it can hurt the original creator's business.

2. International Regulations for SICLD Protection
- ➤ Various international organizations, including the **World Trade Organization (WTO)**, and the **TRIPS** Agreement, formulated rules for the protection of **Semiconductor Integrated Circuits and Layout Designs (SICLD)**.

3. India's Response to SICLD Protection
- ➤ India, as a member of the WTO, passed the **Semiconductor Integrated Circuits Layout-Design Act (SICLD Act), 2000**. This Act ensures compliance with the provisions of the TRIPS Agreement.

4. TRIPS Agreement Compliance
- ➤ The **SICLD Act, 2000** adheres to **Articles 35 to 38** of the TRIPS Agreement, which specifically address the protection of **Semiconductor Integrated Circuits and Layout Designs**. The Act ensures that India's legal framework aligns with international standards for the protection of SICLD.

5.6.7. PLANT VARIETIES

1. Patent Exclusions for Plants and Animals Pre-1970s
- ➤ Before the 1970s, patents, which are legal rights given to inventors to protect their inventions, did not focus much on things that came from animals and plants. This means that if someone discovered something new about animals or plants, they couldn't easily get a patent for it.
- ➤ However, tiny living things called microbes, like bacteria and fungi, and the products or processes made from them, could be patented. This is because microbes are often used in industries, like making yogurt or antibiotics, and people wanted to protect these useful inventions.

2. Expansion of Patent Laws for Biological Materials
- ➤ To include all types of biological materials under patent protection, international discussions led to the enactment of **sui generis laws**. These laws were shaped by the **International Convention for the Protection of New Varieties of Plants (UPOV)**, introduced in 1978 and revised in 1991.

3. Indian Patents Act, 1970 Exclusion
- ➤ In India, the Patents Act of 1970 specifically said that you cannot patent plants and animals, or any part of them, except for microorganisms. This means if you discovered a new type of plant or animal, you couldn't get a patent for it in India.

4. Compliance with TRIPS Agreement
- ➤ To comply with Article 27.3(b) of the TRIPS Agreement, India adopted a sui generis legal framework for plant variety protection. This resulted in the enactment of the Protection of Plant Varieties and Farmers' Rights (PPV&FR) Act, 2001.

5. Key Features of the PPV&FR Act, 2001
- ➤ The PPV&FR Act provides protection not only to new plant varieties but also recognizes and safeguards farmers' rights. It ensures that the protection system is in line with the TRIPS mandate and addresses the concerns of environmental sustainability and public welfare.

5.6.8. TRADITIONAL KNOWLEDGE

1. What is Traditional Knowledge?
  - ➤ **Definition**: Traditional Knowledge (TK) is the wisdom and know-how that has been developed by communities over many generations. It is the knowledge that is passed down from parents to children and is often unique to a specific group of people or culture.
  - ➤ **Oral Tradition**: In the past, this knowledge was not written down. Instead, it was shared through speaking and listening. This means that people would tell stories or teach skills directly to others, who would then remember and pass it on to the next generation.

2. Scope of Traditional Knowledge
  - ➤ TK spans a wide variety of fields and areas, including but not limited to:
    - ❖ Use of plants and their extracts for medical treatments.
    - ❖ Traditional dances and other forms of cultural expression.
    - ❖ Techniques for hunting and other survival skills.
    - ❖ Craft knowledge/skills such as weaving or pottery.
  - ➤ TK often finds expression in culture, stories, legends, folklore, rituals, and songs, although it was not officially recorded.

3. Lack of Early Protection for TK
  - ➤ Previously, there was no mechanism available to protect TK from misuse or misappropriation.

4. Recognition of TK as Intellectual Property
  - ➤ **Traditional Knowledge** has now been recognized as a form **of Intellectual Property Rights (IPR)** under the **TRIPS Agreement.**
  - ➤ This recognition allows TK to be protected in a similar way to other forms of IP.

5. Traditional Knowledge Digital Library (TKDL)
  - ➤ To protect TK, the **Government of India** created the **Traditional Knowledge Digital Library (TKDL).**
  - ➤ The TKDL serves as a repository containing **250,000** formulations from various systems of Indian medicine, helping to document and safeguard India's rich heritage of TK.

5.6.9. INDUSTRIAL DESIGNS

1. Definition of Industrial Design (ID)
  - ➤ An industrial design is a creative idea that comes from a person's mind. It is something that looks nice and catches people's attention. Think of it like a fancy pattern on a dress or a unique shape of a chair. These designs make products more attractive to customers.

2. Early Recognition of Industrial Design Protection
  - ➤ The need to protect Industrial Designs was recognized in the **18th century.**
  - ➤ In India, the first legislation for the protection of designs was the **Patterns and Designs Act, 1872.**

3. Purpose of the Patterns and Designs Act, 1872
  - ➤ This Act was enacted to **protect the rights** over the creation of designs and novel patterns made by inventors.
  - ➤ It provided legal protection to designers and inventors for their **original designs.**

4. Replacement by British Patents and Designs Act, 1907
  - ➤ The **Patterns and Designs Act, 1872** was replaced by the **British Patents and Designs Act, 1907.**
  - ➤ This Act served as the foundation for India's later **Patents and Designs Act, 1911**.

5. Indian Patents and Designs Act, 1911
  - ➤ The Indian **Patents and Designs Act, 1911** was based on the British Act and governed both **patents** and **designs** in India.
  - ➤ It provided a unified legal framework for both patents and industrial designs until 1970.

6. **Separation of Patents and Designs in 1970**
   - ➤ In 1970, a separate **Patent Act, 1970** was enacted, which focused solely on patents.
   - ➤ The **Indian Patents and Designs Act, 1911** continued to govern designs only after this.
7. **Dedicated Industrial Designs Act (2000)**
   - ➤ In 2000, a separate and dedicated **Industrial Designs Act** was passed by the Indian legislature.
   - ➤ The Act came into force in 2001, ensuring comprehensive protection and legal recognition for industrial designs in India.

5.6.10. BIODIVERSITY CONSERVATION

1. **What is Biodiversity?**
   - ➤ **Definition:** Biodiversity refers to the variety of all living things on Earth, including plants, animals, fungi, and microorganisms. It also includes the ecosystems they form, like forests, oceans, and deserts.
   - ➤ **Importance:** Biodiversity is essential because it supports ecosystem services that humans rely on, such as clean water, air, food, and medicine. It also helps in regulating the climate.
2. **Historical Importance of Biodiversity**
   - ➤ Historical records show that efforts to protect biodiversity date back to the times of **Chandragupta** and **Ashoka**.
   - ➤ During these eras, forests and trees were classified into categories like **reserved forests**, indicating early awareness of conservation.
3. **Indian Forest Act, 1927**
   - ➤ The **Indian Forest Act, 1927** was one of the first legislative efforts to provide **legal protection** to biodiversity in India. This Act aimed to regulate forest management and conservation efforts.
4. **Wildlife Protection Act, 1972**
   - ➤ The **Wildlife Protection Act, 1972** was enacted to further strengthen legal protection for India's **wildlife and biodiversity**. It focused on protecting endangered species and conserving wildlife habitats.
5. **National Forest Policy, 1988**
   - ➤ The **National Forest Policy, 1988** brought revolutionary changes in the **conservation and management of biodiversity.** The policy aimed at management and development of forest resources.
6. **Key Acts and Policies for Biodiversity Conservation**
   Several Acts and policies have been introduced in India to protect biodiversity including:
   - ➤ **Mining and Mineral Development Regulation Act, 1957:** Regulated mining activities to ensure minimal impact on biodiversity.
   - ➤ **Water (Prevention and Control of Pollution) Act, 1974:** Aimed at preventing water pollution to protect aquatic ecosystems.
   - ➤ **Forest Conservation Act, 1980:** Provided stricter regulations on the use of forest land and encouraged reforestation.
   - ➤ **Biological Diversity Act, 2002:** A comprehensive law aimed at conserving biodiversity and ensuring sustainable use of its components.
   - ➤ **Scheduled Tribes and Other Traditional Forest Dwellers (Recognition of Rights) Act, 2006:** Recognized the rights of indigenous communities to their traditional forest lands, promoting the sustainable use of biodiversity.
   - ➤ **National Biodiversity Action Plan, 2009:** Laid out a strategic plan for biodiversity conservation.
   - ➤ **National Environment Policy, 2006:** Focused on integrating environmental conservation into developmental policies.
7. **Ongoing Biodiversity Protection Efforts**
   - ➤ India continues to implement and update its legal framework to ensure the protection and sustainable management of its rich biodiversity, aligning with both national interests and global commitments.

5.7. MAJOR AMENDMENTS IN IP LAWS AND ACTS IN INDIA

India has undergone significant reforms in its intellectual property (IP) laws, with a focus on aligning domestic legislation with global standards and fostering innovation. These amendments are primarily driven by the need to adhere to the obligations of international treaties such as the TRIPS (Trade-Related Aspects of Intellectual Property Rights) Agreement. Below is an overview of some major amendments in Indian IP laws and acts:

1. Patents

India's intellectual property (IP) regime, particularly for patents, has undergone significant amendments over the years. These amendments aim to align India's IP laws with international standards, ensure innovation, protect the rights of inventors, and promote economic growth. Below is a comprehensive analysis of key amendments in IP laws and acts concerning patents in India.

Table 5.1. Major Amendments in IP Laws and Acts in India for Patents[16], [17]

Sl. No.	Year	Amendment/Act	Key Features	Impact on Patent Law	Examples/Case Studies
1	1856	**The Patent Act of 1856**	Modeled on the British Patent Law of 1852; first introduction of a patent system in India.	Allowed protection for inventions and innovations, offering exclusive rights for 14 years.	Laid the foundation for modern IP laws in India.
2	1911	**Indian Patents and Designs Act, 1911**	Focused on patents and industrial designs; revised the patent system.	Enhanced patent protection, centralized administration, and shortened patent validity to 16 years.	Influenced by colonial policies and industrial needs of the time.
3	1970	**The Patents Act, 1970**	Introduced post-independence; restricted product patents in specific fields (food, chemicals, and pharmaceuticals).	Shifted focus to process patents, allowing more room for innovation in manufacturing while controlling monopolies in crucial sectors.	Important for domestic industries, particularly generics, allowing companies like Cipla to thrive in the pharma sector.
4	1999	**The Patents (Amendment) Act, 1999**	Aimed at complying with TRIPS (Trade-Related Aspects of Intellectual Property Rights) agreements under the World Trade Organization (WTO).	Allowed for product patents in fields such as chemicals, pharmaceuticals, and food, with retrospective protection from 1995.	Affected pharmaceutical industries like Ranbaxy and Dr. Reddy's, as they transitioned to international patent compliance.
5	2002	**The Patents (Amendment) Act, 2002**	Introduced major changes in the patent filing process, including publication of patent applications, provision for pre-grant opposition, and extension of patent terms to 20 years.	Streamlined the process to bring India in line with global standards; strengthened protection for innovators and inventors.	Enabled Indian IT and pharma companies to protect their innovations more effectively on the global stage.

Sl. No.	Year	Amendment/Act	Key Features	Impact on Patent Law	Examples/Case Studies
6	2005	**The Patents (Amendment) Act, 2005**	Further TRIPS compliance; reintroduced product patents in all fields of technology, including pharmaceuticals and agricultural chemicals.	This landmark amendment reversed earlier restrictions, now allowing product patents on pharmaceuticals and other innovations.	Cipla's legal challenges during this time are a case study in balancing public health and patent rights.
7	2012	**The Patent Rules (Amendment) 2012**	Introduced the provision for filing of patent applications electronically and the Fast Track Patent Examination.	Allowed expedited processes for patent applications, increasing efficiency. It also helped startups by reducing timelines.	Beneficial for innovation-driven startups in sectors such as biotechnology and electronics.
8	2016	**The Patents (Amendment) Rules, 2016**	Introduction of expedited examination for patents filed by startups and small enterprises.	Encouraged more patent filings by reducing the hurdles and introducing online filing systems.	Significant increase in patent applications from Indian startups, particularly in the tech and software industry.
9	2017	**The Patents (Amendment) Rules, 2017**	Focus on speeding up the examination process. Introduced "tatkal" mode of examination.	Further encouraged innovation by reducing patent grant timelines; focused on Make in India initiative.	Impactful in increasing the number of patents filed by Indian startups and research institutions.
10	2021	**The Patents (Amendment) Rules, 2021**	Extended the benefits of expedited examination to female applicants, government institutions, and educational institutions.	Made patent filing more inclusive, encouraging diversity in innovation and intellectual property ownership.	Promoted female innovators, allowing more patent grants for women-led research and innovation in India.

2. Copyrights and Related Rights

Copyright law in India has undergone substantial transformations both before and after independence. These amendments reflect India's evolving understanding of creativity, innovation, and the need to protect creators while adapting to international standards. Below is a detailed overview of key amendments in IP laws and acts concerning copyrights and related rights in India.

Table 5.2. Major Amendments in IP Laws and Acts in India for Copyrights and Related Rights[16].

Sl. No.	Year	Amendment/Act	Key Features	Impact on Copyright Law	Examples/Case Studies
1	1847	**The Copyright Act of 1847**	Modeled after the British Copyright Law of 1842, this was the first legal framework for copyright protection in India.	Granted rights for printed books and literary works for 28 years after the death of the author.	Early colonial framework focused on literary works; had limited scope for other forms of creativity.

2	1914	**The Indian Copyright Act, 1914**	Modeled on the British Copyright Act of 1911, it extended the scope of copyright to cover music, art, and dramatic works.	Expanded protection to include a broader range of creative works, introduced the concept of moral rights, and enhanced duration to 50 years post-author's death.	Encouraged the protection of more forms of intellectual property in India, reflecting the rise of music, art, and theater industries during the colonial period.
3	1957	**The Copyright Act, 1957**	This act was the first post-independence copyright legislation and is still the foundational copyright law in India.	Provided protection for literary, dramatic, musical, and artistic works, as well as cinematographic films and sound recordings. Introduced provisions for fair use.	Marked a major shift by codifying copyright law in India, ensuring better protection for creators, and aligning with India's independence-driven ethos of creativity.
4	1983	**The Copyright (Amendment) Act, 1983**	Addressed issues related to film rights and performers' rights. Introduced statutory licenses for radio broadcasting of literary and musical works.	Allowed for broader licensing, particularly for broadcasting, and recognized performers' rights.	Key for the growth of the Indian film and music industry, which relied on statutory licensing.
5	1994	**The Copyright (Amendment) Act, 1994**	Expanded copyright protection to computer software and databases, included provisions for performers' rights, and enhanced protection for broadcasting and cable transmissions.	Recognized the need to protect emerging technologies, especially in the IT sector, and clarified the rights of performers and broadcasters.	This amendment significantly impacted India's burgeoning IT industry, which started contributing to global software development.
6	1999	**The Copyright (Amendment) Act, 1999**	Introduced the concept of copyright societies for collective management of rights, especially in the fields of music and publishing.	Enhanced the collective management of copyrights through societies, allowing for better revenue collection and distribution for creators.	Key for the Indian music industry, which saw better management of royalties and rights through societies like the Indian Performing Right Society (IPRS).
7	2012	**The Copyright (Amendment) Act, 2012**	Focused on aligning Indian copyright law with the World Intellectual Property Organization (WIPO) treaties. Introduced provisions for fair use	Strengthened the rights of authors and music composers, preventing the assignment of rights in perpetuity and enhancing royalty provisions. Allowed	Beneficial for authors like Javed Akhtar, who were vocal about unfair royalty practices in the film and music industries. This amendment also helped

Sl. No.	Year	Amendment/Act	Key Features	Impact	Examples
			for disabled persons, strengthened the rights of authors and lyricists, and clarified compulsory licensing terms.	the visually impaired to access copyrighted material without infringement.	persons with disabilities access creative content.
8	2016	**The Copyright Rules, 2016**	Introduced reforms in the functioning of copyright societies, making them more transparent and accountable, especially regarding royalty distribution.	Improved the functioning of copyright societies, ensured more transparency, and mandated timely distribution of royalties to authors and artists.	Impactful for the Indian music and publishing industries, where royalty disputes were common.
9	2021	**The Copyright (Amendment) Rules, 2021**	Emphasized the implementation of online dispute resolution (ODR) mechanisms for resolving copyright-related disputes. Expanded digital copyright protections.	Addressed issues of online infringement and the management of digital rights, a crucial step in dealing with growing online piracy. Strengthened the protection for digital works, including online streaming platforms.	Important for platforms like Netflix and Amazon Prime, which increasingly rely on strong copyright protection for digital media.

3. Trademarks

Trademarks play a critical role in the identification of goods and services and are essential in distinguishing one entity's products from another. India's trademark laws have evolved significantly from the colonial era to modern times, aligning with global standards and addressing the changing needs of businesses and industries. Below is a comprehensive overview of the major amendments in IP laws and acts concerning trademarks in India.

Table 5.3. Major Amendments in IP Laws and Acts in India for Trademarks[16].

Sl. No.	Year	Amendment/Act	Key Features	Impact on Trademark Law	Examples/Case Studies
1	1860	**The Trade Marks Act, 1860**	The first legal recognition of trademarks in India, based on British common law.	Allowed the registration of trademarks but lacked formal structure and detailed protection mechanisms.	Limited protection was granted to trademarks, mainly focused on symbols and marks used in trade.
2	1940	**The Trade Marks Act, 1940**	Based on the UK Trade Marks Act, 1938; provided for the formal registration and protection of trademarks.	Introduced the registration of trademarks in India and offered protection for businesses to secure their brand identity.	Marked the first structured system for registering trademarks in pre-independence India.

3	1958	**The Trade and Merchandise Marks Act, 1958**	Replaced the 1940 Act, providing a more detailed framework for trademark registration, protection, and infringement remedies.	Broadened trademark protection, covering deceptive similarity and infringement; enhanced protection for industrial products.	A critical law for post-independence India, it helped streamline trademark registration for growing industries in India.
4	1999	**The Trade Marks Act, 1999**	Comprehensive reform to align with the Trade-Related Aspects of Intellectual Property Rights (TRIPS) Agreement. Extended protection to service marks, collective marks, and well-known trademarks.	Brought Indian trademark law in compliance with international standards, enhancing protection for trademarks across industries, including services.	Important for companies like Infosys and Wipro, which sought trademark protection as their brands expanded globally.
5	2002	**The Trade Marks Rules, 2002**	Implemented the 1999 Act with detailed procedures for registration, opposition, and enforcement of trademark rights.	Provided a clearer framework for registering service marks, geographical indications, and collective marks. Strengthened opposition mechanisms.	Significant for industries like hospitality and software services that needed protection for service-related trademarks.
6	2010	**The Trade Marks (Amendment) Act, 2010**	Introduced the Madrid Protocol, allowing Indian businesses to register trademarks internationally with a single application.	Enabled Indian companies to seek trademark protection in multiple jurisdictions, simplifying the process of protecting trademarks abroad.	Beneficial for Indian companies expanding globally, such as Tata Motors and Mahindra, as it facilitated international trademark protection.
7	2017	**The Trade Marks Rules, 2017**	Simplified the trademark registration process, introduced new categories such as sound marks, and introduced an online filing system.	Made the trademark registration process faster and more efficient, reduced fees for startups and small businesses, and allowed the registration of non-traditional marks like sound.	Increased trademark filings by startups and SMEs, and brands like ICICI used sound marks to differentiate themselves.
8	2019	**The Trade Marks (Amendment) Rules, 2019**	Introduced further simplifications in the registration process, including additional	Focused on making the trademark system more accessible to small businesses, startups,	Boosted trademark registrations among startups, particularly those in the tech sector, who sought IP

Sl. No.	Year	Amendment/Act	Key Features	Impact	Examples
			provisions for startups and individuals.	and individual applicants.	protection at an early stage.
9	2020	**The Trade Marks (Amendment) Rules, 2020**	Enhanced the enforcement mechanisms for trademark infringement and included provisions for faster dispute resolution.	Strengthened the ability of businesses to defend their trademarks against infringement, with quicker resolutions of disputes through fast-track mechanisms.	Important for companies involved in frequent trademark litigation, such as pharmaceutical companies and tech startups.

4. Geographical Indications

Geographical Indications (GIs) are crucial for protecting products that have a specific geographical origin and possess qualities, reputation, or characteristics inherent to that location. India's journey in establishing a robust legal framework for GIs reflects its rich cultural and agricultural diversity. The legal provisions have evolved over time, especially after independence, to comply with international agreements and safeguard the interests of traditional artisans and farmers. Below is a detailed table of major amendments in IP laws and acts in India concerning Geographical Indications (GIs).

Table 5.4. Major Amendments in IP Laws and Acts in India for Geographical Indications[16].

Sl. No.	Year	Amendment/Act	Key Features	Impact on GI Law	Examples/Case Studies
1	1958	**The Trade and Merchandise Marks Act, 1958**	Extended protection to marks that are indicative of geographic origin, preventing misleading claims about the source of goods.	Provided some protection to GIs by linking them to trademarks but did not recognize GIs as a separate category.	Examples include Darjeeling Tea and Basmati Rice, where protection was mainly through trademarks before the GI Act.
2	1999	**The Geographical Indications of Goods (Registration and Protection) Act, 1999**	A landmark law that provided a separate legal framework for GIs in India, protecting goods that possess a specific geographical origin.	Established a formal registration process for GIs, granted exclusive rights to registered users, and prohibited unauthorized use. It was following TRIPS (Trade-Related Aspects of Intellectual Property Rights).	Darjeeling Tea became the first GI registered in India under this Act in 2004, protecting its name and heritage.
3	2002	**The Geographical Indications Rules, 2002**	Implemented the provisions of the 1999 Act, setting out detailed procedures for the registration, opposition, and cancellation of GIs.	Created a structured and transparent process for GI registration, ensuring that stakeholders from different sectors could protect their regional products.	Beneficial for products like Pashmina Shawls and Kanchipuram Silk Sarees, which sought GI protection for their traditional craftsmanship.

4	2010	**Amendments to the GI Act, 2010**	Introduced provisions to streamline the registration process and extended protection to agricultural products, handicrafts, and textiles.	Strengthened the framework for protecting agricultural products and traditional crafts, allowing quicker registration and opposition proceedings.	Helped in the protection of agricultural products like Alphonso Mango and handicrafts like Chanderi Sarees.
5	2013	**The Geographical Indications (Amendment) Rules, 2013**	Enhanced the protection for GIs by simplifying the opposition process and introducing digital filing of applications.	Encouraged more applications for GIs, especially from small-scale producers and traditional artisans, by making the process more accessible.	Boosted the GI registrations of products like Madhubani Paintings and Mysore Silk, making the registration process easier for rural artisans.
6	2017	**Amendments to the GI Act, 2017**	Increased enforcement measures against GI infringement, introduced penalties for unauthorized use, and enhanced international cooperation for GI recognition.	Strengthened protection against counterfeit products, improved enforcement mechanisms, and promoted international recognition of Indian GIs.	Helped Indian GIs like Basmati Rice and Darjeeling Tea gain better recognition in international markets, protecting them from infringement.
7	2019	**The Geographical Indications (Amendment) Rules, 2019**	Focused on easing the procedural requirements for small businesses and cooperatives to file GI applications, and promoted the registration of new GI categories.	Allowed small businesses and rural cooperatives to access GI registration more easily and extended protection to new categories such as non-agricultural goods.	Encouraged the registration of non-agricultural GIs, such as Kolhapuri Chappals, which were registered under this rule.
8	2021	**The GI Amendment Rules, 2021**	Introduced stricter penalties for GI infringement, enhanced the digitization of the registration process, and allowed GI holders to file international applications under the Madrid Protocol.	Improved international cooperation, streamlined registration processes, and strengthened enforcement to prevent misuse of Indian GIs abroad.	Crucial for Indian GIs such as Banarasi Silk and Pashmina, which face competition in global markets where counterfeit goods are prevalent.

5. Designs

Designs are an important category of intellectual property (IP) that protect the visual appearance of products. In India, the legal framework for protecting industrial designs has evolved to keep pace with technological and industrial growth. The amendments over the years reflect India's commitment to promoting innovation and design protection, as well as aligning with international standards. Below is a comprehensive table detailing major amendments in IP laws and acts concerning designs in India.

Table 5.5. Major Amendments in IP Laws and Acts in India for Designs[16].

Sl. No.	Year	Amendment/Act	Key Features	Impact on Design Law	Examples/Case Studies
1	1872	**The Indian Patents and Designs Act, 1872**	The first law regulating designs, providing basic protection for industrial designs.	Provided limited protection to registered designs, mainly in the form of preventing the unauthorized use of visual designs.	Early design protection was limited to specific industries, such as textiles and handicrafts.
2	1911	**The Indian Patents and Designs Act, 1911**	Combined patent and design protection in a single act; it extended protection to new and original designs.	More comprehensive provisions for the registration. Extended the duration of design protection.	Focused on preventing copying in industries like textiles and manufacturing, ensuring that original designs.
3	1970	**The Patents Act, 1970**	Primarily focused on patents but had indirect impacts on the protection of designs, particularly in the fields of engineering and manufacturing.	The act helped clarify the distinction between patents and designs, encouraging innovations in both functional & aesthetic aspects of products.	Applied to industries where functionality and design aesthetics were both important, such as automobiles and machinery.
4	2000	**The Designs Act, 2000**	Replaced the 1911 Act; focused exclusively on design protection. Defined "design" clearly as the features of shape, configuration, pattern, ornamentation, or composition of lines or colors applied to an article.	Aligned Indian design laws with international standards, including the TRIPS Agreement. Provided protection for 10 years, renewable for an additional 5 years. Strengthened the enforcement mechanisms for design infringement.	Promoted design protection in industries like fashion, electronics, and consumer goods, encouraging innovation in product aesthetics. Examples include protection for mobile phone designs and automobile aesthetics.
5	2001	**The Designs Rules, 2001**	Introduced procedural details for filing, examination, and opposition of design registrations.	Simplified the process for registering designs, providing more transparency and accessibility for businesses and designers.	Encouraged a rise in design registrations from small businesses and startups, particularly in sectors like fashion and product design.

Sl. No.	Year	Amendment/Act	Key Features	Impact on Design Law	Examples/Case Studies
6	2008	**The Designs (Amendment) Rules, 2008**	Simplified procedural aspects related to the classification of designs and expedited the design registration process.	Introduced clearer classification systems, making it easier for applicants to register designs under specific categories.	Beneficial for sectors like consumer electronics and household goods, which sought faster design protection for rapidly evolving products.
7	2014	**The Designs (Amendment) Rules, 2014**	Enhanced procedural efficiency in design applications, allowed for electronic filing, and introduced priority examination for certain sectors.	Promoted faster processing of design applications, particularly for startups and SMEs, and reduced bureaucracy.	Encouraged innovation in industries like fashion & consumer goods, where rapid design changes are critical for success.
8	2021	**The Designs (Amendment) Rules, 2021**	Focused on harmonizing design laws with international standards, introduced stricter penalties for design infringement, and enhanced enforcement mechanisms.	Strengthened design protection in India, encouraging businesses to invest in innovative and original product designs. Promoted international cooperation for design protection.	Key for global companies with significant design portfolios in India, such as Samsung and Apple, who rely on robust design protection to prevent counterfeit products.

6. Semiconductor Integrated Circuits Layout Design (SICLD)

The protection of Semiconductor Integrated Circuits Layout Design (SICLD) is a crucial aspect of intellectual property law, especially in the rapidly advancing fields of electronics and technology. In India, the legal framework for protecting semiconductor layout designs has been established to ensure that innovators in this field are granted exclusive rights. Below is a detailes of the major amendments in IP laws and acts concerning SICLD in India.

Table 5.6. Amendments in IP Laws and Acts for Semiconductor Integrated Circuits Layout Design (SICLD)[16].

Sl. No.	Year	Amendment/Act	Key Features	Impact on SICLD Law	Examples/Case Studies
1	1988	**The Semiconductor Chip Protection Act, USA (Indirect Impact)**	Not an Indian law, this U.S. act influenced global policies, by establishing exclusive rights to the creators of semiconductor chip designs.	Prompted India to consider establishing its own legal framework for the protection of semiconductor designs.	The U.S. law inspired India to draft similar legislation to protect domestic innovation in semiconductor design.
2	2000	**TRIPS Agreement Compliance**	As part of India's obligations under the TRIPS Agreement, the need for protecting layout designs of integrated circuits was recognized.	India acknowledged the importance of protecting semiconductor designs as part of its compliance with global IP standards.	This pushed for the development of a specific legal framework for layout designs in India.

3	2000	**The Semiconductor Integrated Circuits Layout Design Act, 2000**	The first Indian law specifically aimed at protecting the layout designs of semiconductor integrated circuits. It provided exclusive rights to creators for original layout designs for a period of 10 years.	Recognized and protected the intellectual property rights of designers of semiconductor layouts. Prohibited the copying, selling, or importing of a layout design without authorization.	Key for India's burgeoning electronics industry. This act provided protection to companies developing integrated circuits, such as Bharat Electronics Limited (BEL) and Semiconductor Laboratory (SCL).
4	2001	**The Semiconductor Integrated Circuits Layout Design Rules, 2001**	Implemented the 2000 Act with detailed rules for the registration process of layout designs.	Provided a structured procedure for filing applications, examining, and registering layout designs. Streamlined the process for protecting layout designs.	Made it easier for semiconductor companies and innovators in India to secure IP protection for their designs.
5	2004	**The Semiconductor Integrated Circuits Layout Design (Amendment) Rules, 2004**	Introduced changes to simplify the registration process, reduced application fees for individuals and startups, and improved the procedural aspects of the act.	Made the process of registering layout designs more accessible to startups and smaller firms, encouraging innovation in the semiconductor industry.	Benefited tech startups working in semiconductor design, allowing easier entry into the market.
6	2017	**The Digital India Initiative and SICLD**	Although not a direct amendment, the government's focus on digital innovation under the Digital India Initiative indirectly impacted the semiconductor industry by promoting research and development.	The emphasis on innovation led to a surge in demand for protecting IP, including layout designs, as new semiconductor technologies were developed domestically.	Encouraged the growth of indigenous semiconductor companies such as SCL and startups in the electronics space.
7	2020	**National Policy on Electronics 2020 (Indirect Impact)**	Focused on boosting electronics manufacturing, including semiconductor fabrication, and	Created a favorable environment for electronics manufacturing in India, increasing the importance of	Stimulated investments in semiconductor manufacturing, driving up patent and design filings for integrated

Sl. No.	Year	Amendment/Act	Key Features	Impact on SICLD Law	Examples/Case Studies
			promoting IP creation. Indirectly influenced the need for strong protection of semiconductor designs.	protecting SICLDs as part of the broader IP strategy for technology-driven industries.	circuits by companies like HCL and Wipro.
8	2021	**The SICLD Rules (Amendment), 2021**	Enhanced procedural clarity in the registration of layout designs and focused on digitization of the process, allowing electronic filing and faster processing of applications.	Made the process of filing for layout design protection more efficient, reducing delays in the approval and registration process.	Helped streamline registration for semiconductor companies focusing on cutting-edge integrated circuit designs, enhancing competitiveness in the global market.

7. Protection of Plant Varieties and Farmers' Rights (PPV&FR)

The Protection of Plant Varieties and Farmers' Rights (PPV&FR) Act, 2001, represents a significant milestone in India's intellectual property regime. It acknowledges both the rights of plant breeders and the contributions of farmers in conserving and improving plant genetic resources. This table provides an overview of the major amendments and developments in IP laws related to the protection of plant varieties and farmers' rights in India.

Table 5.7. Amendments in IP Laws and Acts for Protection of Plant Varieties and Farmers Rights (PPV&FR)[16].

Sl. No.	Year	Amendment/Act	Key Features	Impact on PPV&FR Law	Examples/Case Studies
1	1898	**Indian Patents and Designs Act, 1898**	Did not include any provisions for the protection of plant varieties or farmers' rights. The focus was on inventions in industrial fields.	No impact on plant varieties; plant breeding remained outside the purview of intellectual property protection.	Not applicable to plant variety protection, focused solely on mechanical inventions and industrial designs.
2	1970	**The Patents Act, 1970**	Excluded agricultural and horticultural methods and plant varieties from patent protection.	The exclusion of plant varieties from the Patents Act opened the need for separate legislation for protecting plant breeders and farmers.	Led to the development of later laws specifically addressing plant variety protection.
3	1991	**International Convention for the Protection of New Varieties of Plants (UPOV), 1991**	India did not join UPOV but started discussions on a national law that would balance the rights of breeders and farmers.	Triggered national discussions around the need for a law that not only protects plant breeders but also acknowledges farmers' rights.	India chose a sui generis system instead of joining UPOV, aiming to address its specific agricultural concerns.

4	2001	**Protection of Plant Varieties and Farmers' Rights (PPV&FR) Act, 2001**	Aimed at protecting the intellectual property rights of plant breeders while ensuring that farmers retained their rights to save, use, sow, resow, exchange, and sell farm-saved seeds.	First comprehensive law that acknowledged both the contributions of breeders and farmers. Established a Plant Variety Authority to oversee registration and enforcement.	Rice variety 'Basmati' and wheat variety 'HD 2967' were registered under this act, with recognition to the breeders as well as farmers contributing to the conservation.
5	2003	**The Protection of Plant Varieties and Farmers' Rights (PPV&FR) Rules, 2003**	Laid down detailed procedures for the registration of plant varieties and the filing of claims for compensation by farmers.	Provided a clear and transparent process for the registration of new plant varieties and the recognition of farmers' rights.	Encouraged the registration of traditional varieties, such as Nagpur oranges and Kerala cardamom, safeguarding biodiversity.
6	2011	**Amendments to PPV&FR Rules, 2011**	Introduced provisions for the recognition of farmer-conserved varieties and enhanced the role of farmer participation in the authority.	Strengthened the rights of farmers by providing them more active involvement in the process of registering and protecting their traditional varieties.	Farmers' varieties such as 'Kala Jeera' rice were registered, and farmers were recognized as conservers of biodiversity.
7	2015	**National Biodiversity Authority (NBA) and PPV&FR Collaboration**	Emphasized collaboration between the NBA and the Plant Variety Authority for the protection of traditional knowledge related to plant varieties.	Fostered closer cooperation between the protection of plant varieties and the conservation of biodiversity, acknowledging the role of farmers in both.	Led to the registration and protection of indigenous crops such as 'Black Rice' from Manipur and 'Joha Rice' from Assam.
8	2017	**Amendments to PPV&FR Rules, 2017**	Streamlined the process of filing applications for the registration of new plant varieties and improved procedures for dispute resolution.	Simplified the process of registering new plant varieties, making it more accessible to breeders and farmers alike.	Increased registrations of both commercial and traditional varieties, boosting agricultural innovation.
9	2021	**Digitalization of PPV&FR Authority**	Introduced digital filing of applications and online platforms for dispute resolution and information sharing regarding registered varieties.	Enhanced the efficiency of the application process, making it easier for farmers and breeders to register their plant varieties.	Improved access for farmers and breeders in rural areas, allowing faster registration and protection of new and traditional varieties.

8. Biological diversity

Biological diversity is vital for the ecological balance and sustainability of life. India, as one of the world's most biodiverse countries, has developed comprehensive legal frameworks to protect its biodiversity, with a focus on conservation and sustainable use. Below is a detailed table summarizing the major amendments in IP laws and acts concerning biological diversity in India, pre- and post-independence.

Table 5.7. Major Amendments in IP Laws and Acts in India for Biological diversity[16].

Sl. No.	Year	Amendment/Act	Key Features	Impact on Biological Diversity Law	Examples/Case Studies
1	1894	The Indian Forest Act, 1894	Provided for the conservation of forests and regulated forest produce, focusing on timber and other resources.	Indirectly impacted biodiversity by regulating the use of forest resources, but not includes specific provisions.	Early legal framework for forest management, but limited in scope regarding the protection of overall biodiversity.
2	1972	The Wildlife Protection Act, 1972	Aimed at the protection of wildlife and biodiversity by establishing national parks and sanctuaries.	Marked a shift towards active conservation of biological resources, providing protection for endangered species and habitats.	The creation of protected areas like Corbett National Park and Kaziranga Sanctuary helped conserve species such as tigers and rhinos.
3	1980	The Forest Conservation Act, 1980	Focused on conserving forests by restricting deforestation and land use changes, emphasizing ecological balance.	Enhanced the legal framework for forest conservation, indirectly contributing to biodiversity protection.	Helped reduce deforestation and habitat destruction, promoting the preservation of ecosystems such as the Western Ghats.
4	1992	Ratification of the Convention on Biological Diversity (CBD), 1992	India ratified the CBD, committing to conserving biodiversity, sustainable use of resources, and fair sharing of benefits arising from genetic resources.	Created the need for national legislation to protect biodiversity and ensure equitable access and benefit-sharing.	Led to the creation of a comprehensive legal framework to address issues like biopiracy and the protection of indigenous knowledge.
5	2002	The Biological Diversity Act, 2002	A landmark law to protect India's biological diversity, promote conservation, sustainable use, and ensure fair and equitable sharing of benefits from biological resources.	Established the National Biodiversity Authority (NBA) to oversee biodiversity protection, regulate access to biological resources, and protect traditional knowledge.	Cases like the protection of neem and turmeric helped prevent biopiracy, where foreign companies tried to patent traditional knowledge without benefit-sharing.

6	2004	**The Biological Diversity Rules, 2004**	Implemented the 2002 Act, detailing procedures for access to biological resources and sharing of benefits with local communities.	Provided a detailed regulatory framework to operationalize the 2002 Act, including guidelines for accessing biological resources and sharing benefits with stakeholders.	Promoted the registration of traditional varieties like Basmati rice, ensuring that indigenous communities benefited from their biodiversity-related knowledge.
7	2010	**The Nagoya Protocol on Access and Benefit Sharing, 2010**	India signed the Nagoya Protocol, which further strengthened the international legal framework for access to genetic resources and fair benefit-sharing.	Strengthened India's commitment to protecting its biodiversity and ensuring that benefits derived from biological resources were shared with local communities.	Case study: The use of genetic resources from India for pharmaceuticals and the benefit-sharing mechanisms in place with local communities.
8	2017	**Amendments to the Biological Diversity Rules, 2017**	Focused on streamlining the process for accessing biological resources, with enhanced protections for traditional knowledge and local communities.	Simplified the procedures for accessing biological resources while strengthening the role of state biodiversity boards in regulating access.	Encouraged more participation from local communities in the conservation and sustainable use of biological resources, such as forest-based products from the Nilgiri Hills.
9	2021	**The Biological Diversity (Amendment) Bill, 2021**	Proposed changes to the 2002 Act to promote greater access to biological resources for the AYUSH (Ayurveda, Yoga, Unani, Siddha, and Homeopathy) industry.	Aimed to promote the indigenous AYUSH industry by easing access to biological resources while maintaining the principles of conservation and benefit-sharing.	Controversial as it raised concerns among environmentalists about potential over-exploitation of resources. The bill is still under discussion and review.

Questions

1. Describe Intellectual Property Rights (IPR) and list its types.

2. What is definition of Intellectual Property (IP)? In what way does Intellectual Property contribute to economic growth and cultural development in a society?

3. Discuss the history of Intellectual property in India.

"You should be innovating so fast that you're invalidating your prior patents."

: Elon Musk

Module - 3

Chapter 6:
PATENTS

INTRODUCTION

Intellectual Property (IP) plays a critical role in protecting innovations[15] and ensuring that inventors can benefit from their creations. This chapter introduces the basics of patents, which are a key part of IP. It covers essential topics like the conditions required to obtain patent protection, the decision of whether to patent an invention or not, and the rights that come with holding a patent. We will also explore the process of patenting, the kinds of inventions that can be patented, what is considered non-patentable, and how to enforce patent rights. Additionally, the importance of avoiding public disclosure before filing a patent and understanding patent infringements will be discussed, providing a foundation for students to appreciate the value and complexity of patents in today's world.

6.1. PATENTS

What is a Patent?

➢ A patent is like a special permission or right given to someone who invents something new. This new thing could be a new way to do something or a new solution to a problem. Think of it as a reward for being creative and coming up with something unique.

Exclusive Right

➢ When you have a patent, you have an "exclusive right." This means you are the only one who can use, make, or sell your invention[16]. No one else can use your invention without your permission.

Legal Protection

➢ The patent gives you legal protection. This means the law will help you if someone tries to copy your invention without asking. It's like having a guard who makes sure no one steals your idea.

Example of a Patent

➢ Let's say you invent a new type of umbrella that never flips inside out in the wind. You can apply for a patent. Once you have it, no one else can make or sell your special umbrella without your permission. But you must explain how your umbrella works so others can learn from it.

Benefits of Having a Patent

➢ Having a patent can help you make money from your invention. You can sell your invention or let others use it for a fee.

---

[15] *Innovation: Innovation is the process of translating an invention into commercial entity or widespread use.*
[16] *Invention: Invention is the creation of a new idea or concept.*

6.2. CONDITIONS FOR OBTAINING A PATENT PROTECTION

The **Patents Act, 1970** of India outlines the conditions that must be met for obtaining patent protection for a product or process. These conditions ensure that the innovation qualifies for a patent. As per **Section 2(1)(j)** of the Patents Act[16], [18], the following three key criteria must be satisfied:

1. **Novelty:** *Not part of 'State of the Art'[17]*

    ➢ **Defination:** For an invention to be considered new, it must not be part of the existing **"State of the Art."** This means the invention should be something that nobody else in the world knows about.

    Conditions:

    ➢ **Not in Public Knowledge:** The invention should not be something that people already know about.

    ➢ **Not Published Anywhere:** The invention should not have been written about in any books, articles, or online. If your invention has been described in a magazine or on a website, it might not be considered new.

    ➢ **Not Claimed by Others:** No one else should have applied for a patent for the same invention. If someone else has already claimed it, you can't get a patent for it.

    Purpose: This condition ensures that the invention introduces something genuinely new to the field and is not a duplication of existing knowledge.

2. **Inventive Step:** *Not obvious to the person (s) skilled in the art.*

    ➢ **Defination:** The invention should not be something that is obvious to someone who is skilled in the field. This means it should be a real step forward in technology or knowledge.

    Conditions:

    ➢ **Technical Advancement:** The invention should improve on what already exists. For example, if you create a new type of engine that is more efficient than current engines, that could be a technical advancement.

    ➢ **Economic Significance:** The invention should have some economic value. This means it should be useful in a way that could help make money or save money.

    ➢ **Not Obvious to Experts:** If someone who is an expert in the field could easily think of the invention, it might not qualify. For instance, if a new type of pen is just a slight change from existing pens, it might be considered obvious.

    Purpose: This ensures that the invention is a result of genuine creativity or ingenuity and not just a minor modification of an existing product or process.

3. **Capable of Industrial Application:** *For the benefit of society*

    ➢ **Defination:** The invention should be something that can be made or used in an industry. It should have practical use and benefit society.

    Conditions:

    ➢ **Made or Used in Industry:** The invention should be something that can be manufactured or used in a business setting. For example, a new machine that helps make cars faster would be useful in the car industry.

    ➢ **Benefit to Society:** The invention should help people in some way. This could mean making a process cheaper, faster, or more efficient.

    Purpose: This condition ensures that the invention is not just theoretical but has real-world utility that contributes to society.

> ***Example:*** *Imagine you invent a new type of solar panel that is more efficient than any other. To get a patent, your solar panel must be **new (nobody else has made it), not obvious (it uses a unique technology that experts didn't think of), and useful in industry (it can be used to generate electricity for homes and businesses).***

---

[17] *State of the Art: The most recent stage in the development of a product, incorporating the newest technology, ideas, and features.*

6.3. TO PATENT OR NOT TO PATENT AN INVENTION

When an invention is developed, the inventor must decide whether to patent it, keep it a trade secret, or place it in the public domain. Each option has its own implications regarding commercial gain, societal benefit, and the legal protection of intellectual property. The decision-making process typically involves the following considerations:

1. **Exploitation for Personal or Public Benefit**
   a. **Personal Benefits:**
      - Most inventors prefer to exploit their inventions for personal and financial gain under the protection of statutory laws.
      - By patenting the invention or keeping it a trade secret, the inventor can control how the invention is used and can derive direct monetary benefits.
   b. **Public Domain:**
      - A minority of inventions are placed directly into the public domain, where anyone can use the innovation freely without compensating the inventor.
      - Once in the public domain, the invention can be commercially or societally exploited without paying any royalties to the inventor.

2. **Monetary Gains: Patent vs. Trade Secret**
   a. **Patent:**
      - A patent grants the inventor **exclusive rights** to exploit the invention for a limited period (usually 20 years), during which others cannot make, use, or sell the invention without the inventor's consent.
      - A patent is preferred when:
         - The invention has a relatively **short life span**.
         - It is likely that the invention will be publicly known or that it may be **reverse-engineered** easily.
         - The protection provided by a patent is essential to securing short-term profitability.
   b. **Trade Secret:**
      - A trade secret is a type of intellectual property that allows the inventor to **maintain secrecy** over the invention for an indefinite period, as long as the secret can be protected.
      - A trade secret is preferred when:
         - The inventor is certain they can maintain **absolute secrecy** over the invention for a very long period (potentially 100 years or more).
         - The invention is difficult or impossible to reverse-engineer, reducing the risk of the secret being disclosed.
         - There is no legal requirement to publicly disclose the details of the invention, unlike patents which require full disclosure upon filing.

3. **Key Factors for Decision-Making**
   a. **Life Span of the Invention:**
      - If the invention has a short life span and is likely to become obsolete in a few years, patent protection is preferable due to its limited duration.
      - For inventions with long-term viability, a trade secret may provide better protection.
   b. **Probability of Reverse Engineering:**
      - If there is a **high likelihood** that others could reverse-engineer the invention once it is public, patent protection ensures legal recourse.
      - If reverse engineering is unlikely or impossible, maintaining a trade secret might be a better option.

    c. **Legal Protection and Costs:**
- ➤ Patents require legal filings, fees, and may involve litigation costs to enforce.
- ➤ Trade secrets, while potentially longer-lasting, require rigorous internal controls and strategies to protect the confidential nature of the invention.

6.4. RIGHTS ASSOCIATED WITH PATENTS.

Patents grant inventors specific rights and protections under the law. These rights provide the patent holder with control over the use and commercialization of the patented invention.

1. **Exclusive Rights of the Patent Owner**
   a. **Right to Control Usage:**
      - ➤ The patent owner has the **exclusive right** to decide who may or may not use the patented invention.
      - ➤ Preventing others from commercially making, using, distributing, importing, or selling the patented invention without obtaining consent from the patent holder.
   b. **Licensing to Others:**
      - ➤ The patent owner has the ability to **permit third parties** to use the invention, but this can only happen under **mutually agreed terms**.
      - ➤ Licensing agreements allow the patent holder to generate revenue from their invention while still retaining control over its use.

2. **Nature of Patent Rights: Negative Rights**
   a. **Definition:** Patent rights are considered negative rights, meaning that they do not give the owner the right to use the invention themselves but instead allow the owner to restrict others from using the invention without permission.
   b. **Restricting Usage:**
      - ➤ The primary function of a patent is to **prevent unauthorized usage** of the invention by others.
      - ➤ The owner can block others from making, using, selling, or distributing the patented technology or product without their prior approval.

3. **Legal Recourse in Case of Infringement[18]**
   a. **Suing for Infringement:**
      - ➤ If a third party infringes on the patent rights by using or commercializing the patented invention without permission, the patent owner has the right to **sue the infringer**.
      - ➤ Legal actions can be taken to stop the unauthorized use of the invention, including court injunctions to prevent further infringement.
   b. **Compensation:**
      - ➤ The patent holder may seek **compensation** or damages for the unauthorized use of their patented invention. This includes seeking financial restitution for losses caused by the infringement.

> *Example: If you invented a new type of bicycle. You get a patent for it. Now, you have the right to decide who can make or sell this bicycle. If someone starts making and selling your bicycle without asking you, you can take them to court. You can ask the court to make them stop and also pay you for using your invention without permission.*

4. **Importance of Patent Rights:** Patent rights are crucial because they:
   i. Provide the patent owner with **control** over how their invention is used.
   ii. Ensure that inventors can **monetize** their innovations by either commercializing the invention themselves or licensing it to others.
   iii. Protect inventors from **unfair exploitation** of their work by others.

---

[18] *Infringement: The unauthorized use, sale, or production of a product or material that is protected by intellectual property rights*

6.5. ENFORCEMENT OF PATENT RIGHTS

Enforcing patent rights is essential to protect the patent holder's exclusive control over their invention. This enforcement process involves ensuring compliance with the law and stopping unauthorized use of the patented invention. The following are the key aspects of patent rights enforcement.

1. **Definition of Enforcement**
    - ➢ **Enforcement** refers to the process of ensuring that laws, regulations, and rules are followed.
    - ➢ It involves monitoring, identifying violations, and taking appropriate actions against non-compliance.
    - ➢ In the context of patents, enforcement means ensuring that the patent holder's exclusive rights are upheld and preventing unauthorized use of the invention by others.

2. **Role of the Judicial System**
    - ➢ **Court of Law**:
        - ❖ Patent rights are primarily enforced through the **judicial courts**.
        - ❖ The court has the authority to stop patent infringement by issuing orders, such as injunctions, to prevent further unauthorized use of the patented invention.
        - ❖ Courts can also award **damages** or compensation to the patent holder for losses incurred due to infringement.
    - ➢ Judicial Protection:
        - ❖ Courts play a vital role in safeguarding the patent holder's rights. They act as the primary legal avenue for resolving disputes related to patent infringement.

3. **Responsibility of the Patent Owner**
    - ➢ Monitoring and Identifying Infringement:
        - ❖ The **main responsibility** for detecting and monitoring infringement falls on the **patent owner**.
        - ❖ The patent holder must be proactive in identifying instances where their patented invention is being used or commercialized without authorization.
    - ➢ **Taking Action Against Infringers**:
        - ❖ Once the patent owner identifies an infringement, it is their responsibility to **take legal action** against the infringer.
        - ❖ The patent holder may initiate a lawsuit to enforce their rights, stop the unauthorized use, and seek damages for the infringement.

6.6. INVENTIONS ELIGIBLE FOR PATENTING

1. **Types of Inventions That Can Be Patented**

    Patents can be given for inventions in any field. This means it doesn't matter if the invention is something simple like a paper clip or something complex like a tiny chip used in nanotechnology. Even a special type of mouse used in scientific research, like the Harvard mouse with cancer genes, can be patented.

2. **Common Misunderstanding About Patents**

    Many people think that patents are only for big, groundbreaking scientific discoveries. But this is not true. Most patents are actually given for improvements on things that already exist. This means if you make something a little better or different, you might be able to get a patent for it.

Example of Patented Improvements
Let's look at penicillin, which is a type of medicine that kills germs. Scientists have made small changes to the original penicillin to create new versions with better features. These new versions might be more stable in acid, work at different temperatures, or kill more types of germs. Each of these new versions, called second, third, or fourth generation penicillins, can also be patented.

---

3. **Everyday Items with Patents**

In our daily lives, we use many things that have patents. This includes simple items like toothbrushes and shoes, as well as more complex things like mobile phones and cars. Even a simple pen or a pair of eyeglasses can have a patent.

4. **Complex Products with Multiple Patents**

Some products are made up of many different inventions, each with its own patent. For example, a laptop computer has hundreds of different inventions inside it, all working together. The same is true for cars, mobile phones, and televisions. Each part, like the screen or the battery, might have its own patent.

6.7. NON-PATENTABLE MATTERS

In the **Patent Act of 1970**, there are certain things that cannot be patented[18]. A patent is a legal right given to an inventor to stop others from making, using, or selling their invention without permission. However, not everything can be patented. Let's look at what cannot be patented and why.

1. **Invention Contrary to Public Morality**: Some inventions are not allowed because they go against what society considers right or moral. For example, a method for human cloning or a method for gambling cannot be patented. These are seen as harmful or unethical.

2. **Mere Discovery**: If you find something that already exists in nature, like a new type of micro-organism, you cannot patent it. Similarly, you cannot patent natural laws, like the law of gravity, because they are not inventions; they are discoveries.

3. **Mere Discovery of a New Form of a Known Substance**: If you find a new use for something that is already known, like using aspirin for heart treatment when it was originally used for reducing fever, you cannot patent this new use. The substance itself is not new.

4. **Frivolous Invention**: These are inventions that are not serious or important. For example, adding herbs to dough just to change its taste, or creating a 100-year calendar or a bus timetable, are not considered significant enough to be patented.

5. **Arrangement or Rearrangement**: Simply putting things together in a new way, like attaching a fan to an umbrella or a torch to a bucket, is not enough for a patent. These are just new combinations of existing things.

6. **Inventions Related to Atomic Energy**: According to Section 20(1) of the Atomic Energy Act, 1962, inventions involving certain materials like Uranium or Plutonium cannot be patented. These materials are controlled by the government for safety reasons[19].

7. **Literary, Dramatic, Musical, Artistic Work**: Creative works like books, sculptures, and paintings are protected by copyright, not patents. Copyright is a different type of protection that covers artistic and creative works.

8. **Topography of Integrated Circuits**: The design of integrated circuits, which are tiny electronic circuits used in devices, is protected under a different law called the Semiconductor Integrated Circuit Layout Designs Act, 2000[20].

9. **Plants and Animals**: You cannot patent plants and animals, or any part of them, like seeds or species. This also includes natural processes for growing or breeding them. These are considered part of nature.

10. **Traditional Knowledge**: If an invention is based on traditional knowledge, like using herbs that have been known for centuries for healing, it cannot be patented. This is because it is not a new invention; it is based on what is already known.

6.8. PATENT INFRINGEMENTS

Once you have a patent, you own the rights to your invention. This means you can decide how it is used or sold. No one else can use it without asking you first. ***Patent infringement happens when someone uses your invention without your permission.***

6.8.1. TYPES OF PATENT INFRINGEMENT:

1. **Direct Infringement:** This is when someone makes or sells something very similar to your patented invention without your permission. Imagine if you invented a new kind of toy car, and someone else started selling a car that looks just like yours.
2. **Indirect Infringement:** This happens when someone accidentally uses your invention without knowing it. It's like if someone used your toy car design by mistake, thinking it was okay.

6.8.2. WHAT CAN YOU DO IF SOMEONE INFRINGES YOUR PATENT?

If someone uses your invention without permission, you can take legal action. This means you can go to court to stop them. Here are some things you can ask for:

1. **Interlocutory/Interim Injunction:** This is a temporary order from the court to stop the person from using your invention until the case is decided. It's like a pause button.
2. **Damages or Accounts of Profits:** You can ask for money to make up for any losses you suffered because someone used your invention without permission. It's like getting paid back for what you lost.
3. **Permanent Injunction:** This is a long-term order from the court to stop the person from using your invention forever. It's like a permanent stop sign.

Special Rights of the Government:

Sometimes, the government can use your invention without your permission. This can happen in emergencies, like during a national crisis. But they have to tell you first. This is allowed under specific laws, like Section 100 of the Patent Act, 1970 [21], and Rule 32 of the Patent Rules, 2003[22].

Why Are These Rules Important?

These rules help protect inventors. They make sure that people who create new things can benefit from their hard work. It's like making sure you get to play with your toy first before anyone else can.

> ***Example:*** *Imagine you invented a new kind of smartphone. You get a patent, so only you can make and sell this phone. If someone else starts selling a phone that looks just like yours without asking, that's direct infringement. If a company accidentally uses your phone design because they didn't know it was patented, that's indirect infringement. You can go to court to stop them and ask for money if you lost sales because of them.*

6.9. AVOID PUBLIC DISCLOSURE OF AN INVENTION BEFORE PATENTING

Why Keep Your Invention Secret?

- ➢ **Public Disclosure:** If you show or tell people about your invention before you apply for a patent, it is called public disclosure. This can happen if you publish it in a magazine, show it at a fair, or talk about it in a public meeting. Public disclosure can make your invention lose its novelty.
- ➢ **Novelty Criterion:** For an invention to be patented, it must be new. This is called the "novelty" criterion. If an invention is already known to the public, it is not considered new anymore. This means it cannot be patented.

Grace Period for Patenting

- ➢ **Grace Period:** Sometimes, inventors accidentally or necessarily disclose their invention. The Patents Act allows a grace period of 12 months. This means you have one year from the time you first showed or talked about your invention to apply for a patent. This grace period helps inventors who might have disclosed their invention by mistake or for a good reason.

When Disclosure is Unavoidable

- ➢ **Unavoidable Disclosure:** Sometimes, you might need to tell someone about your invention before you apply for a patent. For example, if you want to sell your invention to an investor or a business partner, they need to know all about it to decide if it is worth investing in.
- ➢ **Non-Disclosure Agreement (NDA):** In such cases, it is important to protect your invention. You can do this by signing a Non-Disclosure Agreement (NDA) with the person you are telling. An NDA is a

legal document where the person agrees not to share your invention with anyone else. This keeps your invention safe until you can apply for a patent.

Examples

Example of Public Disclosure: *Imagine you invented a new type of phone. If you post about it on social media or show it at a tech fair before applying for a patent, anyone can see it. This means it is no longer new, and you might not get a patent.*

Example of Using an NDA: *Suppose you want to sell your new phone idea to a company. Before you tell them all the details, you ask them to sign an NDA. This way, they cannot tell anyone else about your phone idea, keeping it safe until you apply for a patent.*

Questions

1. Define the term patent and what are the conditions that must be met for obtaining patent protection?

2. What types of inventions are eligible for patenting, and which matters are considered non-patentable?

3. What are Patent Infringements? Explain its two categories of Infringements.

4. What are the exclusions (Product and Processes) that cannot be petented? Explain.

"A country without a patent office and good patent laws is just a crab, and can't travel any way but sideways and backways."

: Mark Twain

Module - 3

Chapter 7:
PROCESS OF PATENTING

INTRODUCTION

The journey of transforming an innovative idea into a patented invention involves several well-defined steps known as the Process of Patenting. This chapter explores each stage of this process, starting with a Prior Art Search, which helps determine if an invention is truly novel. It then moves on to the choice of application, filling out the required patent forms, and understanding the jurisdiction for filing. Additionally, we will cover the importance of publication, the role of pre- and post-grant opposition, and how an invention is examined before a patent is granted. Finally, this chapter discusses the commercialization of patents, the need for a patent attorney, and answers questions like whether a worldwide patent can be obtained. Understanding these steps is crucial for effectively protecting and utilizing inventions in today's global economy.

7.1. PROCESS OF PATENTING

The process of patenting involves a series of well-structured steps designed to protect an invention by granting exclusive rights to the inventor. The process of patenting, particularly in India, involves several critical steps that can be time-consuming, often taking 3-4 years or more to complete. Figure 7.1. is a simplified flowchart of the critical steps involved in the patenting process.

1. **Prior Art Search:**

   Before applying for a patent, it is essential to perform a **prior art search**. This search helps determine if an invention is novel and non-obvious by checking existing patents and publications worldwide. A thorough search avoids unnecessary rejections during the patent examination process.

   ➢ **Example**: In the pharmaceutical industry, searching for similar chemical compositions in databases like **Derwent Innovations Index**[19] is critical to ensuring that a drug formula is patentable.

   ➢ **Sources**: Patent databases such as **WIPO**, **Google Patents**, and **Indian Patent Office** databases are used to conduct prior art searches.

2. **Filing the Patent Application:**

   The second step in the patenting process is to file a patent application with the appropriate patent office. This application must include a detailed description of the invention, claims defining the scope of the patent protection sought, and any necessary drawings or diagrams.

---

[19] *Derwent Innovations Index: It is an index of worldwide patents issued since 1963.*

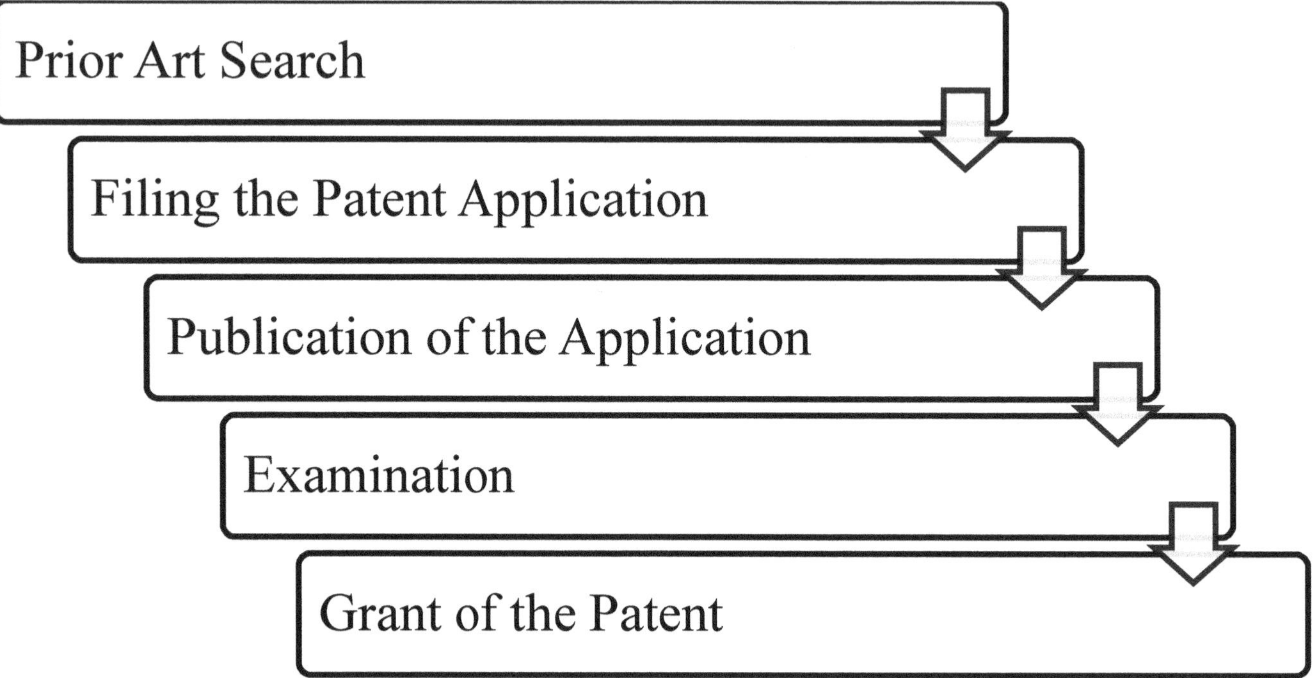

Fig. 7.1 Flowchart of the critical steps involved in the Patenting process.

3. **Publication of the Application:**

After filing, the patent application is typically published by the patent office. This publication usually occurs 18 months from the filing date or the priority date, whichever is earlier. This step makes the details of the invention publicly available.

4. **Examination:**
   - **Examination Request:** A request for examination must be filed to initiate the examination process. This request can be made by the applicant or any other interested party. The examination process involves a thorough review of the application to ensure it meets all legal requirements for patentability.
   - **Examination and Objections:** During the examination, the patent office may raise objections or request clarifications regarding the application. The applicant must respond to these objections, providing necessary amendments or explanations to satisfy the examiner's concerns.

5. **Grant of the Patent:** Once all objections are resolved, and the application is deemed to meet all patentability criteria, the patent is granted. The grant of a patent provides the inventor with exclusive rights to the invention for a specified period, typically 20 years from the filing date.

These steps are crucial for securing patent protection and ensuring that the inventor's rights are legally recognized and enforceable. The process requires careful attention to detail and adherence to legal requirements to successfully navigate the complexities of patent law.

7.2. PRIOR ART SEARCH

When someone invents something new, they often want to protect their idea by getting a patent. A patent is like a special permission that says only the inventor can make, use, or sell their invention. But before they can get this permission, they need to make sure their invention is truly new. This is where a **Prior Art Search** comes in.

What is Prior Art?
   - **Definition**: Prior Art refers to any information that is already available to the public in any form before a patent application is filed. This could be anything from existing patents, scientific articles, books, or even online content.
   - **Purpose**: The main goal of checking Prior Art is to see if the invention is already known. If it is, then it might not be considered new or "novel," which is a key requirement for getting a patent.

Why Conduct a Prior Art Search?

➢ **Avoiding Infringement**: By checking Prior Art, inventors can avoid accidentally copying someone else's idea. This helps them stay out of legal trouble.

➢ **Tracking Research and Development**: It helps inventors understand what has already been done in their field. This can guide them in making improvements or finding new directions for their work.

➢ **Access to Information**: A Prior Art Search provides detailed information about similar inventions. This can be very useful for inventors to refine their ideas.

Parameters of Prior Art Search

➢ **Novelty**: These checks if the invention is new. If something similar already exists, the invention might not be considered novel.

➢ **Patentability**: This assesses if the invention can be patented. It looks at whether the invention meets all the criteria for a patent.

➢ **State of the Art**: This involves understanding the current level of technology in the field. It helps inventors see how advanced their invention is compared to existing technology.

➢ **Infringement**: To checks if the invention might violate existing patents. It helps to avoid legal issues.

➢ **Validity**: This ensures that the invention is strong enough to withstand legal challenges. It checks if the invention can be defended if someone questions its patent.

➢ **Freedom to Operate**: This determines if the invention can be used without infringing on other patents. It helps inventors know if they can freely use their invention.

Where to Conduct a Prior Art Search?

To determine if an invention is novel, inventors must review:

1. **Patent Databases**: These are collections of existing patents. They are a primary source for checking if an invention is already patented.

   Unpaid Databases

   a. **Indian Patent Advanced Search System (InPASS):** This is a tool used in India to search for patents. InPASS helps people find out if an invention is already patented in India.
   URL: http://ipindiaservices.gov.in/publicsearch/

   b. **Patentscope (WIPO):** This is a global tool provided by the World Intellectual Property Organization (WIPO). It allows people to search for patents from many countries. This is useful if you want to know if an invention is patented somewhere else in the world.
   URL: https://www.wipo.int/patentscope/en/

   c. **Espacenet (EU):** This is a European tool that helps people search for patents. It is useful for finding patents that are registered in Europe.
   URL: https://worldwide.espacenet.com/patent/

   d. **USPTO (USA):** The United States Patent and Trademark Office (USPTO) provides this tool. It helps people search for patents in the United States. **URL:** https://www.uspto.gov/

   e. **Google Patents Advanced Search:** Google offers a way to search for patents from many countries. It is similar to using Google to search for websites, but specifically for patents.
   URL: https://patents.google.com/advanced

   Paid Databases

   f. **Orbit Intelligence:** This is a business tool that helps companies understand patents. It is used by businesses to make smart decisions about inventions.
   URL: https://www.questel.com/business-intelligence-software/orbit-intelligence/

   g. **Derwent Innovation:** This tool helps people find and understand patents. It is used by researchers and companies to see what inventions are already out there.
   URL: https://clarivate.com/derwent/solutions/derwent-innovation/

    h. PROQUEST: This is a tool that helps people search for patents and other academic information. It is often used by students and researchers.

    URL: https://about.proquest.com/search/?searchKeyword=patent+

2. **Non-Patent Literature (NPL)**: This includes scientific journals, reports, magazines, and other publications. NPL is important because not all inventions are patented; some might be described in other forms of literature.

    a. Scholarly Publications: These include handbooks, textbooks, and journals. Journals like IEEE and Springer publish articles about new research. Dissertations and conference proceedings are also part of this group. They provide detailed information about research that might not be patented yet.

    b. Industry/Trade Publications: These are publications that focus on specific industries. They include reviews, public disclosures, and even social media posts. For example, a YouTube video explaining a new technology could be considered industry literature.

    c. Others: This includes newspapers, websites, and technology blogs. These sources provide information that might not be found in patents or scholarly publications. For example, a blog post about a new gadget could be useful for understanding current technology trends.

Most non-patent literature is available for free. However, some journals require a subscription, meaning you have to pay to read them. This is important for researchers who need access to the latest information. Major patent offices like the USPTO, EPO, and JPO maintain their own databases of non-patent literature.

7.3. CHOICE OF APPLICATION TO BE FILED

Once an inventor decides to patent an invention, they must choose between filing a **Provisional Patent Application** or a **Complete (Final) Patent Application**. The decision depends on several factors:

1. **Provisional Patent Application**

    A Provisional Patent Application is often preferred due to its flexibility and cost-effectiveness. The key advantages include:

    a. Cost and Time Efficient: Filing a provisional patent application is usually cheaper and faster. It also involves fewer formal steps. This means inventors can save money and time, which is especially helpful if they are just starting out or have limited resources.

    b. Flexibility for Improvements: After filing a provisional application, inventors can still make changes or improvements to their invention. These changes can be added to the final application later. This is useful because sometimes inventors are still working on their ideas and might not have all the details ready at first.

    c. Incomplete Data is Okay: A provisional application doesn't need all the details about the invention. Inventors can file it even if they are still collecting data or doing experiments. This means they don't have to wait until everything is perfect before starting the patent process.

    d. Securing a Priority Date: Filing a provisional application gives the inventor a "priority date." This is like a timestamp that shows when they first claimed their invention. If someone else tries to patent a similar idea later, the priority date can help prove who was first.

2. **Complete (Final) Patent Application**

    a. Mandatory Follow-Up: After filing a provisional application, inventors must file a **complete patent application within one year.** If they don't, the provisional application will be rejected, and they might lose their priority date. This means they could miss out on protecting their invention.

    b. Detailed Information Required: Unlike the provisional application, the complete application needs all the details about the invention. This includes how it works, what it does, and any improvements made since the provisional application. It's like telling the whole story of the invention.

7.4. PATENT APPLICATION FORMS

As per the **Patent Act, 1970** [18] and the **Patents Rules, 2003** [22], filing a patent in India requires submitting specific forms, namely **Form-1** and **Form-2**. These forms play a crucial role in ensuring that the patent filing process is completed with all required information.

1. **Form-1: General Information**

    Form-1 primarily gathers general information about the patent application, refer fig. 7.2 to fig. 7.5. This form includes:

    a. **Title of Application:** The title of the invention being patented.

    b. **Applicant and Inventor Information:** Names and details of the applicant(s) and inventor(s).

    c. **Type of Application:** Different types of patent applications include:

        i. **Ordinary Application:** Direct filing of a patent.

        ii. **Convention Application:** Based on an earlier filing in a convention country.

        iii. **PCT-NP (PCT-National Phase):** Based on an international PCT application.

        iv. **Divisional Application:** Filed when an application needs to be divided into two or more patents.

        v. **Patent of Addition:** Filed for improvements or modifications to an already granted patent.

FORM 1 THE PATENTS ACT 1970 (39 of 1970) and THE PATENTS RULES, 2003 **APPLICATION FOR GRANT OF PATENT** (See section 7, 54 and 135 and sub-rule (1) of rule 20)	(FOR OFFICE USE ONLY)	
	Application No.	
	Filing date:	
	Amount of Fee paid:	
	CBR No:	
	Signature:	

1. APPLICANT'S REFERENCE / IDENTIFICATION NO. (AS ALLOTTED BY OFFICE)

2. TYPE OF APPLICATION [Please tick (✓) at the appropriate category]

Ordinary ( )		Convention ( )		PCT-NP ( )		PPH ( )
Divisional( )	Patent of Addition ( )	Divisional( )( )	Patent of Addition ( )	Divisional( )	Patent of Addition ( )	

3A. APPLICANT(S)

Name in Full	Gender (optional, for individuals)	Nationality	Country of Residence	Age (optional, for natural persons)	Address of the Applicant	
	- Male - Female - Others - Prefer not to disclose			-____ years - Prefer not to disclose	House No.	
					Street	
					City	
					State	
					Country	
					Pin code	
					Email (OTP verification mandatory -will be redacted)	
					Contact number (OTP verification mandatory -will be redacted)	

3B. CATEGORY OF APPLICANT [Please tick (✓) at the appropriate category]

Natural Person ( )	Other than Natural Person ( )		Educational institution ()
	Small Entity ( )	Startup ( )	Others ( )

4. INVENTOR(S) [Please tick (✓) at the appropriate category]

Are all the inventor(s) same as the applicant(s) named above?	Yes ( )	No ( )

Fig. 7.2 Page Number 1 of Patent Form – 1: General Information[23].
URL to download: https://ipindia.gov.in/writereaddata/Portal/IPOFormUpload/1_12_1/form-1.pdf

If "No", furnish the details of the inventor(s)					
Name in Full	Gender (optional, for natural persons)	Nationality	Age (optional, for natural persons)	Country of Residence	Address of the Inventor
	- Male - Female - Others - Prefer not to disclose		- ____ years - Prefer not to disclose		House No. Street City State Country Pin code

5. TITLE OF THE INVENTION

6. AUTHORISED REGISTERED PATENT AGENT(S)	IN/PA No.	
	Name	
	Mobile No. (OTP verification mandatory-will be redacted)	

7. ADDRESS FOR SERVICE OF APPLICANT IN INDIA	Name	
	Postal Address	
	Telephone No.	
	Mobile No. (OTP verification mandatory-will be redacted)	
	Fax No.	
	E-mail ID (OTP verification mandatory-will be redacted)	

8. IN CASE OF APPLICATION CLAIMING PRIORITY OF APPLICATION FILED IN CONVENTION COUNTRY, PARTICULARS OF CONVENTION APPLICATION

Country	Application Number	Filing date	Name of the applicant	Title of the invention	IPC (as classified in the convention country)

9. IN CASE OF PCT NATIONAL PHASE APPLICATION, PARTICULARS OF INTERNATIONAL APPLICATION FILED UNDER PATENT CO-OPERATION TREATY (PCT)

International application number	International filing date

10. IN CASE OF DIVISIONAL APPLICATION FILED UNDER SECTION 16, PARTICULARS OF ORIGINAL (FIRST) APPLICATION

Original (first) application No.	Date of filing of original (first) application

11. IN CASE OF PATENT OF ADDITION FILED UNDER SECTION 54, PARTICULARS OF MAIN APPLICATION OR PATENT

Main application/patent No.	Date of filing of main application

12. DECLARATIONS

Fig. 7.3 Page Number 2 of Patent Form – 1: General Information[23].

(i) Declaration by the inventor(s)
(In case the applicant is an assignee: the inventor(s) may sign herein below or the applicant may upload the assignment or enclose the assignment with this application for patent or send the assignment by post/electronictransmission duly authenticated within the prescribed period).
I/We, the above named inventor(s) is/are the true & first inventor(s) for this Invention and declare that the applicant(s) herein is/are my/our assignee or legal representative.
(a) Date
(b) Signature(s)
(c) Name(s)

(ii) Declaration by the applicant(s) in the convention country
(In case the applicant in India is different than the applicant in the convention country: the applicant in the convention country may sign herein below or applicant in India may upload the assignment from the applicant in the convention country or enclose the said assignment with this application for patent or send the assignment by post/electronic transmission duly authenticated within the prescribed period)
I/We, the applicant(s) in the convention country declare that the applicant(s) herein is/are my/our assignee or legal representative.
(a) Date
(b) Signature(s)
(c) Name(s) of the signatory

(iii) Declaration by the applicant(s)
I/We the applicant(s) hereby declare(s) that: -
☐ I am/We are in possession of the above-mentioned invention.
☐ The provisional/complete specification relating to the invention is filed with this application.
☐ The invention as disclosed in the specification uses the biological material from India and the necessary permission from the competent authority shall be submitted by me/us before the grant of patent to me/us.
☐ There is no lawful ground of objection(s) to the grant of the Patent to me/us.
☐ I am/we are the true & first inventor(s).
☐ I am/we are the assignee or legal representative of true & first inventor(s).
☐ The application or each of the applications, particulars of which are given in Paragraph-8, was the first application in convention country/countries in respect of my/our invention(s).
☐ I/We claim the priority from the above mentioned application(s) filed in convention country/countries and state that no application for protection in respect of the invention had been made in a convention country before that date by me/us or by any person from which I/We derive the title.
☐ My/our application in India is based on international application under Patent Cooperation Treaty (PCT) as mentioned in Paragraph-9.
☐ The application is divided out of my /our application particulars of which is given in Paragraph-10 and pray that this application may be treated as deemed to have been filed on DD/MM/YYYY under section 16 of the Act.
☐ The said invention is an improvement in or modification of the invention particulars of which are given in Paragraph-11.

13. FOLLOWING ARE THE ATTACHMENTS WITH THE APPLICATION
(a) Form 2

Item	Details	Fee	Remarks
Complete/ provisional specification)#	No. of pages		
No. of Claim(s)	No. of claims and No. of pages		
Abstract	No. of pages		
No. of Drawing(s)	No. of drawings and No. of pages		

Fig. 7.4 Page Number 3 of Patent Form – 1: General Information[23].

In case of a complete specification, if the applicant desires to adopt the drawings filed with his provisional specification as the drawings or part of the drawings for the complete specification under rule 13(4), the number of such pages filed with the provisional specification are required to be mentioned here.

(b) Complete specification (in conformation with the international application)/as amended before the International Preliminary Examination Authority (IPEA), as applicable (2 copies).

(c) Sequence listing in electronic form

(d) Drawings (in conformation with the international application)/as amended before the International Preliminary Examination Authority (IPEA), as applicable (2 copies).

(e) Priority document(s) or a request to retrieve the priority document(s) from DAS (Digital Access Service) if the applicant had already requested the office of first filing to make the priority document(s) available to DAS.

(f) Translation of priority document/Specification/International Search Report/International Preliminary Report on Patentability.

(g) Statement and Undertaking on Form 3

(h) Declaration of Inventorship on Form 5

(i) Power of Authority

(j) ....

Total fee ₹ .... in Cash / Banker's Cheque /Bank Draft bearing No......... Date.............on ....
Bank.

I/We hereby declare that to the best of my/our knowledge, information and belief the fact and matters stated herein are correct and I/We request that a patent may be granted to me/us for the said invention.

Dated this .... day of ....20.................

Signature:

Name:

To,

The Controller of Patents

The Patent Office, at.....................................

Note: -

* Repeat boxes in case of more than one entry.
* To be signed by the applicant(s) or by authorized registered patent agent otherwise where mentioned.
* Tick (✓)/cross (x) whichever is applicable/not applicable in declaration in paragraph-12.
* Name of the inventor and applicant should be given in full, family name in the beginning.
* Strike out the portion which is/are not applicable.
* For fee: See First Schedule.

Fig. 7.5 Page Number 4 of Patent Form – 1: General Information[23].

2. Form-2: Technical Information

Form-2 is used to provide technical details about the invention, refer fig. 7.6. The content differs based on whether the inventor is filing a Provisional or Complete application:

a. Provisional Application:
i. Requires only a Description of the Invention and an Abstract.
ii. This allows inventors to file without complete data, enabling them to secure a priority date while continuing to develop the invention.

b. Complete Application:
i. Requires a more comprehensive submission, including the Description of the Invention, Abstract, and most importantly, Claims.
ii. Claims define the boundaries of the invention and specify what aspects of the invention are to be protected under the patent.

3. Importance of Claims

Claims are the most critical part of a patent specification, as they determine the legal scope of the invention. They define what is protected by the patent and outline the boundaries of the invention. Claims are categorized into:

➢ **Independent Claims:** Stand-alone claims that define the essential features of the invention.
➢ **Dependent Claims:** Claims that rely on an independent claim and add additional features or improvements.

FORM 2
THE PATENT ACT 1970
(39 of 1970)
&
The Patents Rules, 2003
PROVISIONAL/COMPLETE SPECIFICATION
(See section 10 and rule13)

1. TITLE OF THE INVENTION

2. APPLICANT (S)
(a) NAME:
(b) NATIONALITY:
(c) ADDRESS:

3. PREAMBLE TO THE DESCRIPTION

PROVISIONAL	COMPLETE
The following specification describes the invention.	The following specification particularly describes the invention and the manner in which it is to be performed.

4. DESCRIPTION (Description shall start from next page.)

5. CLAIMS (not applicable for provisional specification. Claims should start with the preamble — **"I/we claim"** on separate page)

6. DATE AND SIGNATURE (to be given at the end of last page of specification)

7. ABSTRACT OF THE INVENTION (to be given along with complete specification on separate page)

Note: -
*Repeat boxes in case of more than one entry.
*To be signed by the applicant(s) or by authorized registered patent agent.
*Name of the applicant should be given in full , family name in the beginning .
*Complete address of the applicant should be given stating the postal index no./code, state and country.
*Strike out the column which is/are not applicable

Fig. 7.6 Patent Form-2: Technical Information[24].
URL to download: https://ipindia.gov.in/writereaddata/Portal/IPOFormUpload/1_13_1/form-2.pdf

7.5. JURISDICTION OF FILING PATENT APPLICATION

In India, the jurisdiction for filing a patent application is determined by the location of the applicant's residence, place of business, or where the invention originated. The country is divided into four patent jurisdictions, each with its own patent office responsible for receiving and processing applications. These jurisdictions ensure that patent applications are managed systematically and efficiently across regions.

Table 7.1. Territorial Jurisdiction of Appropriate Office for the Applicants[16], [25].

Sl. No.	Region	States covered	Address	Example
1	Northern Region	Haryana, Himachal Pradesh, Punjab, Rajasthan, Uttar Pradesh, Uttarakhand, Delhi and the Union Territory of Chandigarh, Jammu and Kashmir and Ladakh.	Plot No. 32, Sector 14, Dwarka, New Delhi-110078 Phone: 011-28032491 Fax: 011-28034301 Email: delhi-patent@nic.in	A company based in Noida, Uttar Pradesh, will file its patent application with the Delhi Patent Office
2	Southern Region	Andhra Pradesh, Karnataka, Kerala, Tamil Nadu, Telangana and the Union Territories of Pondicherry and Lakshadweep	Patent Office Intellectual Property Building G.S.T. Road, Guindy, Chennai-600032 Phone: 044-22505242 Fax: 044-22502066 Email: Chennai-patent@nic.in	An innovation from a research lab in Bangalore, Karnataka, would be filed at the Chennai Patent Office.
3	Western Region	Maharashtra, Gujarat, Madhya Pradesh, Goa and Chhattisgarh and the Union Territories of Daman and Diu & Dadra and Nagar Haveli	Boudhik Sampada Bhawan, Antop Hill, S. M. Road, Mumbai - 400 037. Phone: 022- 24153651, 24148165 Fax: 022-24130387 Email: Mumbai-patent@nic.i	A tech startup from Pune, Maharashtra, would file their patent application at the Mumbai Patent Office.
4	Eastern Region	Remaining States	Intellectual Property Office Building, CP-2 Sector V, Salt Lake City Kolkata-700091 Phone: 033-23679101, 033-23671987 Fax: 033-23671988 Email: Kolkata-patent@nic.in	An inventor based in Bhubaneswar, Odisha, would submit their patent application to the Kolkata Patent Office.

Foreign Applicants: If you're from another country, you need an address in India. This could be your business address or your patent agent's address. This address decides which office you should use.

Joint Applications: Sometimes, more than one person invents something together. In this case, all inventors have the same rights. They all get equal consideration when filing a patent.

7.6. PUBLICATION

Once a patent application is filed at the **Regional Patent Office** in India, it undergoes a mandatory confidentiality period before being made public. This period is crucial to protect the details of the invention during the early stages of the patenting process.

1. **Secrecy Period**

   After the patent application is filed, it is kept secret for 18 months. This 18-month period begins from the filing date of the application or the priority date (the earlier of the two). During this time, the details of the invention are not disclosed to the public, allowing inventors to safeguard their intellectual property while the patent is being processed.

2. **Publication of the Patent Application**

After the 18-month secrecy period expires, the patent application is published in the Official Journal of the Patent Office. This publication is a crucial step for the following reasons:

- ➤ **Informs the Public:** It alerts the public about the invention and its potential claims. This transparency allows others in the same field to be aware of existing patents.
- ➤ **Mandatory Process:** The publication of the patent application is a legal requirement under Indian patent law, and every patent application must go through this stage unless it has been withdrawn before the publication period.

3. **Access to Published Applications**

The published patent applications are available to the public via the Official Journal of the Patent Office. Interested parties can access the journal online at **https://www.ipindia.gov.in/journal-patents.htm**, where they can view the details of the published inventions, including the abstract, description, and claims.

4. **Purpose of Publication**

The main purposes of publishing a patent application are:

- ➤ **Public Awareness:** It allows individuals, researchers, and companies to stay updated on new technological advancements and inventions.
- ➤ **Opportunity to Oppose:** Once published, any interested party has the opportunity to oppose the patent application if they believe it does not meet patentability criteria (such as novelty or non-obviousness).

5. **Example of Publication Process**

- ➤ A patent application filed on **January 1, 2022**, with no earlier priority date, will be published around **July 1, 2023**. From this point on, the invention will be available for public inspection.

7.7. PRE-GRANT OPPOSITION

Definition: Pre-grant opposition is a process where someone can object to a patent application.

Who Can Object: Anyone who believes the invention is not new or has other issues can challenge it. For example, if someone thinks the invention is already known or not original, they can object.

Time Frame: This objection must be made within 6 months after the patent application is published. This is like a window of time where people can speak up if they have concerns.

1. **Grounds for Pre-grant Opposition**

The opposition can be filed on various grounds, such as:

- ➤ **Lack of Novelty:** The invention is not new or has been disclosed to the public before the filing of the patent application.
- ➤ **Obviousness:** The invention is obvious to a person skilled in the relevant field, lacking an inventive step.
- ➤ **Non-patentable Subject Matter:** The invention does not meet the legal criteria of patentability (for instance, if it falls under non-patentable inventions as per Indian law).
- ➤ **Insufficient Disclosure:** The patent application does not sufficiently describe the invention, making it unclear for others to replicate it.

2. **Process of Pre-grant Opposition**

The process for filing and addressing a Pre-grant Opposition is as follows:

- ➤ **Filing:** The opponent files a formal objection by submitting a written notice to the Controller of Patents, outlining the grounds of opposition.
- ➤ **Consideration:** The Controller examines the opposition, and the applicant is provided an opportunity to respond to the objections raised.
- ➤ **Outcome:** Based on the arguments and evidence presented by both sides, the Controller may either:
  - ❖ Reject the Patent Application: If the opposition is upheld and the patent is deemed unworthy of protection.

❖ Recommend the Application for Examination: If the opposition is overruled, the patent application moves forward to the examination stage.

3. Expedited Publication

Though the patent application is generally kept secret for 18 months, this period can be reduced under special circumstances, particularly when the patentee[20] or applicant plans to:

➢ **Sell or License the Patent:** If the inventor is looking to sell or license the patent rights.

➢ **Seek an Investor:** If the applicant is looking for investment and needs patent protection quickly.

To expedite the publication, the applicant must submit **Form**-9 to the Controller General of Patents, requesting early disclosure of the invention[16].

4. Example of Pre-grant Opposition

➢ A competitor who discovers that a published patent application overlaps with their own prior invention may file a Pre-grant Opposition within the six-month to prevent the grant of the patent.

➢ An inventor who wishes to commercialize their invention quickly can submit **Form-9** to reduce the secrecy period, allowing them to proceed with licensing or sales.

7.8. EXAMINATION

Definition: Patent examination is a very important step in getting a patent. The examination checks if the invention is new and not obvious.

Purpose: The main goal of patent examination is to make sure the invention is truly new and different from what already exists. This helps protect the inventor's idea and ensures that only unique inventions get patents.

1. Key Criteria for Examination

➢ **Novelty:** This means the invention must be new. It should not have been known or used by others before the inventor came up with it.

➢ **Inventive Step:** This means the invention should not be obvious to someone who knows a lot about the subject. It should be a creative step forward.

2. Role of the Examiner

➢ **Scrutiny:** The examiner is a professional who carefully checks the invention against the criteria. They look at the details to see if the invention is truly new and inventive.

➢ **Queries and Doubts:** Often, the examiner will have questions or doubts about the invention. They might ask the inventor to explain certain parts or provide more information.

3. Process of Examination

➢ **Request for Examination:** After the invention is published, it doesn't automatically get examined. The inventor or their representative must ask for it to be examined. This is done by filling out a form called Form-18A.

➢ **Time Frame:** The request for examination must be made within 48 months (4 years) from when the patent application was first filed. This is like having a deadline for submitting a request to check your work[16].

Example: If an inventor files a patent application on **January 1, 2022**, they must submit Form-18A before **January 1, 2026** to initiate the examination process.

4. Outcome of Examination

➢ **Satisfaction of Examiner:** If the examiner is happy with the answers and explanations given by the inventor, they will recommend that the patent be granted. This means the invention has passed all the checks and is considered new and inventive.

➢ **Grant of Patent:** Once recommended, the patent is granted, giving the inventor exclusive rights to their invention. This is like getting a certificate that proves the invention is unique and protected.

---

[20] *Patentee: A person/ Organization who owns the patent (granted)*

7.9. GRANT OF A PATENT

The Grant of a Patent marks the final stage in the patent application process, where the patent is formally awarded to the applicant after meeting all necessary requirements. This step occurs after the resolution of any objections or queries raised by the Patent Examiner or the public.

1. **Fulfillment of Requirements**

   Before the patent can be granted, the applicant must satisfy several conditions:
   - ➤ **Responding to Examiner's Queries:** Any objections or queries raised by the Patent Examiner during the examination stage must be resolved to the examiner's satisfaction. This may involve amending claims, clarifying the invention, or providing additional data.
   - ➤ **Public Opposition:** If any objections are raised through the Pre-grant Opposition process (as filed by the public), they must be adequately addressed.

   Once these requirements are fulfilled, the patent is granted to the applicant.

2. **Publication of the Granted Patent**

   After the patent is granted, it is officially published in the **Official Journal of the Patent Office**. This journal is a resource that disseminates information related to patent applications and grants.

3. **Contents of the Official Journal**

   The **Official Journal of the Patent Office, published every Friday**, contains various details related to patents, including:
   - ➤ **Section 11A Publications:** This section lists patent applications that have been published for public viewing after the 18-month confidentiality period.
   - ➤ **Post-grant Publications:** Newly granted patents are published here to inform the public and interested parties.
   - ➤ **Restoration of Patents:** Information of patents that have been restored after being lapsed.
   - ➤ **Notifications:** Official notifications related to patent laws, guidelines, or procedural changes.
   - ➤ **List of Non-working Patents:** Patents that are not actively in use or not being commercialized.
   - ➤ **Public Notices:** Notices issued by the Patent Office, including policy updates, procedural changes, or other relevant information for applicants and the public.

7.10. FLOWCHART FOR THE PROCESS OF FILING A PATENT APPLICATION

The fig. 7.7. provided flowchart that outlines the process of filing a patent application in India, along with the steps involved in its examination and publication.

1. **Patent Filing Before Indian Patent Office (IPO)**

   The first step is the filing of a patent application, either by claiming priority from an earlier application or as a standalone application. This must be done within **12 months** from the priority date if priority is claimed.

2. **Determine Request for Early Publication**

   After the filing, the applicant can choose whether to request **early publication**. Early publication can fast-track the availability of the application to the public in the **Official Journal**.
   - ➤ **Yes**: If the request for early publication is filed, the patent is **published early** in the Official Journal, speeding up the process.
   - ➤ **No**: If no early publication is requested, the patent application is published **automatically** after a specific period (typically 18 months from the filing date).

3. **Filing for Request for Patent Examination**

   After publication, a **Request for Patent Examination** (RFE) is **mandatory** to initiate the examination process. This request must be filed within a **prescribed time** (generally 48 months from the filing or priority date).
   - ➤ The application will not be examined until this request is made.

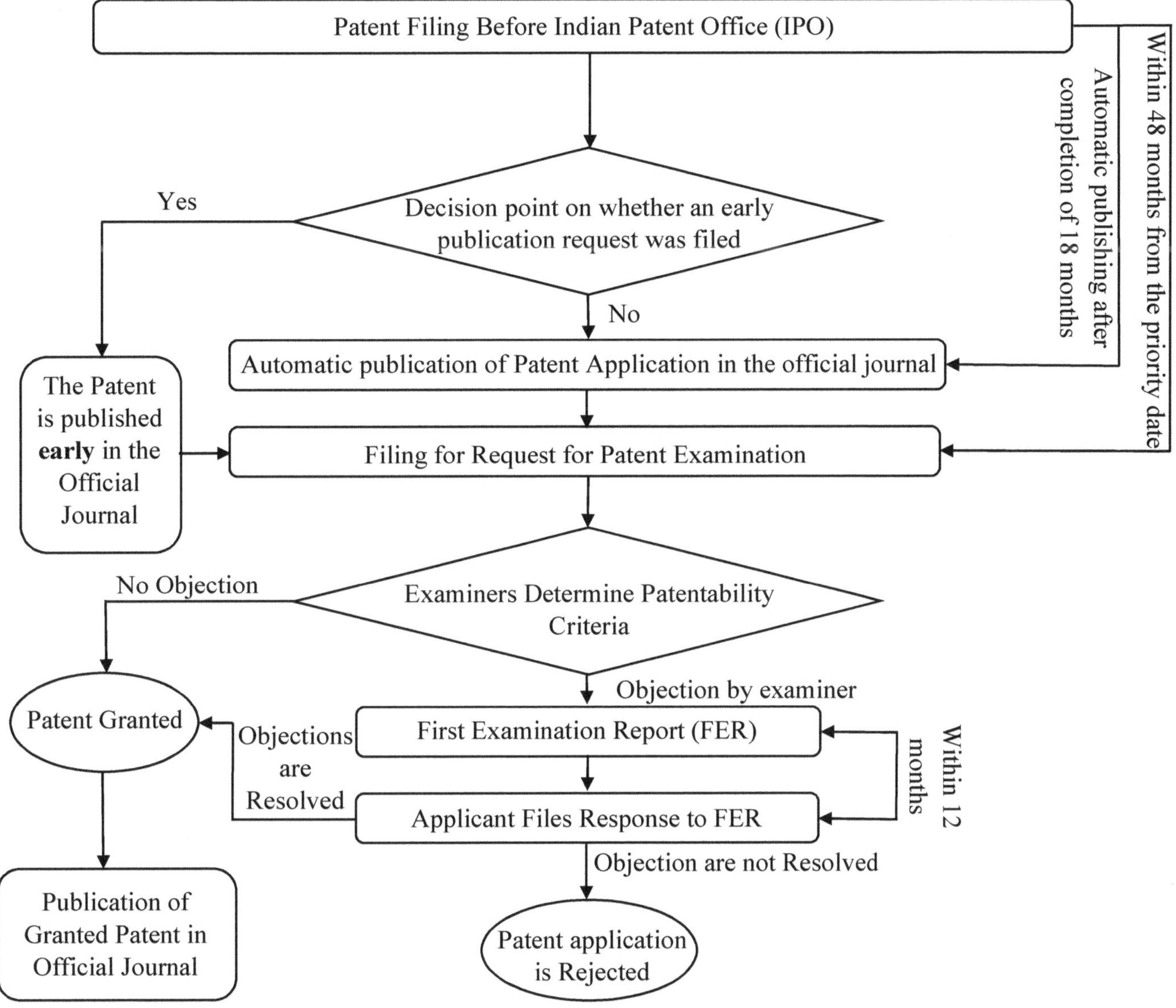

Fig. 7.7. Flowchart for The Process of Filing A Patent Application[16], [26].

4. Examiners Determine Patentability Criteria

Once the request for examination is filed, the **examiners** evaluate the application based on criteria such as **novelty**, **inventiveness**, and **industrial applicability**.

> ➢ If the examiners find **no objections**, the patent proceeds toward **granting**.
> ➢ If there are objections, an **Examination Report (First Examination Report - FER)** is issued to the applicant.

5. Applicant Files Response to FER

The applicant must respond to the objections raised in the FER, either addressing the concerns or amending the claims.

> ➢ After the FER is issued, the applicant generally has **12 months** to respond to the FER.
> ➢ If the **objections are resolved**, the patent proceeds towards **granting**.
> ➢ If the **objections are not resolved**, the patent application is **rejected**.

6. Patent Granted

If there are no objections or the objections are resolved, the **patent is granted**.

> ➢ The granted patent is **published** in the **Official Journal** of the Patent Office.

7.11. VALIDITY OF PATENT PROTECTION

Patent protection is granted to an inventor for a limited period, after this period, the patent enters the public domain unless specific steps are taken to maintain or extend the protection.

1. **Duration of Patent Protection**

   In India, the patent protection period is generally 20 years from the date of filing the application, as per the Indian Patents Act, 1970[18]. This period ensures that the patent holder enjoys exclusive rights to manufacture, sell, and license the invention during this time.

2. **Patent Renewal**

   Once a patent is granted, it is crucial to **renew the patent annually** by paying the Patent **Renewal Fee**. This requirement is outlined under **Section 53, Rule 80 of the Indian Patents Act**[27]. The renewal fee is mandatory from the third year onwards.

   - ➤ **Payment Schedule:** Patent renewal fees must be paid annually to keep the patent in force.
   - ➤ **Non-payment Consequences:** If the renewal fee is not paid, the patent may lapse, and the invention will no longer be protected under patent law.

3. **Extension of Patent Protection**

   In some countries, patent protection can be extended beyond 20 years, particularly in cases where the patent holder has experienced delays due to regulatory or administrative procedures. This extension compensates for the time lost during the approval process, especially for industries like pharmaceuticals, where obtaining marketing approval can take several years after the patent grant.

4. **Global Variation in Patent Extension**

   Indian patent law does not allow for automatic extensions beyond the 20-year term, some countries, like the United States and the European Union, allow **Supplementary Protection Certificates (SPCs)**, which can extend the protection of certain inventions, particularly pharmaceuticals, for an additional **5 years**[28].

7.12. POST-GRANT OPPOSITION

After a patent is granted by the Patent Office, it can still be challenged. This means that even though someone has been given the rights to their invention, others can question if those rights should have been given. This challenge can happen within one year from when the patent is officially published. Anyone can challenge the patent. This means any person or company who believes the patent should not have been granted can step forward.

1. **Filing of Post-grant Opposition**

   A Post-grant Opposition can be filed by any person who believes that the granted patent does not meet the required legal criteria. **The opposition can be filed either with the Patent Office or in a Court of Law.** Upon a successful challenge, the patent may be invalidated or revoked by the concerned body. The opposition must be filed within one year from the publication of the grant in the Official Journal of the Patent Office.

2. **Grounds for Post-grant Opposition**

   The patent can be challenged based on several grounds, including but not limited to the following:

   a. **Wrongful Obtaining of the Invention:** If the applicant wrongfully obtained the invention or any part of it from someone else, the patent may be revoked.

   b. **Prior Publication:** If the invention claimed in the patent has been published anywhere before the priority date of the application, the patent is invalid.

   c. **Public Knowledge or Use:** If the invention was already publicly known or used before the priority date, it is not eligible for a patent.

   d. **Obviousness:** The invention must involve an inventive step that is not obvious to a person skilled in the field. If the invention is deemed obvious, it does not qualify for a patent.

   e. **Non-patentable Subject Matter:** As per Chapter II of the Patent Act, 1970, certain subject matter, such as abstract theories, algorithms, or discoveries of scientific principles, are not patentable[18].

    f.   **Insufficient Disclosure:** The patent specifications must clearly and sufficiently describe the invention. If the description is vague or incomplete, the patent can be opposed.

3. **Process and Outcome**

After filing the Post-grant Opposition, the Controller of Patents or the court evaluates the evidence and arguments presented by both the opposing party and the patent holder. Based on this evaluation, the following outcomes are possible:

> ➢ **Revocation of the Patent:** If the opposition is successful, the patent may be fully revoked.
> ➢ **Amendment of Claims[21]:** In some cases, the claims may be amended to address the objections raised during the opposition process.
> ➢ **Upholding of the Patent:** If the opposition is unsuccessful, the patent is maintained in its original form.

7.13. COMMERCIALIZATION OF A PATENT

Once a patent is granted, the patent owner, patentee holds exclusive rights to their invention. These rights allow them to control how the invention is made, used, and sold. The patentee can choose to exploit the patent themselves or license the invention to third parties for commercialization[22]. Although the patent is valid for **20 years** from the date of filing, the patentee is required to submit annual information regarding the commercialization of the patent. This information is furnished via **Form-27**, as part of the **"Working/Licensing of the Patent"** process. The form ensures that the patent is being used to its full potential and made available to the public[29].

Licensing allows the patent owner to grant permission to another individual, organization, or industry to manufacture, sell, or use the patented invention under agreed terms.

1. **Reasons for Licensing a Patent**

Patent owners may decide to **license** their patent to third parties for various reasons, including:

    a. **Lack of Desire to Commercialize:** For example, a university professor who owns a patent may prefer to focus on academic work rather than commercializing the invention themselves.

    b. **Lack of Manufacturing Facilities:** The patent owner may not have access to the necessary infrastructure to manufacture the invention on a commercial scale.

    c. **Inability to Meet Market Demand:** The patentee may not have sufficient production capacity to meet the demand for the product in the market, prompting them to license the rights to another entity.

    d. **Geographic Focus:** The patent owner may wish to focus on one geographic region while licensing the rights to other geographic markets to third parties.

2. **Types of Licensing**

Licensing can be structured in various ways depending on the nature of the agreement:

    i. **Exclusive License:** In an exclusive license, the patent owner grants rights to **only one party** to use the invention. During the term of the license, no other individual or entity, including the patent owner, can exploit the patent. **Example**: A pharmaceutical company obtains exclusive rights to manufacture and sell a patented drug for a specific period.

    ii. **Non-Exclusive License:** In a non-exclusive license, the patentee can grant rights to **multiple parties**. The patent owner retains the ability to license the invention to as many individuals or organizations as they like. **Example**: A software developer licenses their patented algorithm to multiple companies simultaneously.

3. **Compulsory Licensing**

If the patentee fails to commercialize the patent within **three years** of the grant, third parties can apply for a **compulsory license**. This license allows others to use the patented invention without the patent holder's

---

[21] *Amendment of Claims: The process of modifying or removing certain aspects of a patent claim.*
[22] *Commercialization: The process of bringing new products or services to market.*

consent, subject to specific conditions. The request for compulsory licensing is submitted to the **Controller of Patents**. Conditions that must be met to grant a compulsory license:

> - **Public Demand Not Met:** If the public's requirements for the patented product are not being satisfied.
> - **Excessive Price:** If the patented product is not available at a reasonable price, making it unaffordable for the general public.
> - **Non-working in India:** If the patented invention is not being worked (commercialized) in the territory of India, despite the potential demand.

7.14. NEED FOR A PATENT ATTORNEY/AGENT

While it is possible for inventors to file patent applications on their own, the **complexity** involved in drafting, submitting, and prosecuting patent applications often necessitates the expertise of a **patent attorney[23] or patent agent.** These professionals possess specialized knowledge in patent law and intellectual property, making them valuable assets during the patent application process.

1. **Complexity of Patent Documents**

   Patent documents are often highly technical and legal in nature, requiring precise language to protect the invention effectively. While an inventor may have deep technical knowledge of their invention, they may lack the legal expertise to draft a patent application that meets the stringent requirements of patent law. A patent attorney/agent provides the following advantages:

   a. **Legal Expertise:** Patent attorneys are well-versed in the nuances of patent law, ensuring that the application meets legal standards and avoids rejection due to insufficient claims, improper disclosure, or legal inadequacies.

   b. **Drafting and Claims:** Drafting a patent application involves framing the claims in a way that maximally protects the invention while avoiding any overlap with prior art. A patent attorney can help ensure that the claims are both broad enough to provide meaningful protection and specific enough to prevent legal challenges.

   c. **Navigating the Process:** Patent applications undergo various stages, including examination, opposition, and grant. An attorney/agent can represent the applicant through each stage, responding to objections and queries from the patent office.

2. **Representation Requirements**

   In many countries, patent law mandates that applicants whose **principal place of business or residence** is outside the country must be represented by a patent attorney or agent who is qualified to practice in that country. This requirement ensures that the applicant is represented by someone who understands the local patent laws and procedures. **Example**: An inventor based in the United States wishing to file a patent in **India** must be represented by an Indian patent attorney/agent who is licensed to practice in India.

3. **Advantages of Hiring a Patent Attorney/Agent**

   Some key advantages of seeking professional assistance from a patent attorney/agent include:

   > - **Avoiding Errors:** Patent applications are subject to strict procedural and technical requirements. Even a small error in the application can lead to delays, rejections, or legal challenges. An attorney helps avoid such mistakes by ensuring that all formalities are correctly addressed.
   > - **Patent Strategy:** Attorneys/agents can offer strategic advice on how to maximize the protection of the invention. This might include **filing in multiple jurisdictions, managing timelines, and ensuring compliance** with various international patent treaties.
   > - **Litigation and Enforcement:** In the event of a legal dispute regarding the patent, an attorney can represent the patent owner in court, defending the patent against infringement claims or pursuing legal action against infringers.

---

[23] *Patent attorney: A lawyer who specializes in intellectual property law and helps clients secure and protect their patents*

7.15. CAN A WORLDWIDE PATENT BE OBTAINED?

There is no such thing as a **"Universal Patent," "World Patent,"** or **"International Patent"** since **patent rights** are territorial. This means that patent protection must be sought individually in each country or region where the applicant wishes to protect their invention. Filing for patents in multiple countries can be complex, expensive, and time-consuming, but there are mechanisms that simplify the process for international patent protection.

1. **Territorial Nature of Patents**

   Patents are granted by **national or regional patent offices**, and the rights conferred by a patent are limited to the jurisdiction of the granting authority. As a result, an inventor must file separate patent applications in each country or region where protection is desired. **Example**: If an inventor wants patent protection in both **India** and **the United States**, they need to file applications with both the **Indian Patent Office** and the **United States Patent and Trademark Office (USPTO)**.

2. **Challenges of Filing in Multiple Countries**

   Filing patent applications in several countries can be:

   > **Laborious**: Each country has its own patent laws, procedures, and requirements, making it cumbersome to navigate through different systems.

   > **Time-Consuming**: Filing separate applications in multiple countries involves managing different timelines for examination, opposition, and grant.

   > **Expensive**: Costs associated with translation, legal representation, and official fees can add up significantly when applying for patent protection in numerous jurisdictions.

3. **Regional Patent Offices**

   To streamline the patent application process, some regions have established **Regional Patent Offices** that allow inventors to file a single application to cover multiple countries within the region. These offices simplify the process by offering **regional protection** through one filing.

   > **European Patent Office (EPO)**: The EPO allows an inventor to file a single patent application that covers all member states of the **European Union (EU)**. **Example**: Filing a patent through the EPO provides protection in over 30 European countries.

   > **African Regional Intellectual Property Organization (ARIPO)**: ARIPO is a regional patent office serving several African countries, allowing inventors to obtain protection in multiple member states with a single application.

4. **International Patent Protection under the Patent Cooperation Treaty (PCT)**

   For those seeking patent protection in several countries globally, the **Patent Cooperation Treaty (PCT)** provides an efficient system for international patent filing. The PCT is an international treaty administered by the **World Intellectual Property Organization (WIPO)**. It allows inventors to file a **single international patent application**, which is valid in over **190 countries**, including **India**.

   PCT Process:

   > After filing a **PCT application**, the applicant can later decide in which member countries they want to pursue national patents.

   > This process offers an extended timeline for applicants to evaluate the commercial potential of their invention in different markets before deciding on specific countries for national phase entries.

   > **Example**: An inventor from India can file a PCT application to protect their invention in multiple countries, such as **Germany**, **Japan**, and **Canada**, by entering the **national phase** in those countries after the PCT filing.

5. **Conditions for Filing under PCT**

   To file a PCT application, the applicant's **country of residence** or **principal place of business** must be a member of the PCT. **India**, along with more than **190 countries**, is a member, allowing Indian inventors to use the PCT system for international patent filings.

7.16. DO I NEED FIRST TO FILE A PATENT IN INDIA?

In general, **Indian residents** are required to file their patent applications in **India first** before seeking patent protection in other countries. This requirement ensures that inventions originating in India are initially assessed under the Indian patent system. However, certain exceptions and provisions allow for filing in foreign countries without first filing in India, provided certain conditions are met.

1. **Requirement to File First in India**

   Indian patent law mandates that **Indian residents** must first file their patent application with the **Indian Patent Office**. This process ensures that the Indian government is aware of inventions originating within its territory and that national security or strategic interests are protected.

   Filing Sequence:

   Step 1: File the patent application in India.

   Step 2: After receiving approval or a waiver, file in foreign countries.

2. **Prior Approval for Foreign Filing**

   If an Indian resident wishes to file for a patent in a foreign country without first filing in India, they must obtain **Foreign Filing Permission (FFP)** from the Indian Patent Office. This permission is required to ensure that the invention does not pose any security or strategic concerns for India.

   Approval Process: The applicant must request permission, and the **Controller of Patents** evaluates whether the invention can be filed abroad.

3. **Exceptions to Filing First in India**

   There are several circumstances under which the requirement to first file in India may be waived. These include:

   - **Non-Indian Resident Applicants**: If the applicant is not an Indian resident, they are not bound by the requirement to file in India first. They can directly file for patent protection in other countries.
   - **Six-Week Waiting Period**: If six weeks have passed since the patent application was filed in India, the applicant may file for patent protection in other countries without additional approval. This waiting period allows the Indian Patent Office to evaluate whether there are any security concerns.
   - **Joint Inventions with Foreign Inventors**: If an invention is developed through international collaboration, and one of the inventors is an Indian resident, the resident must seek **Foreign Filing Permission** (FFP).

     Example: If an Indian researcher collaborates with a team in the United States to develop an invention and wishes to file the patent in the U.S., the Indian researcher must first seek permission from the Indian Patent Office.
   - **Invention Not Marketable in India**: If the invention has no potential market in India, the Indian resident may seek FFP to file directly in foreign countries without filing in India. However, the Indian resident must provide a justification for why the invention is not being filed in India.
   - **International Collaboration**: In cases of **international collaboration**, if any part of the invention originated in India, the Indian inventor must obtain FFP before filing the patent application abroad.

     Example: If part of the invention was developed in India and another part in Germany, the Indian inventor must seek permission to file in Germany.

4. **Special Cases for Defense and Atomic Energy Inventions**

   Certain inventions, such as those related to **defense**, **atomic energy**, or **utility models**, are not patentable in India due to national security concerns. In such cases, Indian inventors must seek permission from the Indian Patent Office before attempting to file for a patent abroad.

   Example: If an Indian scientist develops a technology related to atomic energy, they must obtain special permission from the Indian Patent Office before filing a patent application in any other country.

7.17. PATENT RELATED FORMS

In the Indian patent system, there are more than 30 forms associated with different stages of the patent application process. These forms are designed to handle various aspects of patent filing, opposition, licensing, and management. Below is a summary of some of the most important forms used in patent-related procedures.

Table 7.2. Important Patent Application Forms in India[16], [29].

Sl. No.	Form No.	Title of Form	Purpose
1	**Form 1**	Application for Grant of a Patent	Used to initiate the patent application process, including general information about the applicant, inventor(s), and the invention.
2	**Form 2**	Provisional/Complete Specifications	Filed to submit the specifications of the invention. Provisional provides a basic description, while complete specifications include detailed information and claims.
3	**Form 4**	Request for Extension of Time	To request an extension for filing any document or completing any action as per the Patent Act.
4	**Form 5**	Declaration as to Inventorship	To declare the true and first inventor(s) of the invention.
5	**Form 7**	Notice of Opposition on Grant of a Patent	Filed by individuals or organizations to oppose the grant of a patent. It is used to challenge a granted patent based on specific grounds.
6	**Form 7A**	Representation Opposing Grant of a Patent	Allows third parties to file a pre-grant opposition against a patent application, citing reasons such as lack of novelty or inventive step.
7	**Form 9**	Request for Early Publication	To request the early publication of a patent application (standard publication time is 18 months from the date of filing).
8	**Form 17**	Application for Compulsory License	Filed to request a compulsory license for a patented invention if the patent holder is not sufficiently exploiting the invention.
9	**Form 18**	Request for Examination of the Application for Patent	This form is used to formally request the patent office to examine the patent application, a mandatory step in the patent process.
10	**Form 18A**	Request for Expedited Examination	To request an expedited examination of the patent application (usually for start-ups and certain government institutions).
11	**Form 19**	Request for Hearing	To request a hearing during the examination process of the patent application if required by the applicant or the Controller.
12	**Form 21**	Request for Termination of Compulsory License	Used to request the termination of a previously granted compulsory license.
13	**Form 22**	Application for Registration of Patent Agent	Filed by individuals who wish to be registered as a patent agent to represent clients in patent matters.
14	**Form 24**	Request for Post-Dating Patent	To post-date the patent application (extend the filing date) in specific circumstances as allowed by the Controller of Patents.

15	**Form 26**	Power of Attorney	To authorize a patent agent or legal representative to act on behalf of the applicant in patent proceedings.
16	**Form 27**	Statement Regarding the Working of the Patented Invention on a Commercial Scale in India	Submitted annually to disclose the extent to which the patented invention is being commercially worked in India.
17	**Form 30**	Miscellaneous Form	Used when no specific form is prescribed for a particular action related to patent procedures.

7.18. FEE STRUCTURE

As per the **Patent Act, 1970** and **The Patents Rules (1972)**, the fees for filing patent applications and other related processes are categorized based on the type of applicant: **natural person/startup**, **small entity**, or **others**. Filing electronically provides a **10% discount** compared to physical filing. Below table 7.3 is outlining the fee structure for electronically filed patent applications.

Table 7.3. Detailed table of fee structure for electronically filed patent applications[16], [29].

Sl. No.	Fee Type	Natural Person / Startup (₹)	Small Entity alone or with Natural Person / Startup (₹)	Others alone or with Natural Person / Startup / Small Entity (₹)
1	Application Filing Fee	1,600	4,000	8,000
2	Provisional/Complete Specifications	1,600	4,000	8,000
3	Request for Early Publication	2,500	6,250	12,500
4	Request for Examination	4,000	10,000	20,000
5	Express Request for Examination	5,600	14,000	28,000
6	Fee for Filing Opposition	2,400	6,000	12,000
7	Request for Amendment to Patent	800	2,000	4,000
8	Fee for Assignment/License	800	2,000	4,000
Renewal Fees (Annually)				
9	3rd to 6th Year	800	2,000	4,000
	6th to 10th Year	2,400	6,000	12,000
	11th to 15th Year	4,800	12,000	24,000
	16th to 20th Year	8,000	20,000	40,000
10	Surcharge for Delayed Payments	10% of the applicable fee	10% of the applicable fee	10% of the applicable fee

7.19. TYPES OF PATENT APPLICATIONS

In the Indian patent system, different types of patent applications cater to the specific needs of inventors depending on the stage of development of their invention or their international patent filing strategy. Here is a detailed explanation of the key types of patent applications.

1. **Provisional Application:** A **Provisional Application** is filed when the invention is not yet fully developed or finalized. This type of application allows the inventor to establish an **early priority date** for their invention, which can be crucial for securing patent rights. A provisional application does not require complete specifications, and the inventor can continue experimenting and refining the invention after filing. The inventor must file a **Complete Specification** within **12 months** of filing the provisional application to move forward with the patent process.

   Key Benefits:
   - Gives the inventor time to complete the invention and gather data.
   - Less formal requirements compared to a complete application.

2. **Ordinary Application:** An **Ordinary Application** is filed when the invention is fully developed, and the inventor has all the necessary information and claims ready. This type of application does not claim any priority from earlier filings, meaning it is a **standalone application**. The ordinary application includes a complete description of the invention and the claims outlining the scope of protection being sought.

   Key Features:
   - Contains complete specifications and claims.
   - No priority date is claimed from any earlier applications.

3. **PCT Application:** A **PCT (Patent Cooperation Treaty) Application** is an international application filed under the **Patent Cooperation Treaty**. It allows inventors to file a single application that is valid across multiple countries that are PCT members (over 150 countries, including India). The PCT application gives inventors up to **30 months** from the priority date to decide in which member countries they wish to pursue national patents. Although the PCT application itself does not grant a patent, it streamlines the process of seeking patent protection in multiple jurisdictions.

   Key Features:
   - A single application can cover multiple countries, reduce cost and effort of filling multiple forms.
   - Offers an extended timeline to decide on specific countries for national patents.

4. **Divisional Application:** A **Divisional Application** is filed when a patent application contains more than one invention, and the applicant is required to split the application to meet the **plurality of inventions** objection. Alternatively, the applicant may voluntarily divide the application. Each divisional application retains the **same priority date** as the original (parent) application, which is essential for maintaining the earliest possible patent protection for all inventions.

   Key Features:
   - Filed to divide a single application into multiple applications if it contains more than one invention.
   - Retains the same priority date as the original (parent) application.

5. **Patent of Addition Application:** A **Patent of Addition** is filed when an inventor makes a slight improvement or modification to an invention that has already been patented or is covered under an ongoing patent application. The improvement must be **new** and distinct from the original invention. One key benefit of a patent of addition is that it does not require a separate renewal fee and will expire with the **main patent**.

   Key Features:
   - Filed for modifications or improvements to an already patented invention.
   - Does not require a separate renewal fee.
   - Expires along with the main patent.

6. **Convention Application:** A **Convention Application** is filed by an applicant who has already filed a patent application in one country and wishes to file the same invention in one or more **Convention countries,** such as those under the **Paris Convention**. The key feature of a convention application is that it allows the applicant to claim the **priority date** of the first application, provided that the convention application is filed within **12 months** of the original filing.

Key Features:
> ➢ Allows the applicant to claim the priority date of an earlier filing in another country.
> ➢ Must be filed within 12 months of the original application to claim the priority date.

7.20. COMMONLY USED TERMS IN PATENTING

In the field of patenting, several terms are frequently used to describe the processes, people, and entities involved in the creation, application, and management of patents. Understanding these terms is crucial for navigating the patent system effectively. Below is a detailed explanation of the key terms used in the domain of patenting.

1. **Inventor:** An **Inventor** is the creator or developer of a new invention. The inventor is responsible for coming up with the original idea and developing it into a patentable product or process.
2. **Applicant:** An **Applicant** is the person, organization, or industry that files a patent application. The applicant may or may not be the inventor. In many cases, companies file patent applications on behalf of their employees who are inventors.
3. **Patentee:** The **Patentee** is the individual or organization that holds the granted patent. Once the patent is approved and granted, the patentee gains exclusive rights to the invention for the duration of the patent.
4. **Licensee:** A **Licensee** is an individual or entity that obtains the rights to use or commercialize a patented invention from the patentee. Licensing is a common way to commercialize patented inventions.
5. **Assignee:** An **Assignee** is a person or organization to whom the ownership of the patent is legally transferred. The assignee holds the legal rights to the patent after the transfer.
6. **In Force:** A patent is considered **In Force** when the patentee continues to pay the required **annuity (renewal fee)** to keep the patent active. If the renewal fee is not paid, the patent may lapse.
7. **Working of a Patent:** The **Working of a Patent** refers to the commercial exploitation of the patented invention. This includes the sale or licensing of the invention to a third party for commercial purposes.
8. **Patent Specification:** The **Patent Specification** is the written document that describes the invention in detail. It includes the technical aspects of the invention, how it is made, and how it can be used. This document is a key part of the patent application.
9. **Priority Right:** A **Priority Right** or **Right of Priority** allows the applicant to claim an earlier filing date from another patent application. This right is time-limited and is generally used to file subsequent applications in other countries.
10. **Priority Date:** The **Priority Date** is the date on which the first application for the invention is filed. This date is crucial because it establishes the timeline for determining the novelty of the invention against other applications.
11. **Patent Claims:** The **Patent Claims** define the legal scope of protection that the patent provides. The claims specify what aspects of the invention are protected and are critical in determining whether someone is infringing the patent.
12. **National Phase Application:** A **National Phase Application** refers to an application filed in individual countries based on a **PCT (Patent Cooperation Treaty)** application. This process allows inventors to file for protection in multiple countries simultaneously after the international phase.
13. **Patent Revocation: Patent Revocation** refers to the cancellation of a granted patent. This can occur due to reasons such as lack of novelty, non-patentability, or wrongful obtaining of the patent.
14. **Restoration of Patent:** If a patent lapses due to non-payment of renewal fees, it can be restored within a specific period by paying the requisite fees. **Restoration of Patent** is a process that brings the patent back into force.

7.21. NATIONAL BODIES DEALING WITH PATENT AFFAIRS

In India, several government organizations and bodies handle various aspects of patent administration, promotion, and commercialization. These institutions play a crucial role in managing the country's intellectual property (IP) landscape, including patent filings, assessments, and commercialization of innovations. Below is an overview of the key national bodies involved in patent affairs.

1. **Indian Patent Office (IPO):** The **Indian Patent Office (IPO)** is the primary body responsible for administering the patent system in India. It operates under the **Department for Promotion of Industry and Internal Trade (DPIIT)** and is responsible for:
   - **Filing and Granting of Patents**: IPO handles the examination, opposition, and grant of patent applications.
   - **Publication**: It publishes patent applications and granted patents in the **Official Journal** of the Indian Patent Office.
   - **Patent Revocation and Restoration**: The IPO also manages processes related to revocation or restoration of patents.

2. **Department for Promotion of Industry and Internal Trade (DPIIT):** The **DPIIT** is a government department under the **Ministry of Commerce and Industry**. It plays a significant role in formulating policies related to **intellectual property** and **industrial promotion**. The DPIIT oversees the Indian Patent Office and helps shape India's IP policies, ensuring that they align with national interests and international agreements. Its Key Responsibilities is to:
   - Overseeing the functioning of the IPO.
   - Promoting **innovation** and **entrepreneurship** by creating a supportive patent ecosystem.
   - Ensuring India's compliance with international IP treaties like the **TRIPS Agreement**.

3. **Technology Information, Forecasting and Assessment Council (TIFAC):** TIFAC is an autonomous body under the **Department of Science and Technology (DST)**. Its main function is to:
   - **Provide Policy Advice**: TIFAC advises the Indian government on science and technology trends, including the development and commercialization of patented technologies.
   - **Patent Facilitation Centers**: TIFAC supports inventors by providing patent information, guidance on patent filings, and assessing the commercialization potential of technologies.

4. **National Research Development Corporation (NRDC);** The **National Research Development Corporation (NRDC)** is a government enterprise under the **Ministry of Science and Technology**. It focuses on:
   - **Technology Transfer**: NRDC helps transfer technologies developed in Indian research institutions to industries for commercialization.
   - **Patent Commercialization**: The NRDC actively promotes the commercialization of patents, helping inventors and organizations bring their patented inventions to the market.
   - **Licensing and Partnerships**: It also facilitates licensing agreements between inventors and industries, ensuring the effective exploitation of patented technologies.

7.22. UTILITY MODELS

A **Utility Model**, sometimes referred to as a **Petty Patent** or **Innovation Patent**, provides a form of legal protection for inventions that involve minor improvements over existing products. These incremental innovations may not meet the stringent requirements of **novelty** and **non-obviousness** needed for a patent but still offer valuable technical improvements. Utility models are recognized in many countries to protect such small-scale innovations.

1. **Criteria for Utility Models:** Unlike patents, utility models typically have relaxed requirements for **novelty** and **non-obviousness**. However, the invention must still demonstrate **industrial applicability** or **utility**, which is the same criterion as that for patents. **Example**: A minor modification to an existing smartphone camera that improves performance may qualify for a utility model but might not meet the strict criteria for a full patent.

2. **Utility Models and MSMEs:** Utility models are particularly advantageous for **Micro, Small, and Medium Enterprises (MSMEs)**, which often lack the resources for intensive research and development (R&D).

Many MSMEs innovate by improving existing products or processes, but their innovations may not qualify for patent protection due to the stringent novelty and inventive step requirements.

Benefits for MSMEs:

> ➢ Utility models provide quicker and less expensive protection for small innovations.
> ➢ They allow MSMEs to safeguard their innovations and reap financial rewards without the heavy costs associated with patent filings.

3. **Life of Utility Models:** The **duration** of protection for utility models is shorter than that of patents. Depending on the country, the protection period ranges from **7 to 15 years**, compared to the 20-year duration for patents. This shorter protection period aligns with the less rigorous examination process and the incremental nature of the innovations being protected.

4. **Countries Recognizing Utility Models:** Approximately **80 countries** recognize utility models as part of their intellectual property (IP) system. These countries include major economies such as: **France, Germany, Japan, South Korea, China, Finland, Russian Federation** and **Spain.** These nations use utility models to encourage small innovations, especially in industries where incremental improvements are common.

5. **India's Stance on Utility Models:** India does not currently recognize utility models under its intellectual property laws. However, introducing utility models could significantly increase the number of patents filed and granted annually in India, as many small and incremental innovations could then receive legal protection. Recognizing utility models would particularly benefit India's **MSME** sector, which is known for small-scale innovations but often lacks the resources to file patents.

Potential Benefits for India:

> ➢ Utility models could help **boost innovation** by providing easier access to legal protection for small inventions.
> ➢ It would create an opportunity for **MSMEs** to protect their innovations, leading to **economic growth** and **technological advancement.**

Questions

1. Explain the step by step process of obtaining a patent. From the initial idea to the grant of the patent.

2. What are the commonly used terms in the field of patenting and how do they contribute to effective communication in this domain.

3. Explain the different types of patent applications.

4. What strategies are involved in the commercialization of a patent?

5. What are utility models, and how do they differ from patents?

6. Explain the following major steps involved in the process of patent registration.

   (i) Prior Art Search (ii) Choice of Application to be Filed (iii) Pre-grant Opposition

7. In which circumstances Indian residents are not required to file a patent application first in India to get patent protection in another country? Explain.

8. Name the four national bodies dealing with patent affairs

"Copyright? Copy RIGHT: Steal ideas, steal facts but do not steal words."

: Dan Poynter

Module - 4

Chapter 8:
COPYRIGHTS AND RELATED RIGHTS

INTRODUCTION

Copyrights and related rights form the foundation of intellectual property protection in creative works. This chapter will explore key aspects such as the various classes of copyrights, the criteria for obtaining copyright, and the rights granted to authors. It will also delve into important legal concepts, including copyright infringements, which can be treated as criminal and cognizable offences. Topics such as fair use, the role of copyrights in the digital age, and non-copyright works will be examined. Additionally, the chapter will cover copyright registration, ownership, judicial powers, and international agreements that govern the protection of creative content globally.

8.1. COPYRIGHTS AND RELATED RIGHTS

What are Copyrights?

- ➢ **Definition:** Copyrights are legal protections given to people who create original works. These works can be in literature, like books and poems, or in computer software, like apps and programs.
- ➢ **Purpose:** The main goal of copyrights is to protect the creator's work from being used without permission. This means others can't copy, share, or sell the work without the creator's consent.
- ➢ **Example:** If you write a book, copyright laws ensure that no one else can publish or sell your book without your permission.

What are Related Rights?

- ➢ **Definition:** Related Rights are similar to copyrights but cover different types of creative work. These include plays, music recordings, movies, paintings, and even buildings.
- ➢ **Purpose:** Like copyrights, Related Rights protect the creator's work, ensuring they have control over how it's used and shared.
- ➢ **Example:** If you make a movie, Related Rights ensure that no one can show or sell your movie without your approval.

The Copyright Act, 1957 of India

- ➢ **What it is:** This is a law in India that governs how copyrights and Related Rights work. It sets the rules for what creators can do with their work.
- ➢ **Rights Provided:** The Act gives creators several rights, including:
    - ❖ **Reproduction:** The right to make copies of their work.
    - ❖ **Communication to the Masses:** The right to share their work with the public, like broadcasting a song on the radio.
    - ❖ **Adaptation:** The right to change their work, like turning a book into a movie.

- ❖ **Translation:** The right to translate their work into different languages.

Understanding 'Author' and 'Work'

- ➢ **Author:** This term refers to the person who creates the work. An author can be:
  - ❖ A **writer** who writes books or articles.
  - ❖ A **computer programmer** who creates software.
  - ❖ A **composer** who writes music.
  - ❖ A **producer** who makes films or records music.
  - ❖ A **photographer** who takes pictures.
- ➢ **Work:** This term refers to the actual creation. It can be:
  - ❖ **Literary work:** Like novels or essays.
  - ❖ **Dramatic work:** Like plays or scripts.
  - ❖ **Musical work:** Like songs or symphonies.
  - ❖ **Artistic work:** Like paintings or sculptures.
  - ❖ **Cinematograph film:** Like movies or videos.
  - ❖ **Sound recording:** Like music albums or podcasts.

8.2. CLASSES OF COPYRIGHTS

Copyrights are legal protections given to creators for their original works. In India, there are several types of copyrights, each covering different kinds of creative work. Let's explore each type in detail.

1. **Literature:** This category includes written works like books, essays, and research articles. It also covers oral speeches and lectures, which means if someone gives a speech, they have rights over it. Computer programs and software are included here, meaning the code written by programmers is protected. Databases, which are organized collections of data, are also covered. For example, a library catalog or a customer list in a business.

2. **Dramatics:** This includes screenplays, which are scripts for movies or TV shows. If someone writes a script, they have rights over it. Dramas, which are plays performed on stage, are also protected. This means the script and the performance are covered.

3. **Sound Recordings:** This category protects recordings of sounds, no matter how they are stored. For example, a song recorded on a CD or a digital file. A **phonogram**, which is an old-fashioned term for a sound recording, is also included. This means any sound recording, like a podcast or an audiobook, is protected.

4. **Artistic:** This includes visual works like **drawings and paintings**. If someone creates a painting, they have rights over it. **Logos**, which are symbols used by companies, are protected. This means a company's logo cannot be used without permission. **Maps and charts**, which are visual representations of areas or data, are also covered. **Photographs**, which are pictures taken with a camera, are protected. **Works of architecture**, like building designs, are included. This means the design of a building is protected. **Engravings and craftsmanship**, which are detailed artistic works, are also covered.

5. **Musical:** This category includes musical notations, which are written symbols representing music. The music itself is protected, not the lyrics or actions performed with it. A musical work does not need to be written down to be protected. For example, a melody played on a guitar is protected even if it's not written as sheet music.

6. **Cinematograph Films:** This includes visual recordings made by any medium, like movies or TV shows. It covers the process of making the film and includes sound recordings. Motion pictures, which are movies, are protected. This means the film and its soundtrack are covered. TV programs, which are shows broadcast on television, are included. Visual recordings, which are any recorded images, and sound recordings, which are any recorded sounds, are protected.

8.3. CRITERIA FOR COPYRIGHT

Copyright is a legal mechanism that protects the creators of original works. To qualify for copyright protection, a work must satisfy specific criteria, such as tangibility, originality, and creativity.

1. **Physical or Tangible Form**
   - **Requirement**: For a work to be eligible for copyright protection, it must exist in a tangible form. This means it should be something that can be perceived, either visually or audibly.
   - **Duration of Tangibility**: The period during which the work exists in tangible form may vary—ranging from a brief moment to several years.
   - **Examples**: Music, books, speeches, paintings, and sculptures all qualify if they are in a form that can be experienced by others.
   - **Reference**: According to Section 13 of the Copyright Act, 1957 (India), protection is extended to all original literary, dramatic, musical, and artistic works, among others[30].

2. **Originality of Work**
   - **Definition**: To qualify for copyright protection, the work must be original. This means the creator must produce the work through independent thinking and without copying from another source.
   - **Original Work of Authorship (OWA)**: Even if the final product appears similar to existing works, as long as the work is independently created and not duplicated, it is considered an Original Work of Authorship (OWA).
   - **Quality and Aesthetic Merit**: Copyright law does not judge the quality, quantity, or aesthetic value of the work. Therefore, even a work lacking in these aspects may still qualify for protection.

3. **Creativity in Copyrighted Works**
   - **Minimal Creativity**: Copyright protection requires at least some level of creativity. There is no fixed minimum level of creativity needed, and it is subject to the judgment of the Registrar of Copyright.
   - **Subjective Nature of Creativity**: The level of creative effort required for protection is highly subjective and varies on a case-by-case basis.
   - **Example of Ineligible Works**:
     - ❖ **Dimension Changes**: Changing the dimensions of a book alone is not considered a creative alteration and hence would not qualify for copyright.
     - ❖ **Non-Creative Listings**: An address book with telephone numbers arranged alphabetically does not qualify, as it lacks a creative arrangement, being simply a straightforward listing.

8.4. OWNERSHIP OF COPYRIGHT

Copyright ownership determines who holds the exclusive rights to use, distribute, and license a copyrighted work. Understanding copyright ownership is essential for ensuring proper legal adherence and protection of intellectual property. The law provides clarity on who the initial and subsequent owners of copyright are, depending on the nature of creation and employment conditions.

1. **First Owner of Copyright**
   - **Creator as the Original Owner**: The general rule is that the individual who creates the work (the author) is considered the first and original owner of the copyright.
   - **Examples**: A photographer automatically owns the copyright to the photos they take unless an agreement specifies otherwise.

2. **Employer Ownership in Work for Hire**
   - **Work Created Under Employment**: If an employee creates the work as part of their job duties under a contractual agreement, the copyright ownership typically belongs to the employer.
   - **Example**: A software developer employed by a company to write code will not own the copyright to the software; the company will.

> **Legal Reference**: According to **Section 17 of the Indian Copyright Act, 1957**, in cases of works made during the course of employment, the employer (proprietor) holds the copyright unless agreed otherwise in a written contract[31].

3. **Government Ownership of Copyright**
   > **Government Works**: In the absence of any special arrangement, the government automatically holds the copyright for works created by its employees in the course of their official duties.
   > **Examples**: Reports, publications, and educational materials generated by government employees for government purposes fall under government copyright.
   > **Legal Framework**: **Section 28 of the Copyright Act, 1957**, designates the government as the owner of copyright in government works[32].

4. **Copyright in Speeches**
   > **First Owner of Speech**: The person delivering a speech is automatically the first owner of the copyright for that speech. The speaker retains the exclusive rights to reproduce and distribute the speech.
   > **Examples**: If a politician gives a public address, they hold the copyright to the speech.

5. **Requesting Permission to Use Copyrighted Material**
   > **Who Can Grant Permission?** To use copyrighted material legally, one must obtain permission from the rightful copyright holder. This may include the original author, legal heirs (if the author is deceased), the publisher, or other designated rights holders.
   > **Details to Include in Permission Request**:
   > ❖ **Title, Author, and Edition**: Clearly mention the title of the work, the author's name (and editor if applicable), and the specific edition of the material to be used.
   > ❖ **Precise Material**: Specify the exact sections or portions of the work you intend to use.
   > ❖ **Number of Copies**: Indicate the quantity of copies that will be distributed.
   > ❖ **Purpose of Use**: Clearly state the purpose, such as for educational or research use.
   > ❖ **Form of Distribution**: Specify whether the material will be distributed in physical format (e.g., printed books) or digitally (e.g., on the internet).
   > ❖ **Commercial Use**: If the material is to be sold, such as in a course pack, this must also be indicated.
   > **Example**: If a professor wishes to include a copyrighted article in a course pack, they must send a formal request to the publisher or author outlining these details.

8.5. COPYRIGHTS OF THE AUTHOR

The rights of the creator or author of a work are protected by **Section 14 of the Copyright Act, 1957 (India)**. Copyright law ensures that no one can use or publish the author's work without their permission. This legal framework grants the copyright owner exclusive control over various uses of their creation.

1. **Types of Rights in Copyright:** A copyright owner enjoys two main types of rights:
   i. **Economic Rights (Proprietary Rights)**
   ii. **Moral Rights (Personal Rights)**

These rights protect the financial and personal interests of the creator, allowing them to maintain control over both the economic benefits and the integrity of their work.

   i. **Economic Rights (Proprietary Rights)**

   Economic rights are associated with the financial benefits that can be earned through the sale, licensing, or use of the copyrighted material. These rights enable copyright owners to either authorize or prohibit specific actions involving their work. As outlined in the Copyright Act, 1957, the following are protected under economic rights[33]:

   > **Reproduction**: Copyright holders can prevent or permit the reproduction of their work in any form. This includes printed publications, sound recordings, and digital copies.

- ➤ **Distribution**: Authors can control the distribution of copies of their work, whether in physical or digital formats.
- ➤ **Public Performance**: The right to perform or display the work publicly (e.g., a play, musical performance) is reserved for the copyright owner.
- ➤ **Broadcasting and Communication**: Authors can authorize or restrict the broadcasting of their work over media such as television, radio, or the internet.
- ➤ **Translation**: The work cannot be translated into other languages without the copyright owner's permission.
- ➤ **Adaptation**: Copyright owners retain the exclusive right to allow adaptations of their work, such as converting a novel into a movie or screenplay.
- ➤ **Example**: A filmmaker cannot create a film based on a novel without the permission of the author or copyright owner.
- ➤ **Reference**: The Copyright Act, 1957 defines economic rights under Section 14, highlighting the financial and commercial control that copyright owners possess[33].

ii. Moral Rights (Personal Rights)

Moral rights protect the personal connection between the creator and their work, ensuring that their name and reputation remain intact, regardless of who holds the copyright. The two main moral rights are:

- ➤ **Right of Paternity**: This right ensures that the original author retains the right to claim authorship of the work even if the copyright is transferred to another party (e.g., a publisher). The author's name must always be associated with the work.
- ➤ **Right of Integrity**: The original creator has the right to prevent any distortion, mutilation, or modification of the work that would harm their reputation or misrepresent the original creation.
- ➤ **Example**: If an author licenses their book to a publisher, the publisher cannot alter the book in a way that misrepresents the original intent of the author, nor can they remove the author's name from the work.
- ➤ **Legal Reference**: Section 57 of the Copyright Act, 1957 provides detailed provisions for moral rights, protecting the personal and reputational interests of creators[34].

2. Multiple Rights Holders

In some cases, a single work may have multiple copyright holders. This is common in collaborative works where different contributors hold rights to different aspects of the work. **Example**: For a movie, the screenplay writer, director, actors, music composer, and editor may all have distinct rights to their contributions to the overall work.

8.6. COPYRIGHT INFRINGEMENTS

Copyright infringement occurs when the exclusive rights granted to a copyright owner are violated. Under the **Copyright Act, 1957 (India)**[33], any unauthorized use of a copyrighted work that conflicts with the rights of the copyright owner is considered an infringement. This legal framework helps protect the financial and moral interests of the original creator.

1. **Acts Constituting Copyright Infringement:** The Copyright Act, 1957 outlines specific actions that are deemed to be infringements of copyright. These include unauthorized copying, distribution, and public performance of a work, among other activities. Below are acts considered as infringements:
   a. **Making Copies for Sale or Hire without Permission:** It is an infringement to reproduce a copyrighted work in any form, such as making physical or digital copies, without the explicit permission of the copyright holder.
   b. **Selling or Renting Out Unauthorized Copies**: Selling or renting out copies of copyrighted work without the author's permission is also considered a violation.
   c. **Permitting Public Performance without Authorization**: Allowing the performance of copyrighted works in public spaces without proper licensing constitutes infringement.

    d. Distributing Infringing Copies: Distributing unauthorized copies of a work for trade, especially when it adversely affects the financial interests of the copyright owner, is an infringement.

    e. Public Exhibition of Infringing Copies: Exhibiting unauthorized copies of copyrighted works in public spaces for commercial purposes is a form of infringement.

    f. Importing Infringing Copies: Importing unauthorized or pirated copies of copyrighted material from another country without permission from the copyright owner is also an infringement.

    g. Translating a Work without Permission: Translating a copyrighted work into another language without the consent of the original author or copyright holder is an infringement.

2. Impact of Copyright Infringement

- **Legal Consequences**: Copyright infringement can lead to civil and criminal penalties, including fines, damages, and imprisonment. The copyright owner may seek legal recourse to recover lost revenue and stop further infringement.
- **Economic and Moral Harm:** Infringements not only cause financial losses to the author but also affect the moral rights, especially when the work is distorted or used without due credit.

8.7. COPYRIGHT INFRINGEMENT AS A CRIMINAL OFFENCE

- **Legal Framework**: According to Section 63 of the Copyright Act, 1957, knowingly infringing on copyright constitutes a criminal offence in India. This section outlines the penalties and legal consequences that infringers face if found guilty[35].
- **Punishment for Copyright Infringement**:
  - **First Conviction**: If a person is convicted of copyright infringement for the first time, they are subject to a minimum imprisonment of six months along with a fine of ₹ 50,000.
  - **Second and Subsequent Convictions**: In case of a repeat offence, the punishment increases to a minimum imprisonment of one year and a fine of ₹ 1,00,000.
- **Dedicated IP Division and Copyright Board**:
  - **IP Division:** There is a specialized Intellectual Property (IP) division established to handle copyright infringement cases, ensuring swift legal proceedings.
  - **Copyright Board:** Constituted by the Central Government in 1958, the Copyright Board is responsible for adjudicating disputes related to copyright claims, resolving conflicts between copyright holders and infringers.

8.8. COPYRIGHT INFRINGEMENT AS A COGNIZABLE OFFENCE

- **Definition of a Cognizable Offence**: A cognizable offence allows law enforcement officers to act without a warrant. Under the Copyright Act, 1957, copyright infringement qualifies as a cognizable offence, meaning authorities can take immediate action against the infringer.
- **Authority of Police Officers:**
  - A police officer of the rank of sub-inspector or higher has the authority to confiscate infringing material without needing to issue a warrant.
  - **Confiscation and Legal Proceedings**: Once confiscated, the infringing material must be presented in court for further legal proceedings.

8.9. FAIR USE DOCTRINE

The Fair Use Doctrine provides certain exceptions to the rights granted under copyright law. While copyright holders generally have exclusive control over their works, Section 52 of the Copyright Act, 1957 outlines specific circumstances where copyrighted material can be used without infringing on these rights. This doctrine is crucial for educational and research purposes, allowing limited use of protected material under specific conditions[36].

1. **Conditions for Fair Use**

The Fair Use Doctrine is assessed through a **four-part test**, which determines whether the use of a copyrighted work is permissible without violating the law:

    i. **Character of the Use:** The use must be educational, non-profit, or personal in nature. If the work is used in a classroom setting or for individual study, it is typically considered fair use. **Example**: A student copying a short section of a textbook for personal study purposes.

    ii. **Nature of the Work**: The work being used must be factual rather than imaginative or creative. Factual works, such as research articles or news reports, are more likely to fall under fair use compared to fictional or creative works like novels or films.

    Example: Quoting from a scientific journal article for a research paper.

    iii. **Amount of the Portion Used**: Only a small portion of the copyrighted work should be used. The law permits limited copying, though the definition of a "small portion" may be subject to debate and interpretation. **Example**: Quoting a paragraph from a book for academic research.

    iv. **Impact of Use on the Value of the Copyrighted Material**: The use must not negatively impact the economic or moral rights of the copyright holder. If the use does not affect the market value of the work, it is more likely to be considered fair use. **Example**: Quoting a few lines from a book in a review without affecting the book's sales.

2. **Examples of Fair Use under Section 52 of the Copyright Act[36]**

The following examples illustrate situations where the Fair Use Doctrine applies:

- **Personal Use**: Using copyrighted material for personal study or research is allowed under fair use. **Example**: A researcher copying a few pages of a book for their personal study.
- **Quotations**: Short quotations from copyrighted works are permitted, especially in academic and research. **Example**: Quoting a few sentences from a novel in a literary analysis.
- **Media Reporting**: Reporting on current events, such as news in newspapers, magazines, or on radio/television, is protected under fair use. **Example**: A news channel showing brief clips of a movie as part of a review.
- **Educational Reproduction**: Teachers and scientific researchers can reproduce parts of copyrighted works for academic purposes. **Example**: A teacher making copies of a research paper for classroom discussion.
- **Government Officials and Judicial Use**: Government officials performing their duties, including during judicial proceedings, are allowed to reproduce copyrighted works. **Example**: Reproducing a legal document for use in a court case.
- **Use by Legislatures**: Work prepared by the Secretariat of a Legislature can be used without permission. **Example**: Government reports shared with legislative bodies for review.
- **Certified Copies**: Making certified copies of documents as required by law falls under fair use. **Example**: A court producing certified copies of legal judgments.
- **Limited Copies**: Making up to three copies of a book, pamphlet, music sheet, map, chart, or plan is allowed. **Example**: A student making two photocopies of a book for reference.
- **Religious and Cultural Events**: Copyrighted works used in bonafide religious ceremonies, including marriage functions, are protected under fair use. **Example**: Playing copyrighted music at a wedding ceremony.

8.10. COPYRIGHTS AND INTERNET

The digital age has revolutionized how copyrighted materials are shared and accessed, particularly through the internet. As more content is uploaded, shared, and downloaded online, understanding the legal boundaries of copyright in the digital space has become crucial. The Copyright Act, 1957 has undergone amendments to accommodate these changes, ensuring that the principles of copyright protection extend to the digital environment.

1. **Transmission of Copyrighted Data Online**
   - **Ease of Data Transmission**: The internet has made it easier and faster to transmit copyrighted materials globally. However, this ease of access raises concerns about potential copyright infringement. **Example**: Downloading an eBook without proper authorization from the publisher or author can be considered a violation of copyright laws.

2. **Copyright and Fair Use Online**
   - **Fair Use Concerns**: Individuals must be mindful of copyright and fair use principles when downloading materials from the internet. Not all content available online is free for use.
   - **Unauthorized Uploads**: Materials may be placed online without the copyright owner's consent, which complicates the issue of legality. Users should verify material they access is legally available for use.

3. **Personal vs. Commercial Use of Online Material**
   - **Rights for Personal Use**: When the copyright owner uploads material to the internet, users generally have the right to access and use that material for personal. **Example**: An individual may download a PDF for personal study but cannot sell or distribute copies of that PDF for profit without violating copyright laws.
   - **Important Disclaimer for Educational Distribution**: When distributing copyrighted work electronically for educational purposes, it is required to include a clear copyright statement. A typical disclaimer might be: *"This work is protected by copyright laws and is provided for educational instruction only. Any infringing use may be subject to disciplinary action and/or civil or criminal liability as provided by law."*

4. **Literary Works and Digital Copyright (Including Software)**
   - **Definition of Literary Work**: Under Section 2(o) of the Copyright Act, 1957[37], "Literary Work" extends beyond traditional writings to include computer programs, tables, and compilations such as computer databases. This definition ensures that digital content, including software and data compilations, receives the same copyright protection as other.
   - **Source Code and Object Code Registration**: When registering a copyright for a computer program, it is mandatory to provide both the source code and the object code along with the application. This ensures that both the readable and executable forms of the program are protected. **Example**: A software developer seeking copyright protection for a new application must include both the source code (human-readable code) and the object code (machine-readable format) during the copyright registration process.

8.11. NON-COPYRIGHT WORK

Not all creations and information are protected by copyright law. The Copyright Act, 1957 specifically outlines what does not fall under the jurisdiction of copyright protection. This helps differentiate between original works that can be protected and other forms of information or content that remain outside the scope of copyright.

1. **Ideas, Concepts, and Principles:** Copyright does not protect ideas, concepts, or principles themselves. Only the specific expression or form in which these ideas are conveyed can be copyrighted. **Example**: A theory on physics or a new business idea cannot be copyrighted, but a book explaining that theory or idea in a detailed manner can be protected[30].

2. **Facts and Discoveries:** Factual information, such as scientific or historical discoveries, is not eligible for copyright protection. This is because facts are considered to be common knowledge that anyone can use. **Example**: An author may spend years researching Buddhism, gathering facts from various sources. However, after publishing the book, anyone else can use those facts, provided they express them in their own words or format.

3. **Titles, Names, and Short Phrases:** Titles, names, slogans, short phrases, and word combinations are generally not copyrightable. This is because these elements do not contain sufficient creativity to warrant protection. **Example**: A title of a book or a short slogan used in advertising cannot be copyrighted.

4. **Certificates:** Certificates and similar documents are not considered copyrightable because they lack sufficient scope for creativity. These are typically standard forms with minimal original content. **Example**: A birth certificate or a diploma cannot be copyrighted, though the form or template may be protected.

5. **Digitally Created and Transformed Works:** Works created digitally or works that are transformed into digital formats are eligible for copyright protection. **Example**: If a physical book is converted into an eBook and distributed online, both the original and digital versions are protected under copyright.

6. **Copyright Registration for Websites:** The Copyright Act does not allow copyright registration for an entire website. However, different components of the website may be copyrighted individually.
   Copyrightable Components:
   - ➢ **Computer Programs/Software**: Considered literary works.
   - ➢ **Photographs, Maps, and Diagrams**: These are classified as artistic works.
   - ➢ **Music**: Musical compositions and graphical notations fall under musical works.
   Example: A website may contain code, images, and text, each of which can be copyrighted separately. However, a separate application must be filed for each component.

7. **Copyright for Mobile and Computer Applications:** A mobile or computer application qualifies for copyright registration. Applications are self-contained programs designed to perform specific tasks and are dynamic in nature, often requiring user interaction. **Example**: A mobile app that tracks fitness activity or a software program used for data analysis can be copyrighted, including its code and graphical elements.

8. **Copyright Infringement on the Internet:** If someone uses copyrighted material (like a picture, song, or video) from the internet without the owner's permission, it is considered copyright infringement. The same rule applies if someone takes another person's work and uses it for their own purposes. **Example**: Downloading and using a song for a personal video without permission from the copyright holder is copyright infringement.

8.12. COPYRIGHT REGISTRATION

1. **Automatic Copyright Protection:** Under the Copyright Act, 1957, it is not necessary to register a work to claim copyright protection. Once a work is created and fixed in a tangible medium (e.g., written, recorded, or otherwise produced), it automatically receives copyright protection. **There is no requirement to submit a formal request to the copyright office to acquire copyright protection.** As soon as a work is completed, it is protected. **Example**: A writer's poem, once written down or typed, automatically receives copyright protection.

2. **Copyright Registration:** While registration is not mandatory to claim copyright, it can provide additional legal benefits. Registration does not grant rights beyond those conferred by the creation of the work; instead, it serves as evidence of the work's existence and ownership. A registered copyright is prima facie evidence in legal disputes. The registration certificate is proof of an entry in the Copyright. **Example**: If a dispute arises over the ownership of a copyrighted work, the certificate of registration can be used in court to support the creator's claims.

3. **Legal Benefits of Registration:**
   - ➢ **Evidence in Court**: Registration is particularly useful in cases involving disputes over copyright ownership, financial matters, or the transfer of rights.
   - ➢ **Example**: In case of plagiarism or unauthorized use, a registered copyright holder will have a stronger case in court than an unregistered one.

4. **Copyright Administration in India**
   - ➢ **Governing Laws**: Copyright matters in India are governed by the Copyright Act, 1957 and the Copyright Rules, 2013. These laws cover copyright protection, registration, enforcement, and penalties for infringement.

> **Copyright Office**: The office of the Registrar of Copyrights, under the Department for Promotion of Industry and Internal Trade (DPIIT), manages copyright-related matters.
> **Online Access**: Detailed information, including forms and procedures for registration, is available on the official website https://copyright.gov.in/.

5. **Prominent Forms for Copyright Registration**
> **Form XIV**: For literary, dramatic, musical, and artistic works.
> **Form XV**: For registering computer software, including programs and databases.
> **Form XII**: For cinematograph films.
> **Form IX**: For sound recordings.
> **Form I**: For registering miscellaneous works.

8.13. JUDICIAL POWERS OF THE REGISTRAR OF COPYRIGHTS

The Registrar of Copyrights in India holds the powers of a civil court while handling cases under the Code of Civil Procedure. These powers enable the Registrar to function as a quasi-judicial authority, ensuring the proper enforcement and adjudication of copyright-related disputes. The following are the key powers exercised by the Registrar:

> **Summoning and Enforcing Attendance**: The Registrar can summon individuals and enforce their attendance for examination under oath.
> **Requiring Discovery and Production of Documents:** The Registrar can require the discovery and submission of documents that are relevant to the case.
> **Receiving Evidence on Affidavit:** Evidence can be submitted in the form of affidavits, which are legal written statements made under oath.
> **Issuing Commissions:** The Registrar can issue commissions for the examination of witnesses or documents, enabling the gathering of testimonies and additional evidence from external parties.
> **Requisitioning Public Records:** The Registrar has the authority to request public records or copies of such documents from any court or public office to aid in decision-making.
> **Other Prescribed Matters:** The Registrar may exercise additional powers as prescribed by the rules governing copyright.

1. **Application Process for Copyright Registration**
> **Filing the Application**: To register a work for copyright, the applicant must submit a duly filled **Form XIV** to the Copyright Office. Applications can be submitted via post or through the online e-filing system at https://www.copyright.gov.in/.
> **Eligibility**: Both the author of the work and the assignee (if the rights have been transferred) are eligible to file for copyright registration.
> **Submission Address**: The physical address for submission of the form is: The Registrar of Copyright, Plot no. 32, Boudhik Sampada Bhawan, Sector 14, Dwarka, New Delhi - 110075.

2. **Copyright Registration Timeline**
> **Processing Time**: The process typically takes around **2-3 months** to complete. After submission, there is a **mandatory waiting period of 30 days**, during which objections may be raised by any party.
> **Objection Handling**: If any individual objects to the claims made in the copyright application, they can approach the office of the Registrar of Copyrights. Both the applicant and the objector are given the opportunity to present their case.
> **Hearing and Decision**: The Registrar conducts hearings and evaluates the evidence from both parties. The decision may be made in favor of or against the applicant.
> **Examination and Objections**: Once any objections are resolved, the application is examined by copyright examiners. If the examiners raise any queries, the applicant is given around **45 days** to respond and resolve these issues.

3. **Steps in the Copyright Filing Process**
   Step 1: Submit the application (Form XIV) along with the required documents to the Copyright Office.
   Step 2: Wait for the mandatory **30-day objection period**.
   Step 3: If objections arise, both parties present their arguments before the Registrar.
   Step 4: After objections are cleared, the work is examined by officials.
   Step 5: Any further doubts or queries must be cleared by the applicant within **45 days**.
   Step 6: Once all steps are completed, the copyright is officially registered.

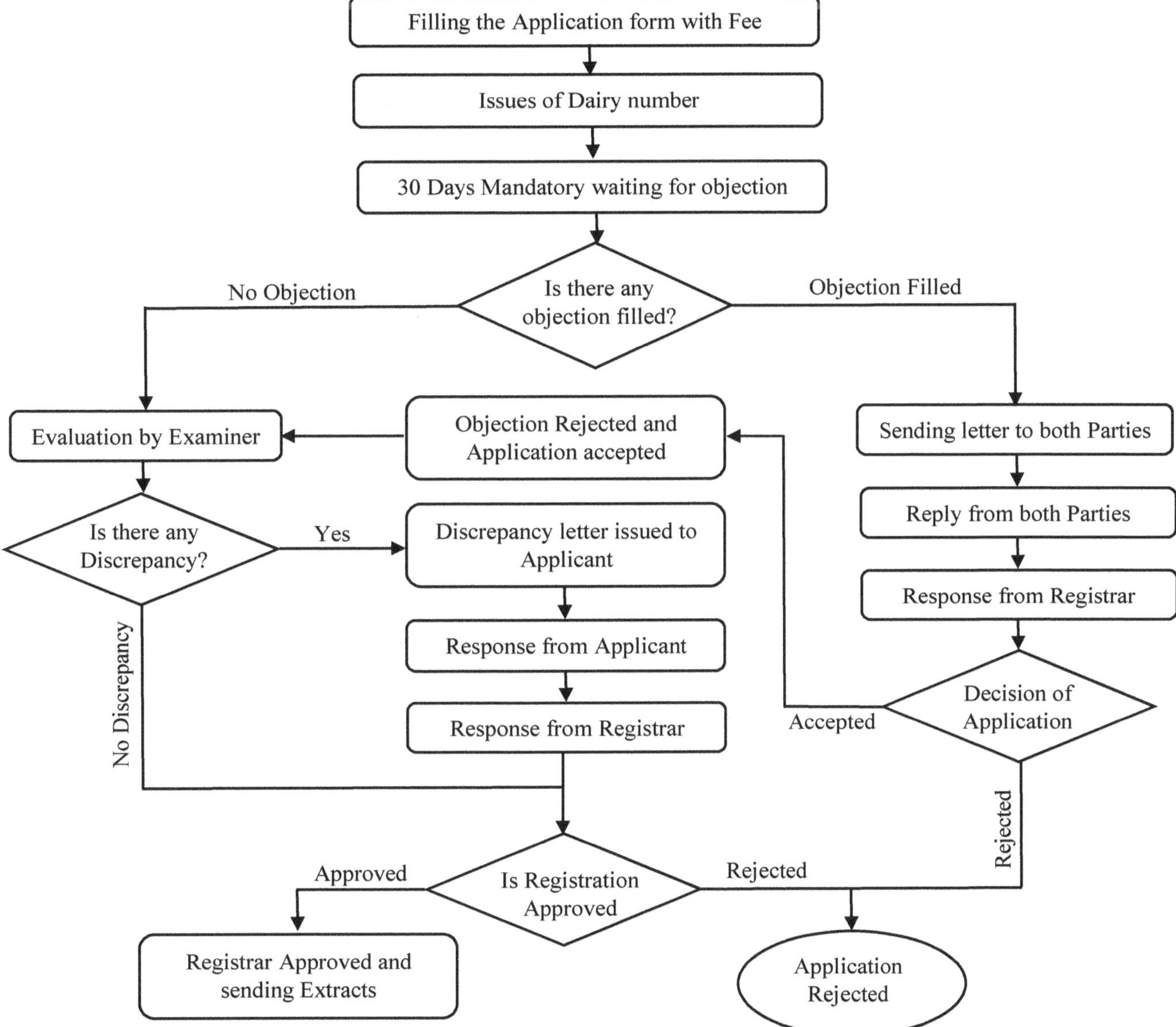

Fig. 8.1. Flow chart for the process of Copyright registration[38].

8.14. FEE STRUCTURE

For each type of copyright registration, a separate application form needs to be submitted. It is important to note that the fee paid for these applications is non-refundable, even in cases where the application is rejected.

Key Points:
1. Separate applications are required for each work.
2. The fee is non-reimbursable in case of application rejection.
3. Fees vary depending on the type of work (literary, artistic, sound recording, etc.).

Table 8.1. Fee Structure for Copyrights[39].

Attribute	Fee (₹)
For an application for registration of Copyright in	
➢ Literary, Dramatic, Musical, or Artistic work	500/- per work
➢ Cinematograph Film	5,000/-
➢ Sound Recording	2,000/-
For a Literary or Artistic work used or capable of being used in relation to goods or services	2,000/-
For making any change in	
➢ Literary, Dramatic, Musical, or Artistic work	200/-
➢ Literary or Artistic work used in relation to goods or services	1,000/-
For registration of changes in particulars of Copyright in	
➢ Cinematograph Film	2,000/-
➢ Sound Recording	1,000/-
For prevention of importation of infringing copies per place of entry	1,200/-

This table provides a clear breakdown of the fees associated with various types of copyright registration, changes, and the prevention of copyright infringement through importation.

8.15.   COPYRIGHT SYMBOL

The use of the copyright symbol (©) is not a legal requirement for obtaining copyright protection. Once a work is created and fixed in a tangible form, it automatically receives copyright protection under the Copyright Act, 1957. However, placing the copyright symbol on your work can provide certain legal advantages, particularly when pursuing cases of copyright infringement in court.

1. **Purpose and Advantages of the Copyright Symbol**
   - ➢ **Legal Protection**: While it is not mandatory to use the copyright symbol, adding it to your work can make it easier to enforce your copyright in legal proceedings. It serves as a visible notice to others that the work is protected and that unauthorized use may result in legal action.
   - ➢ **Example**: Adding "© [Your Name], 2024" to the bottom of a published article helps inform readers that the work is copyrighted.
2. **Elements of a Copyright Notice**
   When choosing to display a copyright notice, the following elements should be included for clarity and legal strength:
   - ➢ **The Copyright Symbol:**
     - ❖ **Options**: You can use the standard copyright symbol © (the letter C in a circle), the word "Copyright," or the abbreviation "Copr.".
     - ❖ **Example**: "© 2024 John Doe" or "Copr. 2024 John Doe" can be used as valid copyright notices on creative works.
   - ➢ **Year of Creation or Publication:**
     - ❖ **Requirement for Compilations/Derivative Works**: In the case of compilations or derivative works that incorporate previously published materials, the year of the first publication of the compilation or derivative work should be included in the copyright.

- ❖ **Exemption for Certain Works**: For pictorial, graphic, or sculptural works, as well as items like greeting cards, postcards, stationery, jewellery, dolls, and toys, the year of publication may be omitted from the copyright notice.
- ❖ **Example**: "© 2024 John Doe" for a book published in 2024. For a compilation of articles published in previous years, it would be "© 2024, John Doe, incorporating materials from 2021."
- ➢ **Name of the Copyright Owner:**
  - ❖ **Identification**: The name or a recognizable abbreviation of the copyright owner should be included in the copyright notice. If the work is owned by a company or organization, a generally known alternative designation of the owner can also be used.
  - ❖ **Example**: "© 2024 ABC Publishing Co." or "© 2024 J. Doe."
- ➢ **Special Case: Sound Recordings**
  - ❖ **Symbol for Sound Recordings**: For sound recordings, the symbol used is ℗ (the letter P in a circle), which stands for "phonogram" (a recording of sound).
  - ❖ **Requirements**: Similar to other works, sound recordings require the inclusion of the year of publication and the name of the copyright owner.
  - ❖ **Example**: "℗ 2024 XYZ Records" on a music album.

8.16. VALIDITY OF COPYRIGHT

Copyright protection provides creators with exclusive rights over their works for a specific period. After the expiration of this period, the work enters the public domain, meaning it can be freely used by others without permission from the original copyright owner. The duration of copyright protection varies depending on the type of work and the circumstances of its creation or publication.

1. **General Duration of Copyright Protection**
   - ➢ **Standard Duration**: In India, the standard duration of copyright protection is **60 years**. This ensures that the creator and their heirs benefit from the work during the specified period.
   - ➢ **Start of the 60-Year Period**:
     - ❖ **Literary, Dramatic, Musical, and Artistic Works**: For these types of works, the 60-year period begins after the death of the author. This provides the author's estate with continued protection for a substantial time following the author's death. **Example**: If an author of a novel dies in 2024, the copyright on that work will remain valid until the end of 2084.
     - ❖ **Cinematograph Films, Sound Recordings, Photographs, Posthumous Publications[24], Government Works, and Works of International Organizations**: For these works, the 60-year period begins from the date of publication. **Example**: A film released in 2024 will have copyright protection until the end of 2084.

8.17. COPYRIGHT PROFILE OF INDIA

The data from 2018 to 2023 provides an overview of copyright applications, examinations, registrations, and disposals in India. This period reflects significant changes in the volume of copyright-related activities, indicating both growth and variability in the process of managing intellectual property rights. The fig. 8.2. illustrates key trends in copyright activity in India from 2018 to 2023, covering four major areas: total applications received, applications examined, Registers of Copyright (ROC) generated, and total disposal of applications.

1. **Total Applications Received** The number of copyright applications received increased steadily over the five-year period, reflecting a growing interest in copyright registration. The rise in applications indicates a greater awareness among creators to protect their intellectual property, with the peak occurring in 2021-2022.

---

[24] *Posthumous publication: refers to publishing of creative work after the creator's death.*

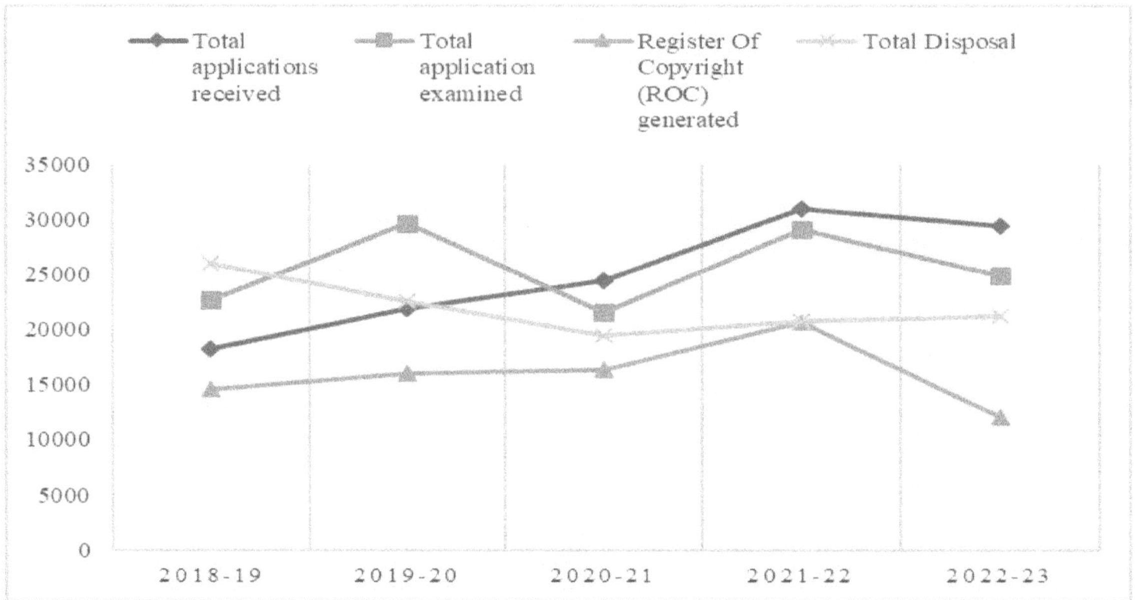

Fig. 8.2. Chart for Copyrights profile of India for the period 2018-23[40].

2. **Total Applications Examined:** The number of applications examined reflects the processing capacity of the copyright office, which fluctuated over the years. The examination process peaked in 2019-20, followed by a reduction in 2020-21 and then a recovery in 2021-22, indicating variability in processing efficiency.

3. **Register of Copyright (ROC) Generated:** The number of Registers of Copyright (ROC) generated, which represents the official registration of copyright works, has shown variability. After reaching a peak in 2021-22, there was a significant drop in the number of ROCs generated in 2022-23, suggesting possible bottlenecks or changes in the registration process.

4. **Total Disposal:** The total disposal of applications, which includes the resolution or final handling of copyright applications, fluctuated over the years. The peak disposal rate occurred in 2018-19, followed by a decline in the following years, before stabilizing in 2021-22 and 2022-23.

8.18. COPYRIGHT AND THE WORD 'PUBLISH'

In the context of copyright, the term "publish" has a specific legal meaning. A work is considered published when it is made available to the public without any restrictions on its access. This means that the work must enter the public domain in a manner that allows anyone to access, use, or view it freely. The act of publishing places the work in the public domain, granting the public unrestricted access to it.

Example: A book that is printed and sold in bookstores or an article posted on a public website is considered published because there are no restrictions on who can access the content.

1. **Restricted Distribution and Its Implications:** If a work is distributed only to a few people or organizations with restrictions, it is not considered published under copyright law. Such restrictions might include confidentiality clauses or non-disclosure agreements that prevent further sharing of the content.

   Example: If an author writes an article titled "Mystery of Sahyadri" and distributes it to selected individuals or organizations with explicit instructions that the content should not be disclosed, the work is not regarded as published in the legal sense.

2. **Transition from Unpublished to Published:** A work can transition from being unpublished to published when the restrictions on its distribution are lifted. Once the work is shared freely with the public, either by posting it online or distributing it in an unrestricted manner, it is then considered published.

   Example: If the author of "Mystery of Sahyadri" decides to remove the non-disclosure restrictions and posts the article on a public website, the work is now considered published because it is accessible to anyone.

3. **Copyright Protection for Published and Unpublished Works:** It is important to note that both published and unpublished works are eligible for copyright protection. Copyright does not depend on whether the work has been made publicly available. The moment a work is created and fixed in a tangible medium, it is automatically granted copyright protection, regardless of whether it has been published.

   Example: A personal diary or an unpublished manuscript still enjoys copyright protection, even if it is never shared with the public. The creator retains exclusive rights over the work, including the right to publish it at a later date if desired.

8.19. TRANSFER OF COPYRIGHTS TO A PUBLISHER

Copyright is a legal framework that grants creators exclusive rights. However, in many cases, authors transfer their copyrights to publishers for financial gains, which can involve receiving a one-time payment, royalties, or a combination of both. This transfer of rights is usually formalized through a contract or agreement, but it is important for authors to carefully consider the terms of such agreements, as they can have significant long-term implications.

1. **Reasons for Transferring Copyright:** Many authors may not have the resources or networks to effectively market and distribute their work. Publishers play a crucial role in publicizing, printing, and distributing the work to a broader audience, which is the primary reason authors transfer their rights. The financial incentives involved in the transfer may include:
   - **Lump Sum Payment:** A one-time payment made by the publisher for the rights to the work.
   - **Royalties:** A percentage of the sales revenue generated by the published work.
   - **Combination of Both:** An agreement that involves both a lump sum payment and royalties.

2. **Implications of Transferring Copyright:** While transferring copyrights can offer immediate financial benefits, it can also have several consequences that authors should be aware of:
   - **Loss of Control:** The publisher may restrict the author's ability to display the work on institutional or personal websites.
   - **Limitations on Revisions:** Once the copyright is transferred, the author may no longer have the right to revise or update the work.
   - **Distribution Issues:** Some publishers may not print sufficient hard copies or fail to upload the digital version online, reducing the work's reach.

3. **Careful Consideration in Signing Agreements:** It is essential for authors to be cautious when signing copyright transfer agreements. Some important points to consider include:
   - **Partial Transfer of Rights:** Authors can retain certain rights, such as digital rights, while transferring only the rights to print and sell hard copies.
   - **Time-Limited Transfer:** Authors can place a time limit on the publisher's right to print and sell the work, after which the rights revert to the author.
   - **Digital Era Impact:** The rise of the internet has lessened authors' reliance on traditional publishers. Many authors now have the option to bypass publishers and directly disseminate their work online.

4. **Statutory Rights under Copyright Law:** Even after transferring their copyrights, authors have certain protections under the law:
   - **Termination of Transfer:** The Copyright Act allows authors to reclaim their rights after a certain period, typically 35 years from the date of the agreement. This provision applies even if it is not explicitly stated in the agreement.

8.20. COPYRIGHTS AND THE WORD 'ADAPTATION'

The term 'Adaptation' in the context of copyright refers to the process of creating a derivative work based on an existing work. It involves transforming or reworking the original content to create something new while retaining essential elements of the original.

The Copyright Act provides specific instances where adaptation is considered valid:
- **Transformation of a dramatic work into a non-dramatic work:** This could involve converting a play into a novel or short story.
- **Changing a literary or artistic work into a drama:** For example, turning a novel into a theatrical performance or film script.
- **Re-arrangement of a literary or dramatic work:** This refers to modifying the structure or organization of the original work, like updating sequence of events or characters in a novel.
- **Depiction through pictures of a literary or dramatic work:** This includes illustrations or visual representations of written work, like turning a novel into a comic book or storyboard.
- **Making a cinematograph film:** Adaptation here refers to creating a movie or audiovisual content based on literary, dramatic, or musical works. For instance, adapting a novel or stage play into a film.

These adaptations are subject to the protection provided by copyright law, ensuring the original creators' rights are safeguarded while permitting derivative creative endeavors. **Example:** An example of adaptation would be the transformation of J.K. Rowling's literary work "Harry Potter" into films, where the books (literary works) were adapted into a series of movies (cinematograph films).

8.21. COPYRIGHTS AND THE WORD 'INDIAN WORK'

The term 'Indian Work' pertains to literary, dramatic, or musical works that meet certain criteria under the Indian Copyright Act:
- **The author is an Indian citizen**: The creator of the work must hold Indian citizenship at the time of creation.
- **The work is first published in India**: The initial publication or release of the work should take place in India.
- **For unpublished works**: If the work remains unpublished, the author must have been a citizen of India when the work was created.

These conditions ensure that Indian works are protected under Indian copyright law, allowing Indian creators to safeguard their intellectual property. **Example**: A novel written by an Indian author, published for the first time in India, qualifies as an 'Indian Work' under copyright law.

8.22. JOINT AUTHORSHIP

A work of 'Joint Authorship' refers to creative content developed collaboratively by two or more authors, where the individual contributions are inseparable and indistinct from one another.

Key characteristics of joint authorship:
- **Collaboration between multiple authors**: The work is a result of joint efforts, and no single author's contribution can be identified as separate from others.
- **Indistinct contributions**: The combined input of the authors blends into a single cohesive work, without clear divisions of responsibility or authorship for different sections.
- **Equal copyright protection**: Each author shares copyright protection for the entire work, and decisions related to the work (e.g., publication, adaptations) typically require the consent of all authors.

Example: An academic research paper jointly written by multiple researchers where the ideas, writing, and research are merged in a way that the individual input cannot be distinguished.

8.23. COPYRIGHT SOCIETY

Copyright societies play a crucial role in managing and protecting the rights of authors and other copyright owners. Given the complexities involved in tracking all uses of their work, collecting royalties, and dealing with copyright infringements, these societies help alleviate the burden on individual creators.

As per **Section 33 of the Copyright Act, 1957**[41], a Copyright Society is a **registered collective administration society**. It is formed by authors and other copyright holders to manage their rights effectively. Copyright societies act as intermediaries between copyright owners and those seeking to use copyrighted works, ensuring that the rights of the owners are protected, and they receive due compensation.

1. **Functions of a Copyright Society:** Copyright Societies perform several critical functions to aid copyright holders:

    - **Track Rights and Infringements**: The society monitors and keeps records of all the rights related to the works of its members, including potential infringements.

    - **Issue Licences**: Copyright societies have the authority to issue licences for the use of the works they manage. This could include licensing music for public performance, films for television broadcasting, or literary works for adaptation.

    - **Collect Fees**: Once licences are issued, the society collects the relevant fees or royalties from users (e.g., broadcasters, publishers, or event organizers) on behalf of the copyright holders.

    - **Distribute Fees**: After deducting administrative expenses, the society distributes the collected fees among the copyright holders.

2. **Formation and Duration:** A Copyright Society can be formed by a group of **seven or more copyright holders**. Once registered, the term of the society's registration is valid for five years, after which it must be renewed to continue its operations.

    Examples of Registered Copyright Societies in India

    i. **Society for Copyright Regulation of Indian Producers for Film and Television (SCRIPT)**
       Address: 135 Continental Building, Dr. A.B. Road, Worli, Mumbai 400 018
       Purpose: Manages copyrights for cinematograph and television films.

    ii. **The Indian Performing Right Society Limited (IPRSL)**
       Address: 208,Golden Chambers, 2nd Floor, New Andheri Link Road, Andheri (W), Mumbai- 400058
       Purpose: Manages copyrights for musical works.

    iii. **Phonographic Performance Limited (PPL)**
       Address: Flame Proof Equipment Building, B.39, Off New Link Road, Andheri (West), Mumbai 400 053
       Purpose: Manages copyrights for sound recordings.

8.24. COPYRIGHT BOARD

The Copyright Board is a regulatory body established by the Indian government to perform judicial and administrative functions under the **Copyright Act of India**. It serves as an adjudicatory body to resolve disputes and oversee matters related to copyright issues. The Board is composed of a **Chairman** (who holds a position equivalent to that of a High Court judge) and **2 to 14 members** appointed by the government.

Functions and Powers of the Copyright Board: The Copyright Board has several critical judicial and administrative roles under the Copyright Act:

- **Hearing Appeals:** The Board hears appeals against decisions made by the Registrar of Copyrights, allowing copyright holders to challenge or seek revisions on copyright-related orders.

- **Rectification of Register of Copyrights:** The Board is authorized to hear applications to rectify or correct entries in the Register of Copyrights if there are errors or discrepancies.

- **Dispute Resolution on Copyright Assignment:** In cases where disputes arise concerning the assignment (transfer) of copyrights, the Board steps in to arbitrate and settle such matters.

- **Granting Compulsory Licences:**
    - **For Publishing or Republishing Works:** Under certain conditions, the Board can issue compulsory licences to publish or republish works. For example, if a work is not readily available to the public, a compulsory licence may be granted to ensure accessibility.

❖ **For Translations:** The Board can grant compulsory licences to translate a literary or dramatic work into any language after seven years from its first publication. This ensures that important works are made accessible to diverse linguistic audiences.

> **Adjudicating Disputes on Publication:** The Board can adjudicate disputes regarding whether a work has been published, its date of publication, or the term of copyright for works from other countries.
> **Fixing Royalty Rates:** The Board has the authority to set royalty rates for sound recordings under the cover-version provision (i.e., when a version of a song is re-recorded by a different artist).
> **Resale Share Right for Original Works:** The Board can fix the resale share right (a portion of the resale price) for the creators of original works, such as paintings, sculptures, drawings, and original manuscripts of literary, dramatic, or musical works.

8.25. COPYRIGHT ENFORCEMENT ADVISORY COUNCIL (CEAC)

The Copyright Enforcement Advisory Council (CEAC) was established in 1991 by the Government of India to review the implementation and enforcement of the Copyright Act and to recommend measures for improvement. The council plays a key advisory role in ensuring effective enforcement of copyright laws in the country.

Functions of CEAC:

> **Periodic Review:** The CEAC regularly reviews the progress made in the enforcement of the Copyright Act and evaluates how well copyright laws are being upheld.
> **Advisory Role:** It provides advice to the government on strategies and actions that can enhance the enforcement of copyright laws, ensuring that copyright holders' rights are better protected and respected.

Term and Reconstitution:

> The term of the CEAC is **three years**, after which it is reconstituted. The council is periodically re-established to ensure it remains effective in keeping up with the evolving copyright landscape.

8.26. INTERNATIONAL COPYRIGHT AGREEMENTS, CONVENTIONS AND TREATIES

Copyright laws are **territorial** in nature, meaning they are only valid within the borders of the country where they were created. As a result, a creative work is not automatically protected worldwide. To ensure copyright protection for an Indian work in foreign countries, the author must apply for protection separately in each country. However, many countries have simplified this process by becoming members of international **copyright conventions** and **treaties**, which provide reciprocal copyright protection among member countries.

India's Participation in International Copyright Conventions

India is a member of several international agreements that facilitate the protection of Indian copyrights abroad and foreign copyrights within India. These conventions set global standards for copyright protection, ensuring that creative works are protected across borders. The major international agreements to which India is a signatory include:

1. **Berne Convention for the Protection of Literary and Artistic Works (1886)**
   > **Overview**: The Berne Convention is one of the oldest and most important international copyright agreements. It ensures that works created by nationals of any member country receive the same protection in other member countries as they would in their home country[42].
   > **Key Feature**: Protection is automatic upon creation, without the need for formal registration.
2. **Universal Copyright Convention (1952)**
   > **Overview**: This convention provides an alternative to the Berne Convention, especially for countries that may not have been part of Berne. It offers minimum protections for literary, artistic, and other creative works[43].
   > **Key Feature**: It requires a formal copyright notice to claim protection.
3. **Rome Convention for the Protection of Performers, Producers of Phonograms, and Broadcasting Organizations (1961)**

> **Overview**: This convention focuses on protecting the rights of performers, record producers, and broadcasting organizations[44].
> **Key Feature**: Provides protection for performers' live performances, sound recordings, and broadcasts.

4. **Multilateral Convention for the Avoidance of Double Taxation of Copyright Royalties (1979)**
   > **Overview**: This treaty addresses the issue of double taxation on royalties earned from copyrighted works[45].
   > **Key Feature**: Ensures that copyright owners are not taxed multiple times in different countries on royalties earned from their works.

5. **Trade-Related Aspects of Intellectual Property Rights (TRIPS) Agreement (1995)**
   > **Overview**: The TRIPS Agreement, administered by the World Trade Organization (WTO), sets comprehensive international standards for intellectual property rights, including copyright[46].
   > **Key Feature**: It ensures that all member countries provide a minimum level of protection for intellectual property, including enforcement mechanisms.

International Copyright Order in India

India protects the copyrights of foreign authors from countries that are members of the **Berne Convention (1886)**, the **Universal Copyright Convention (1952)**, and the **TRIPS Agreement (1995)** through the **International Copyright Order**. This order ensures that foreign works receive the same protection in India as Indian works, provided the country of origin is a member of these international agreements.

8.27. INTERESTING COPYRIGHTS CASES

1. **R.G. Anand vs. Delux Films (1978) – India**

   In Indian jurisprudence, **R.G. Anand vs. Delux Films** is one of the landmark cases involving copyright infringement in the context of cinematic works. The plaintiff, R.G. Anand, was a playwright who claimed that his play was copied by Delux Films in the movie New Delhi[47].
   > **Key Issue**: Whether the storyline of the movie substantially copied the plaintiff's play.
   > **Outcome**: The Supreme Court of India ruled in favor of Delux Films, stating that although there were some similarities, the movie was not a direct copy of the play, and the expression of the ideas was sufficiently different.
   > **Importance**: The ruling reinforced the idea that copyright does not protect ideas themselves, but the specific expression of those ideas. It established important boundaries for copyright protection in Indian creative industries.

2. **David vs. Macaques, Indonesia, 2011**

   In 2011, a legal debate arose over a photograph clicked by a monkey, leading to a complex copyright case. UK-based photographer **David Slater** set up his camera on a tripod in a wildlife sanctuary, intending to photograph **macaque monkeys**. Fascinated by the equipment, one of the monkeys clicked a selfie. The photo quickly became famous, sparking a legal battle regarding ownership of the copyright. The key question was whether the **monkey or David Slater** owned the copyright to the photograph[48].
   > **Legal Controversy:** Under copyright law, ownership is typically granted to the creator of the work, which theoretically would be the monkey. However, David Slater, who set up the equipment and facilitated the photograph, claimed copyright ownership.
   > **People for the Ethical Treatment of Animals (PETA)** entered the dispute, arguing on behalf of the monkey, claiming that the monkey should hold the copyright.
   > **Resolution:** The case was ultimately settled out of court. David Slater was recognized as the copyright holder due to his substantial contribution to creating the photo. However, in a compromise, he agreed to donate 25% of the royalties to the wildlife sanctuary where the monkey lives.

3. **'Happy Birthday to You' Case Law**

The famous song **"Happy Birthday to You"** is one of the most recognized tunes in the world, according to the **Guinness World Records (1998)**. Its melody originally comes from a song titled **"Good Morning to All,"** composed by American sisters **Patty Smith Hill and Mildred J. Hill in 1893**. They created the melody to make it easier for children to learn and sing[49].

➤ **Copyright Journey:** In 1935, the **Summy Company** registered the copyright for the piano arrangement of the song. In **1999, Warner/Chappell** Music acquired the company and began charging royalties for the song. Warner/Chappell earned substantial amounts by collecting licensing fees from individuals and organizations using the song.

➤ **Legal Dispute:** A legal dispute arose over the song's copyright, particularly over the fact that only the melody was registered, not the lyrics. In 2015, a Federal court mediation led to Warner/Chappell agreeing to pay a settlement to individuals and entities who had paid licensing fees. As a result, the song is now in the public domain, meaning no royalties are required for it.

4. **Amitabh Bachchan to Lose Copyright Over His Father's Works in 2063**

Renowned actor Amitabh Bachchan will lose the copyrights to the works of his father, Harivansh Rai Bachchan, by the year 2063. Harivansh Rai Bachchan, a celebrated Hindi poet and recipient of prestigious awards like the Sahitya Akademi Award and the Padma Bhushan, is best known for his work Madhushala (1935) and Hindi translations of Shakespeare's Macbeth and Othello[50].

Copyright Duration: According to the Copyright Act, 1957, an author retains copyright over their work for their lifetime plus 60 years. Harivansh Rai Bachchan passed away on January 18, 2003, meaning the copyright for his works will expire in the year 2063, after which his works will enter the public domain.

Questions

1. Define the term Copyright and write its classes.

2. What are the two exclusive rights owned by the copyright owner? Explain briefly.

3. What are the roles and functions of the copyright board and the copyright society in administering copyright laws and regulations?

4. What are the key considerations and tests for determining fair use doctrine under copyright law? Explain with examples.

5. Using a Flow chart, explain the important steps involved in the process of Copyright Registration.

6. What were the key events and circumstances surrounding the copyright dispute between photographer David Slater and the macaques in Indonesia in 2011? Explain.

7. Explain the criteria that an original work must meet to quality for copyright protection

8. Explain the process of copyright registration? What are the benefits for the copyright

"A great trademark is appropriate, dynamic, distinctive, memorable and unique."

: *Primo Angeli*

Module - 4

Chapter 9:
TRADEMARKS

INTRODUCTION

A trademark is a unique symbol, word, or design that identifies and distinguishes the goods or services of one company from another. In this chapter, we will explore the key aspects of trademarks, including the eligibility criteria for registration, who can apply, and the various laws and acts governing trademarks in India. We will also discuss the different types of trademarks, the process of registration, and the role of the Trademark Registry. Additionally, this chapter highlights a famous case, Coca-Cola Company vs. Bisleri International Pvt. Ltd., to demonstrate the importance of trademarks in protecting business identity.

9.1. TRADEMARK

A **trademark** is like a special badge or symbol that helps people know which company made a product or offers a service. Think of it as a unique stamp that tells you who the product belongs to. This symbol can be anything that makes a product stand out. It could be a picture, a word, a phrase, or even a sound. Example: the golden arches of McDonald's or the swoosh of Nike are trademarks.

1. **Purpose of a Trademark**
   - The main job of a trademark is to identify and differentiate. This means it helps people recognize a product and see how it is different from other similar products. For instance, when you see a bitten apple logo, you know it's an Apple product, not a Samsung.
   - Trademarks make it easier for customers to find the products they like and trust. If you love a certain brand of shoes, the trademark helps you find them quickly among many other shoes.

2. **Components of a Trademark**
   - The word 'Mark' in trademark refers to anything that can be used as a sign. This includes:
     - **Sign:** A simple mark or symbol, **Example:** This stylized "T" is widely recognized and associated with the Tata Group's various businesses.
     - **Design:** A unique pattern or artwork. **Example:** The Tanishq jewelry brand's logo, which features a stylized design element representing elegance and luxury.
     - **Phrase:** A catchy line or slogan. **Example:** "Yeh Dil Maange More!" – Pepsi's iconic Indian slogan that became hugely popular.
     - **Slogan:** A memorable saying that represents the brand. **Example:** " Dar ke aage jeet hai" – the slogan used by Mountain Dew, a popular Indian soft drink brand.
     - **Symbol:** A recognizable image or icon. **Example:** The Air India mascot, "Maharaja," a cartoon character symbolizing royalty and hospitality.

- ❖ **Name:** The brand name itself, **Example:** Amul, a household name in India for dairy products, is registered as a trademark.
- ❖ **Numeral:** Numbers that are associated with a brand. **Example:** 555, a well-known trademark associated with ITC's Wills Navy Cut cigarettes, is protected as a numeral trademark.
- ❖ **Device:** A combination of these elements to create a unique brand identity. **Example:** The Bajaj logo combines text, a symbol, and a design to form a distinctive identity for the automotive brand.

3. **Why are Trademarks Important?**
  - ➢ Trademarks are crucial because they protect the brand's identity. They stop other companies from using the same or similar symbols, which could confuse customers.
  - ➢ They also add value to a company. A strong trademark can make a brand more popular and trusted, leading to more sales and success.

4. **How Trademarks Help Consumers**
  - ➢ Trademarks help consumers by making shopping easier. When you see a trademark, you know what to expect in terms of quality and service.
  - ➢ They also help in building trust. If you have a good experience with a product, the trademark helps you find it again in the future.

9.2. ELIGIBILITY CRITERIA

To legally classify goods or services as a trademark, they must meet certain criteria. These conditions ensure that the trademark is distinct, non-descriptive, and unique compared to existing marks.

1. **Distinctiveness**
  - ➢ **Definition:** A trademark must have sufficient distinctiveness to differentiate it from other goods or services. It should be able to identify the source of the product or service in the market.
  - ➢ **Importance:** Distinctiveness helps consumers recognize the origin of the goods or services and distinguishes them from those of competitors.
  - ➢ **Example:** The trademark "Nike" for sportswear is distinct and immediately identifies the source as the Nike company, which helps in brand recognition and consumer loyalty.

2. **Descriptiveness**
  - ➢ **Definition:** A trademark should not merely describe the goods or services it represents. Descriptive marks are generally not protected under trademark law unless they have acquired a "secondary meaning."
  - ➢ **Explanation:** Descriptive marks describe the characteristics or qualities of the goods or services, which does not meet the uniqueness required for trademark protection.
  - ➢ **Secondary Meaning:** A descriptive term can be registered if it has gained secondary meaning through extensive use and consumer recognition, indicating that it has become associated with a particular source.
  - ➢ **Example:** The brand name "Apple" is descriptive of the fruit, but it has acquired secondary meaning and is recognized as a trademark for electronics due to its widespread use and consumer association with the Apple Inc. company.

3. **Similarity to Prior Marks**
  - ➢ **Definition:** The trademark must be sufficiently unique and not too similar to existing trademarks.
  - ➢ **Importance:** This criterion prevents confusion in the market by ensuring that new trademarks do not closely resemble existing ones, which could mislead consumers.
  - ➢ **Example:** If a new brand of clothing tried to use the name "Addidas," it would be too similar to "Adidas" and likely be rejected due to the similarity to the existing trademark.

9.3. WHO CAN APPLY FOR A TRADEMARK

Following are Eligibility for Trademark Application

1. **Proprietorship:** Any individual or entity who owns the trademark can apply for its registration. This means that the applicant must be the actual owner of the trademark.

2. **Collective Applications:** A trademark application can be filed jointly by multiple applicants. In such cases, supporting documents that outline the joint ownership and purpose must be provided.

3. **Organizations and Associations:** Organizations or associations can also apply for trademarks. This includes filing for a collective mark that can be used by all members of the organization or association.

   Example: The "Reliance" symbol, used by Reliance Industries, represents a collective mark. It indicates all products and services falling under the Reliance brand umbrella, and is utilized by various divisions within the organization.

9.4. ACTS AND LAWS

1. **Legislation**
   - ➢ **Trademarks Act, 1999:** This Act provides the legal framework for the registration and protection of trademarks in India. It outlines the procedures for trademark registration, protection, and enforcement[51].
   - ➢ **Trademarks Rules, 2002:** These rules govern the procedures for trademark registration and related processes. They detail the requirements for application, examination, and opposition[52].

2. **Amendments**
   - ➢ **Recent Amendments:** The Trademarks Act and Rules have been amended periodically to address changes in the legal landscape and to enhance the trademark registration process. The latest amendments occurred in 2010 and 2017.

3. **Administration**
   - ➢ **Office of CGDPDTM:** The administration and enforcement of trademark matters are handled by the Controller General of Patents, Designs, and Trademarks (CGDPDTM), Government of India.

9.5. DESIGNATION OF TRADEMARK SYMBOLS

1. **TM (Trademark)**
   - ➢ **Meaning:** The TM symbol is used to indicate that a trademark is not yet registered but is being used to promote the goods of the company. It signals that the user claims rights to the mark, but legal protection has not been granted.

2. **SM (Service Mark)**
   - ➢ **Meaning:** The SM symbol functions similarly to the TM symbol but is used for services rather than goods. It indicates that the mark is being used to promote services and is not yet registered.

3. **R (Registered Trademark)**
   - ➢ **Meaning:** The R symbol signifies that the trademark has been officially registered with the relevant trademark office. The registered trademark is legally protected, and the owner has exclusive rights to its use.

9.6. CLASSIFICATION OF TRADEMARKS

The classification of trademarks helps in categorizing goods and services for trademark registration. This is done under internationally recognized systems to ensure consistency across different jurisdictions.

1. **Nice Agreement (1957)**
   - ➢ **Introduction:** The Nice Agreement, established in 1957 and administered by the World Intellectual Property Organization (WIPO), provides a standardized classification system for goods and services under trademarks[53].

> **Global Adoption:**
>   - ❖ The Nice classification system is currently followed by 149 countries. These include 84 state parties who are signatories to the agreement and 65 additional states that adopt this classification system without being signatories[53].
>   - ❖ Organizations such as the African Intellectual Property Organization, the African Regional Intellectual Property Organization, and the European Union Intellectual Property Office also use this system for trademark classification.
> **Structure:**
>   - ❖ The classification consists of 45 classes, which are divided into two broad categories:
>   - **i. 34 classes for goods**
>   - **ii. 11 classes for services**
>   - **i. Example of Goods Class (Class 35):** Chemicals used in industry, science, and photography; Unprocessed artificial resins; Unprocessed plastics; Fire extinguishing and prevention compositions; Fertilizers and biological preparations for use in industry and science.
>   - **ii. Example of Services Class (Class 11):** Legal services; Security services for the protection of tangible property and individuals; Personal and social services to meet individuals' needs.

2. **Vienna Codification (1973)**

> **Introduction:** The Vienna Agreement of 1973 established the Vienna Codification, which provides an international classification system specifically for figurative elements in trademarks (such as logos, symbols, or images). This classification ensures that figurative elements are consistently categorized for trademark purposes across countries[54].
> **Structure:**
>   - ❖ The system divides figurative elements into categories (1 to 29), divisions (1 to 19), and sections (1 to 30), creating a structured approach to identifying these elements.
>   - ❖ **Example of Figurative Classification:** A representation of "a little girl eating" belongs to:
>   - ▪ **Category 2:** Human beings
>   - ▪ **Division 5:** Children
>   - ▪ **Main Section 3:** Girls
>   - ❖ If additional details are provided (e.g., "Children drinking or eating"), the figurative element can also be identified with an auxiliary section, in this case, **Auxiliary Section 18**. The full codification of this example would be represented as **2.5.3, 18** (main and auxiliary sections).
> **Examples of Trademark Classes:**
>   - ❖ **Class 1 (Goods):** Chemicals for industrial use, fire prevention compositions, adhesives for industry, fertilizers, and biological preparations for science.
>   - ❖ **Class 45 (Services):** Legal services, security services for the protection of property and individuals, and personal services to meet social needs.

9.7. REGISTRATION OF A TRADEMARK IS NOT COMPULSORY

While the registration of a trademark is not legally mandatory, it provides substantial benefits and legal protections for the proprietor. The key advantages of registering a trademark include legal security, exclusive rights, brand recognition, and asset creation. Understanding these benefits can help businesses make informed decisions about trademark registration[16].

1. **Legal Protection**

> **Prevention of Unauthorized Use:** A registered trademark safeguards the owner from exploitation by other companies, organizations, or individuals who might use the mark without permission.
> **Evidentiary Value:** In legal disputes, the registered trademark serves as evidence of lawful ownership, making it easier for the proprietor to claim and protect their rights in court.

2. **Exclusive Right**
   - ➢ **Full Control Over Usage:** A registered trademark grants the owner the exclusive right to use the mark in connection with their goods or services. The owner can promote their business and prevent others from using a similar or identical mark.
   - ➢ **Legal Enforcement:** The registered owner has the legal authority to prevent third parties from using the mark without permission, which strengthens the business's legal standing.

3. **Brand Recognition**
   - ➢ **Building Brand Identity:** A trademark helps businesses create and maintain brand recognition. Customers associate the logo or trademark with the company's products or services.
   - ➢ **Market Advantage:** Early registration and consistent use of a trademark enhance goodwill, attracting new customers and retaining existing ones. Over time, this builds a strong market position and boosts business growth.

4. **Asset Creation**
   - ➢ **Intangible Asset:** A registered trademark is an intangible asset that adds value to the business. It becomes part of the company's intellectual property and can be monetized or used as leverage in business deals.
   - ➢ **Brand Equity:** The trademark strengthens the business's brand identity, fostering loyalty among customers. It also enhances the company's reputation, which can lead to long-term financial benefits. **Example:** Well-known brands like **Coca-Cola** or **Apple** have leveraged their trademarks to create immense brand equity that drives customer loyalty and business success.

5. **Common Law Trademarks**
   - ➢ **Unregistered Trademarks:** Although unregistered trademarks (also known as common law trademarks) can still be used, they do not offer the same level of legal protection as registered trademarks.
   - ➢ **Passing Off:** An unregistered trademark owner can file a legal action against individuals that attempt to "pass off" their goods or services as those of the unregistered owner. However, the owner must demonstrate the goodwill or reputation associated with their mark in order to succeed in such cases.

9.8. VALIDITY OF TRADEMARK

In India, the **validity period** of a registered trademark is 10 years. After this initial period, the registration can be **renewed perpetually** in increments of 10 years. To maintain the registration, a renewal request must be filed before the expiry date[55].

1. **Renewal Process**
   - ➢ **Application Form TM-R:**
     - ❖ To renew a trademark, the proprietor must submit the form 'TM-R' within **one year before the expiry** of the last registration.
     - ❖ This process ensures that the trademark remains active and protected under the law.
     - ❖ **Example:** If a trademark was registered in 2015, it would be valid until 2025. The renewal request should be submitted between 2024 and 2025 to maintain the trademark's validity.

2. **Legal Basis**
   - ➢ The renewal process is governed by the **Indian Trademarks Act,** which specifies the legal requirements for extending the validity of trademarks.

9.9. TYPES OF TRADEMARK REGISTERED IN INDIA

There are several types of trademarks that can be registered in India. The selection of a trademark should follow certain guidelines to ensure uniqueness and memorability. A carefully chosen trademark can help build brand recognition and protect business interests.

1. **Criteria for a Good Trademark**
   - ➢ **Memorability:** A trademark should be **easy to pronounce**, **spell**, and **remember**. Ideally, it should be an **invented word** or a **unique geographical name** that stands out from common terms.
   - ➢ **Avoid Common Terms:** Trademarks should avoid:
     - ❖ **Common geographical names** (e.g., "Delhi")
     - ❖ **Personal names** (e.g., "John")
     - ❖ **Praising words** (e.g., "best", "perfect", or "super")
   - ➢ **Market Survey:** Before finalizing a trademark, it's recommended to conduct a **market survey** to ensure that no similar mark exists. This helps avoid potential legal conflicts and ensures the distinctiveness of the chosen mark.

2. **Examples of Registerable Trademarks**
   - ➢ **Personal or Surname of the Applicant:**
     - ❖ A trademark can be based on a personal or surname, provided it has a historical or business connection.
     - ❖ **Example:** The trademark '**BAJAJ**' is named after the Indian industrialist Mr. Jamnalal Bajaj, representing a well-known brand in India.
   - ➢ **Word Not Related to Product/Service:**
     - ❖ A word that has no direct relevance to the product or service can be an effective trademark.
     - ❖ **Example:** '**INDIA GATE**' is a registered trademark for food grains and allied products, even though the name originally refers to a national monument.
   - ➢ **Letters, Numerals, or Combinations:**
     - ❖ Trademarks can also consist of letters, numerals, or their combination.
     - ❖ **Example:** '**YAHOO**' an abbreviation of 'Yet Another Hierarchical Officious Oracle' started as a phrase and has become a globally recognized trademark.

3. **Types of Marks Commonly Used:**
   - ➢ **Word Marks:** Invented or creative words that do not directly describe the product (e.g., 'Apple' for electronic goods).
   - ➢ **Figurative Marks:** Logos or symbols that represent the brand.
   - ➢ **Combination Marks:** Words, letters, or numerals combined with figurative elements (e.g., the "Starbucks" logo with the name).

Table 9.1. Example of famous trademarks according to different types

Sl. No.	Type of Mark	Trademark	Company Name
1	Sign	Stylized "T"	Tata Group
2	Design	Tanishq Logo	Tanishq (Titan)
3	Phrase	"Yeh Dil Maange More!"	Pepsi (India)
4	Slogan	"Dar ke aage jeet hai"	Mountain Dew (PepsiCo)
5	Symbol	Air India "Maharaja"	Air India
6	Name	Amul	Amul (GCMMF)
7	Numeral	555	ITC (Wills Navy Cut)
8	Device	Bajaj Logo	Bajaj Auto

9.10. TRADEMARK REGISTRY

In India, the **Trademark Registry** is responsible for overseeing the registration and management of trademarks. The registry operates through **five cities**: Delhi, Mumbai, Ahmedabad, Kolkata, and Chennai. Each city serves a designated territorial region, and businesses must file for trademarks at the appropriate office based on their location. Each of these offices has jurisdiction over a specific region, and businesses must use the services of the office assigned to their state. **Foreign applicants** must file in the jurisdiction where their attorney or agent is located.

Table 9.2. Jurisdiction by Region for trademark

S. No.	Office Location	States/Regions Covered
1	Mumbai	Maharashtra, Madhya Pradesh, Chhattisgarh, Goa
2	Ahmedabad	Gujarat, Rajasthan, and Union Territories of Daman, Diu, Dadra and Nagar Haveli
3	Kolkata	Arunachal Pradesh, Assam, Bihar, Orissa, West Bengal, Manipur, Mizoram, Meghalaya, Sikkim, Tripura, Jharkhand, Union Territories of Nagaland, Andaman & Nicobar Islands
4	New Delhi	Jammu & Kashmir, Punjab, Haryana, Uttar Pradesh, Himachal Pradesh, Uttarakhand, Delhi, Union Territory of Chandigarh
5	Chennai	Andhra Pradesh, Telangana, Kerala, Tamil Nadu, Karnataka, Union Territories of Pondicherry, Lakshadweep Islands

Example: A company based in **Maharashtra** must file its trademark at the **Mumbai Trademark Office**, while a company based in **Kolkata** would register at the **Kolkata Office**.

i.   **Foreign Applicants:** For **foreign applicants**, the territorial jurisdiction is determined by the **location of their legal representative** (agent or attorney) in India. For instance, if a foreign business's attorney is based in Delhi, the trademark application must be filed in the **New Delhi office**.

ii. **Importance of Territorial Jurisdiction:** Understanding the territorial jurisdiction is crucial because **applicants can only use the services of the designated office** for their region. This ensures the correct processing of applications and prevents delays.

9.11. PROCESS FOR TRADEMARK REGISTRATION

To register a **Trademark** in India, the applicant must go through a systematic process, starting from conducting a **prior art search** to obtaining the **Trademark registration certificate**. The applicant may either apply directly or through an authorized agent.

1. Prior Art Search

Before applying for a Trademark, it is crucial to conduct a **prior art search** to ensure that the intended mark is **distinctive** and not already registered. This step helps in avoiding conflicts with existing trademarks. The following platforms are available for conducting such searches:

i.   Public search for Trademarks by CGPDTM:
(Link: https://ipindiaservices.gov.in/tmrpublicsearch/frmmain.aspx)

ii. WIPO's Global Brand Database: (Link: https://www.wipo.int/branddb/en/)

iii. Trademark Electronic Search System (TESS):
(Link http://tmsearch.uspto.gov/bin/gate.exe?f=tess&state=4805:za847u.1.1)

iv. MARKARIA Trademark Search Engine:
(Link: https://trademark-search.marcaria.com/en/asia/india-trademark-search)

v.   VAKIL Search: (Link: https://trademarks.vakilsearch.com/)

Once the **prior art search** confirms the uniqueness of the intended Trademark, the applicant can move forward with the filing of the **TM-A application form**.

2. **Steps for Trademark Registration:** The process of registering a Trademark involves several key steps:
    i. **Application Filing**: The applicant may file the application individually or with the assistance of a certified agent. The application is filed at **Trademarks Office** based on the applicant's jurisdiction.
    ii. **Application Number**: Upon filing, the applicant receives an **application number**, which can be tracked online through link: https://ipindiaonline.gov.in/tmrpublicsearch/frmmain.aspx.
    iii. **Examination**: The application is examined by a professional examiner. If all requirements are met, the application is **published** in the official Trademark journal. If there are objections, the examiner sends them to the applicant for correction. A revised application is submitted after rectifications, and based on the response, the examiner decides whether to recommend the mark for publication.

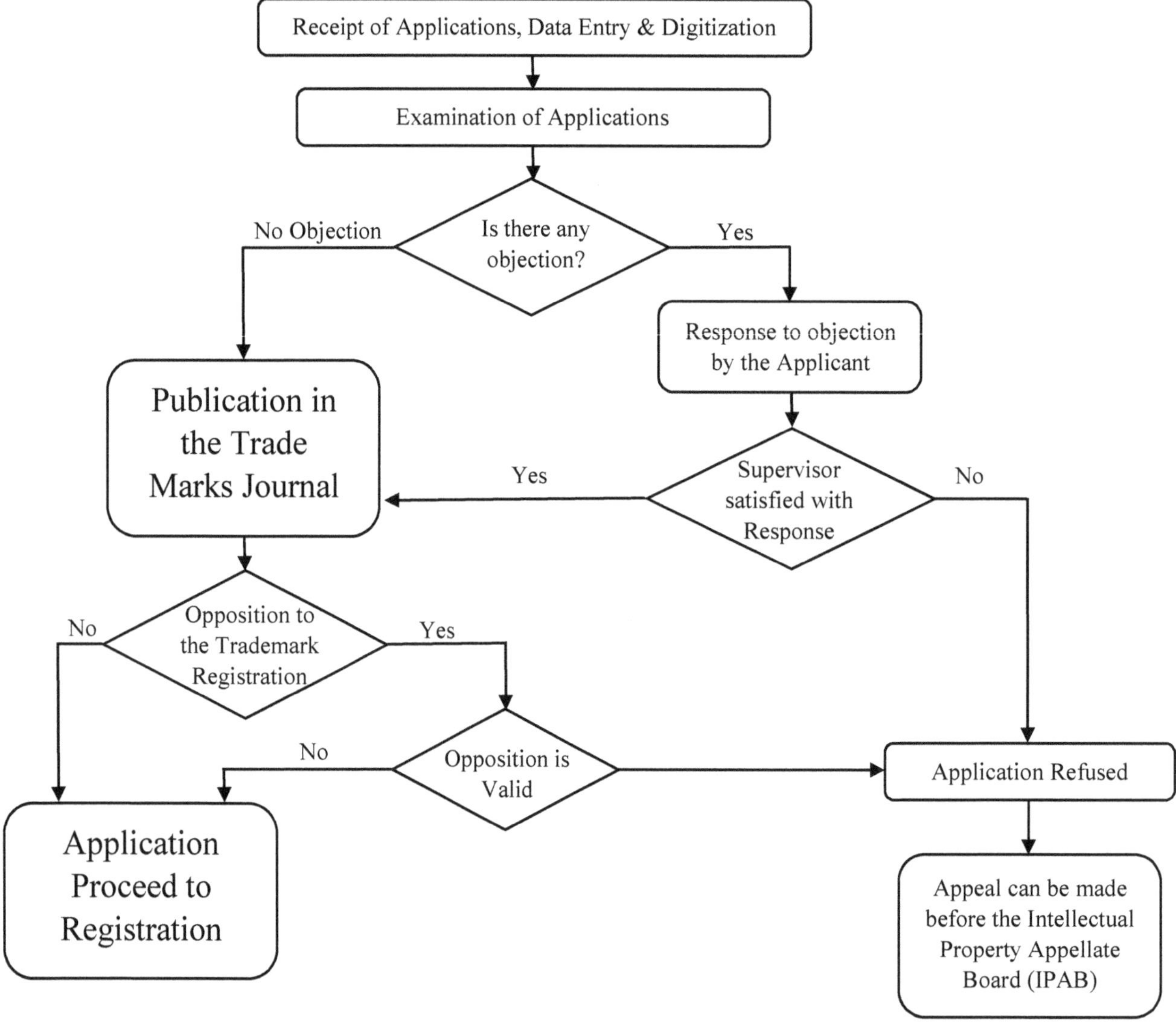

Fig. 9.1. Flowchart of Process for Trademark Registration[56].

3. **Publication in Journal:** After being scrutinized, the details of the application are published in the official **Trademark journal link:** http://www.ipindia.nic.in/journal-tm.htm.
    After publication, the public has **90 days** to file objections, if any. A hearing is conducted to resolve the objections, and the final decision is made by the officer.
4. **Issuance of Registration Certificate**: If the application successfully passes through all formalities, the applicant receives the **Trademark registration certificate**.
5. **Handling Objections:** If the Trademark application is **rejected** at any stage, the applicant has the right to **challenge** the decision in front of the **Intellectual Property Appellate Board (IPAB)**.

6. **Special Considerations:** Applicants must provide an **English translation** of any non-English words included in the application. If the applicant is claiming **priority** from an earlier-filed application, they must provide relevant details such as the **application number, filing date, country**, and **goods/services** mentioned in the prior application.

9.12. FAMOUS CASE LAW: COCA-COLA COMPANY VS. BISLERI INTERNATIONAL PVT. LTD.

This case revolves around **Trademark infringement** and the concept of **passing-off** in relation to the popular beverage brand **MAAZA**. It highlights the complexities of **Intellectual Property Rights (IPR)** when companies transfer ownership of a brand or product to another entity, as well as the consequences of violating such agreements.

1. **Background of the Case:**
   - **Trademark**: The **Trademark 'MAAZA'**, a mango-flavored fruit drink, was originally owned by **Bisleri International Pvt. Ltd.**, an Indian company.
   - **Transfer of Rights**: Bisleri transferred the rights of 'MAAZA' (including the **formulation, IPR, and goodwill**) to **Coca-Cola Company** for use within the Indian territory.
   - **Infringement Issue**: In **2008**, despite the transfer of rights to Coca-Cola for the Indian market, Bisleri **applied for Trademark registration of 'MAAZA' in Turkey** and began exporting the product using the same mark.

2. **Legal Action:**
   - **Filing of Petition**: Coca-Cola filed a **petition for permanent injunction and damages** against Bisleri in 2008, accusing the company of **Trademark infringement** and **passing-off** the 'MAAZA' brand.
   - **Claims by Coca-Cola (Plaintiff)**: Coca-Cola argued that the **Trademark 'MAAZA' for the Indian market** had been fully assigned to them, and thus **any use of the mark by Bisleri**, either within India or for export purposes, would be considered an **infringement**.
   - **Coca-Cola's Stance**: Since Bisleri no longer had rights over 'MAAZA' for India, they were not permitted to use or export the product under that name, as it violated the **exclusive ownership rights** Coca-Cola had acquired.

3. **Court's Decision:**
   - **Interim Injunction**: The court ruled in favor of **Coca-Cola**, granting an **interim injunction** that prohibited Bisleri from using the **Trademark 'MAAZA'** in India and from exporting the product under that name.
   - **Key Reasoning**: The court considered Bisleri's continued use of the mark as a clear case of **Trademark infringement**. The fact that Bisleri was exporting the product using the 'MAAZA' mark, despite having transferred rights to Coca-Cola for Indian territory, was determined to be a violation of the agreement and Coca-Cola's Trademark rights.

4. **Key Legal Concepts:**
   i. **Trademark Infringement**: Involves the unauthorized use of a registered Trademark that causes confusion or deception among consumers. In this case, Bisleri's use of the 'MAAZA' mark outside India was considered an infringement because it was linked to Coca-Cola's rights over the brand.
   ii. **Passing-Off**: A legal principle aimed at preventing one business from misrepresenting its goods or services as those of another. Bisleri's export of 'MAAZA' created confusion about the ownership of the brand, constituting an act of passing-off.
   iii. **Transfer of Rights**: This case underscores the importance of properly defining the territorial limits and conditions of **IPR transfers**. In this instance, Coca-Cola's exclusive rights to 'MAAZA' within India extended to the **export market**, which was upheld by the court.

5. **Implications of the Case:**
   - ➢ **Reaffirmation of IPR in Global Trade**: The court's decision reinforces the importance of honoring **Trademark transfer agreements** and protecting **IPR** in the context of **international trade**.
   - ➢ **Export Market Restrictions**: The ruling clarified that **exporting products** under a Trademark assigned to another party can still be considered **infringement**, even if the exporting company originally owned the Trademark.

Questions

1. What are the key eligibility criteria that a mark must meet to qualify for trademark protection? List advantages that a proprietor gains through trademark registration

2. Using a flowchart, explain the steps involved in the process of Trademarks Registration

3. What are the different categories of trademarks recognized under Indian law, and tabulate the famous trademark types with examples.

"Design is not just what it looks like and feels like. Design is how it works."

: Steve Jobs

Module - 5

Chapter 10:
INDUSTRIAL DESIGNS

INTRODUCTION

Industrial Designs: Eligibility Criteria. Acts and Laws to Govern Industrial Designs. Design Rights. Enforcement of Design Rights. Non-Protectable Industrial Designs India. Protection Term. Procedure for Registration of Industrial Designs. Prior Art Search. Application for Registration. Duration of the Registration of a Design. Importance of Design Registration. Cancellation of the Registered Design. Application Forms. Classification of Industrial Designs. Designs Registration Trend in India. International Treaties. Famous Case Law: Apple Inc. vs. Samsung Electronics Co.

10.1. INDUSTRIAL DESIGNS

Definition: An industrial design refers to the aesthetic features of an article, including its **shape, configuration, pattern, ornamentation**, or the **composition of lines or colors** applied to the article. These features can be:

a. One-dimensional, two-dimensional, or three-dimensional.
b. A combination of one, two, or three dimensions.

Industrial designs are applied to a finished product, and they are judged solely based on **visual appeal**. It is important to note that a "design" does not include any functional or mechanical aspects of a product, nor does it cover principles of construction.

Example: The sleek design of a smartphone may be protected as an industrial design, but its internal mechanical components would not be.

Creation Process: Industrial designs may be created by any of the following processes:

1. Manual
2. Mechanical
3. Chemical
4. Any combination of these processes

The final appearance of the product must be visually appealing to qualify for protection.

Purpose of Design Registration: The primary goal of industrial design registration is to:

1. **Protect the creator's original work:** Ensuring that the unique aesthetic of the design remains exclusive to the creator.
2. **Incentivize creativity:** By protecting designs, it encourages individuals and companies to invest in creating new and innovative designs.
3. **Foster innovation:** Protection of designs motivates others to work towards original and artistic creations.

10.2. ELIGIBILITY CRITERIA

For an industrial design to be eligible for protection, it must meet the following criteria:

1. **Novelty or Originality:**
   - ➢ The design must be **new or original** and should not have been **disclosed to the public** through prior publication, use, or any other means. **Example:** A company that reveals a new product design at a public exhibition before filing for design registration risks losing the protection of that design.

2. **Distinctiveness:**
   - ➢ The design must be **significantly different** from any existing registered designs or those available in the public domain.
   - ➢ The goal is to ensure that the design brings something new to the marketplace, not just a minor variation of existing designs.

3. **Key Considerations:**
   - ➢ Designs that are purely **functional or mechanical** are not eligible for protection.
   - ➢ The design must **appeal to the eye** and should be judged based on **aesthetic** considerations rather than practical functionality.

10.3. ACTS AND LAWS TO GOVERN INDUSTRIAL DESIGNS

1. **Governing Legislation in India:** Industrial designs in India are governed by two primary legislative frameworks:
   - ➢ **The Designs Act, 2000:** Provides legal protection for industrial designs and outlines the process of registration and protection of designs in India[57].
   - ➢ **The Design Rules, 2001:** Complement the Designs Act and define the procedural aspects of industrial design registration. These rules have undergone amendments in 2008, 2013, 2014, and 2019[58]. Both the act and rules aim to protect and regulate industrial designs to promote innovation and creativity.

2. **Key Characteristics of a Protected Industrial Design**

   For an industrial design to be eligible for legal protection under Indian law, it must possess the following characteristics:
   - ➢ **Novelty and Originality:** The design must be new and unique, not previously disclosed or published. **Example:** A new car design that hasn't been released to the public would meet this criterion.
   - ➢ **Applicability to a Functional Article:** The design must be applicable to a practical and functional object. **Example:** The design of a smartphone, which is not only aesthetically pleasing but also functional, would qualify.
   - ➢ **Visibility on a Finished Article:** The design must be clearly visible on the finished product. **Example:** The unique shape of a Coca-Cola bottle is instantly recognizable and visible.
   - ➢ **No Prior Publication or Disclosure:** The design must not have been published or disclosed before its registration. **Example:** A chair design exhibited at a trade show before applying for registration would lose eligibility for protection.

3. **Examples of Famous Industrial Designs**

   Several iconic products serve as benchmarks in the field of industrial design. These examples highlight the importance of aesthetics and functionality:
   - ➢ **Coca-Cola Bottle (1915):** Designed with a contoured shape, this glass bottle has become a classic example of industrial design, widely recognized for its visual appeal.
     Key Design Features: Curved body, easily identifiable shape.
   - ➢ **Piaggio Vespa (1940s):** A scooter designed by the Italian company Piaggio, characterized by its sleek design and practicality.
     Key Design Features: Painted steel body, flat floorboard for comfort, protection from wind.

- ➤ **iPhone (Apple Inc.):** Known for its slim, rectangular body with smooth, rounded corners, the iPhone has become a globally recognized design.
  Key Design Features: User-friendly interface, compact design, aesthetic appeal.
- ➤ **Mini Cooper (Late 20th Century):** A small car designed by the British Motor Corporation, known for its unique structure, which optimizes space for passengers and luggage.
  Key Design Features: Compact size, spacious interior despite small external dimensions.
- ➤ **Rocking Wheel Chair:** A modern chair design featuring a sleek, circular shape that provides a smooth rocking motion.
  Key Design Features: Sleek, circular design, provision for a headlight.
- ➤ **Juicy Salif (Citrus Juice Squeezer):** A striking design in the shape of a squid, made from alumina, considered iconic in the realm of product design.
  Key Design Features: Unique, squid-like shape, functional design for juice extraction.

10.4. DESIGN RIGHTS

Monopolistic Rights Conferred by Design Registration

When an industrial design is registered, the proprietor is granted **exclusive rights** over the design. These rights enable the owner to legally exclude others from:

- ➤ **Reproducing** the design
- ➤ **Manufacturing** products based on the design
- ➤ **Selling** products incorporating the design
- ➤ **Dealing** in any manner with the registered design

This monopoly is particularly beneficial for companies that produce items where the shape or aesthetics of the product contribute significantly to its market appeal. It ensures that the proprietor can maintain **exclusivity** over the novel and original design applied to their product.

Example: A fashion company with a unique shoe design can prevent other brands from copying and selling the same shoe design without consent.

Key Benefits of Design Rights:

- ➤ Protection of **aesthetic value** of a product.
- ➤ Establishment of a **competitive advantage** in the market.
- ➤ Encouragement of **innovation and creativity** by securing exclusivity.

10.5. ENFORCEMENT OF DESIGN RIGHTS

Legal Actions for Infringement

Once an applicant has successfully registered a design, they gain the **right to take legal action** against any party that uses or reproduces the design without permission. If unauthorized copies or "pirated products" of the registered design are discovered, the proprietor can:

- ➤ **File an infringement case** in a court (not lower than a District Court).
- ➤ Seek an **injunction** to stop further use of the design.
- ➤ **Claim damages** for losses incurred due to the infringement.

Court Procedure:

Before any legal action is taken, the court first verifies if the design is registered under **The Designs Act, 2000**. If the design is **not registered**, no legal action can be pursued. However, if the infringer is found guilty of piracy or infringement, the court may order them to:

- ➤ Pay **damages** of ₹50,000 for each registered design infringed.
  Example: If a company unlawfully reproduces the registered design of a mobile phone case without consent, the design owner can sue for damages and prevent further sales.

Key Points of Enforcement:
- ➢ **Only registered designs** are protected under law.
- ➢ Legal action can be initiated only in **District Courts** or higher.
- ➢ The infringer may be required to pay **financial compensation** to the proprietor.

10.6. NON-PROTECTABLE INDUSTRIAL DESIGNS INDIA

Certain industrial designs cannot be registered for protection in India, primarily due to their nature or because they fall under specific legal exclusions. These categories of designs include:

1. **Designs Against Public Moral Values:** Any design that is contrary to **public morality** cannot be registered. This serves to prevent the registration of designs that may offend societal norms or ethical standards.
2. **Flags, Emblems, and Signs:** Designs that incorporate **flags, emblems, or insignia** of any country cannot be registered. This prohibition ensures that national symbols remain free from commercial exploitation. **Example:** The design of a product that includes the Indian national flag cannot be registered.
3. **Integrated Circuits: Designs of integrated circuits (ICs)** are not eligible for protection as industrial designs. IC designs are protected under a different legal framework known as the Semiconductor Integrated Circuits Layout Design Act, 2000.
4. **Design Describing a Manufacturing Process:** Any design that merely describes the **process of making an article** cannot be protected. Industrial designs are focused on the visual or aesthetic appearance of products, not the processes used to create them.
5. **Specific Items Not Eligible for Protection:** The following items cannot be registered as industrial designs:
   - ➢ **Books, calendars, certificates, forms,** and other similar documents.
   - ➢ **Dressmaking patterns, greeting cards, leaflets, maps, plan cards, postcards, and stamps**.
   - ➢ **Medals:** Designs related to medals or other similar objects are excluded from registration.
6. **Artistic Works (Copyright Act, 1957):** Artistic works as defined under **Section 2(c) of the Copyright Act, 1957** are not eligible for industrial design registration[59]. Such works are already protected under copyright law. This includes:
   - ➢ **Paintings, sculptures, and drawings** (e.g., maps, charts, or plans).
   - ➢ **Photographs and architectural works.**
   - ➢ **Artistic craftsmanship,** i.e., items that fall under artistic creativity.

   Example: A sculpture or a unique painting cannot be registered as an industrial design since it falls under copyright protection.
7. **Trademarks:** Industrial designs do not include **trademarks**. Any design that functions as a trademark (e.g., logos, symbols) cannot be registered under the **Designs Act, 2000**, as trademarks have their own protection regime.

10.7. PROTECTION TERM

The design or outer shape of a product contributes significantly to its **aesthetic appeal** and adds value in the marketplace. To safeguard this design from unauthorized use, the **Designs Act, 2000** provides protection to registered designs[60].

Duration of Protection:
- ➢ Registered designs in India are protected for an **initial term of 10 years.**
- ➢ This protection can be **extended by 5 years** upon filing a renewal application.

This system ensures that the creator has **exclusive rights** over the design for a substantial period, during which they can prevent others from using, reproducing, or selling the design without permission. **Example:** A company designing a new type of furniture can protect the design for 10 years and further extend the protection for 5 more years, giving it a competitive advantage in the market.

10.8. PROCEDURE FOR REGISTRATION OF INDUSTRIAL DESIGNS

The registration of industrial designs in India involves a structured process to ensure that the design is novel and eligible for protection under the **Designs Act, 2000**. The steps include conducting a **prior art search**, filing an application, and the subsequent examination and publication of the design. Below is a detailed explanation of the procedure:

10.8.1. PRIOR ART SEARCH

Before filing an application for the registration of industrial designs, it is essential to verify that the design or a similar design has not been previously registered. A **prior art search** helps in determining the novelty and originality of the design. Various databases are available for conducting this search:

1. **Design Search Utility (CGPDTM):** The Indian Controller General of Patents, Designs, and Trademarks provides a platform for design search at https://ipindiaservices.gov.in/designsearch/[61].
2. **Global Design Database (WIPO):** The World Intellectual Property Organization (WIPO) offers a global design database for comprehensive international design searches. It is available at https://www3.wipo.int/designdb/en/index.jsp[62].
3. **Hague Express Database (WIPO):** Another WIPO database specifically for designs filed under the Hague System can be accessed at https://www3.wipo.int/designdb/hague/en/#[63].
4. **Design View (EUIPO):** The European Union Intellectual Property Office (EUIPO) offers a database for searching industrial designs registered within the European Union. It is available at https://www.tmdn.org/tmdsview-web/welcome#/dsview[64].

Conducting a prior art search ensures that the design is **novel** and does not conflict with any existing registered design. Failure to do so could result in the rejection of the application.

10.8.2. APPLICATION FOR REGISTRATION

Once the prior art search confirms the novelty of the design, the next step is filing an **application for registration**. The following points outline the process:

1. **Who Can Apply:** An application for design registration can be filed by:
    - Individuals
    - Small entities
    - Institutions or organizations
    - Industries

    If the applicant is not a resident of India, a registered **patent agent** or legal practitioner residing in India must be appointed to file the application.
2. **Filing Design Application:** This is the initial step where the application is submitted for registration.
    Where to Apply: The application is submitted to the **Deputy Controller of Patents & Designs** at the **Patent Office**, Intellectual Property Office Building, **Salt Lake City, Kolkata**.
3. **Formality Check:** The application undergoes a formality check to ensure all required documents and forms are correctly filled. If there are issues, amendments can be made.
4. **Application Examination:** An examiner assesses the application to determine if it meets the eligibility criteria laid out in the **Designs Act, 2000**. If the examiner raises objections, the applicant is required to respond to the queries within **six months**. Failure to respond may result in the application being abandoned.
5. **Substantive Examination:** Following the application examination, a more detailed substantive examination occurs to further ensure all registration criteria are met. If not accepted, amendments may be made.
6. **Publication and Objection:** Once accepted, the design and its details are published in the Official Journal of the Patent Office. The public can raise objections during this phase. If no objections are raised within the prescribed period, the process moves to the next step.

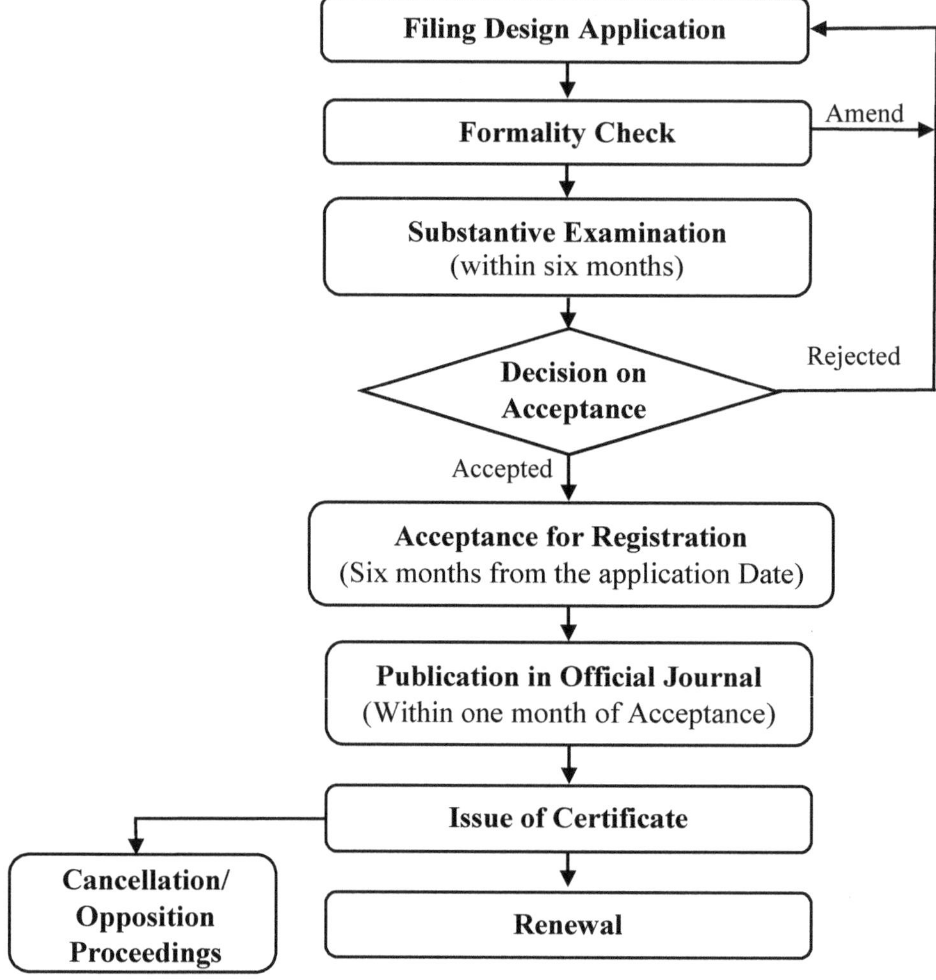

Fig. 10.1. Flowchart of Process for Industrial Design Registration[65].

7. **Issue of Certificate:** Assuming no objections or successful resolution of any objections, a certificate of registration is issued to the applicant, granting exclusive rights to use the design.

8. **Cancellation/Opposition Proceedings:** Even post-registration, there may be legal proceedings such as cancellation requests or oppositions that could challenge the validity of the registration.

9. **Renewal:** The registration is valid for 10 years but can be extended for an additional 5 years.

Example: A company designing a novel bottle shape for its new beverage line would conduct a prior art search, ensuring that the design has not been registered before. Upon satisfying the novelty requirement, the company files the application, and after examination and public scrutiny, the design is registered, granting the company exclusive rights to the bottle shape.

10.9. DURATION OF THE REGISTRATION OF A DESIGN

1. **Initial Duration:** The registration of an industrial design is valid for an initial period of **10 years** from the date of registration. In cases where a **priority date** is claimed (for example, under international agreements like the **Paris Convention**), the duration is calculated from that **priority date**.

2. **Extension**: After the initial 10-year period, the registration can be extended for an additional **5 years**. To do so, an application must be filed in **Form-3** along with the prescribed fee, which must be submitted to the **Controller General of Designs** before the expiry of the initial registration period.

   Example: If a design is registered on January 1, 2025, it remains valid until January 1, 2035. The proprietor can extend this by another 5 years, up to January 1, 2040, by filing the necessary documents.

10.10. IMPORTANCE OF DESIGN REGISTRATION

The registration of a design plays a crucial role in safeguarding the originality and commercial value of a product. Some key benefits include:

1. **Exclusive Rights**: The owner of a registered design holds the exclusive right to use the design on the product. This **exclusivity** allows the owner to prevent others from reproducing or imitating the design without consent, thereby maintaining a competitive edge.

2. **Prevention of Piracy and Imitation**: Registered designs are protected against **piracy** or unauthorized copying. This ensures that the original creator's efforts are rewarded and that their designs cannot be freely copied by competitors.

3. **Market Goodwill**: Legal protection helps the design owner build **goodwill** and **brand reputation** in the market, as the unique design contributes to consumer recognition and product differentiation. The protection helps boost sales by creating a unique identity in the marketplace.

    Example: A company designing a novel and aesthetically pleasing **mobile phone case** can prevent competitors from copying the design. By protecting the design through registration, the company can enhance its product's market appeal and trust among consumers.

10.11. CANCELLATION OF THE REGISTERED DESIGN

The registration of a design is not permanent and may be **cancelled** under certain circumstances. A petition for cancellation can be submitted using **Form-8**, along with the prescribed fee, to the **Controller of Designs**. The cancellation can occur on the following grounds:

1. **Design Already Registered**: If it is proven that the design had already been registered by another party, the current registration can be cancelled.

2. **Design Previously Published**: If the design was published in India or elsewhere before the official date of registration, it is ineligible for protection, and the registration can be revoked.

3. **Lack of Novelty or Originality**: The design may be cancelled if it is found to be **not novel** or original. Designs that resemble prior registered designs or known designs in the public domain may be invalidated.

4. **Not a Design Under Clause (d) of Section 2**: If the design does not fit the definition of "design" as per **Clause (d) of Section 2** of the **Designs Act, 2000**[66], its registration may be revoked. According to this clause, a design must focus on aesthetic features and not on functionality or technical processes.

    Example: If a company registers a **furniture design**, and it is later discovered that the design had been published in a catalog before its registration, another entity can file a cancellation petition on the grounds of prior publication.

10.12. CLASSIFICATION OF INDUSTRIAL DESIGNS

Industrial designs are classified under specific categories to streamline the registration process and facilitate design searches. This classification system is regulated by the **Locarno Agreement, 1968**, a global agreement that establishes an internationally accepted system for classifying goods concerning their industrial designs.

1. **Locarno Agreement**: The **Locarno Agreement** (available at: https://www.wipo.int/classifications/locarno/locpub/en/fr/) defines **32 classes** and **237 subclasses** of goods for registering and searching industrial designs. It also mandates that all **signatory parties** (countries that have signed the agreement) use these classifications in their official design registration documents.

2. **Examples of Classes**:
    i.   **Class 1** includes industrial designs related to **foodstuffs for humans, animals, and dietetic foods**. However, containers or packaging materials are not included in this class.
    ii. **Class 9** comprises **bottles, flasks, pots, and pressurized containers**.
    iii. **Class 32** is assigned to **graphic symbols, logos, surface patterns, and ornamentation**.

These classifications allow for easier categorization of industrial designs and enhance the searchability of registered designs.

Example: A designer seeking to register a unique bottle design for a new beverage will classify the design under **Class 9**.

10.13. APPLICATION FORMS

A detailed collection features 24 unique forms related to Industrial Designs. A listing of important forms is outlined below.

Table 10.1. List of important form related to Industrial Designs[16].

Sl. No.	Name of the Form	Form No.	Fee (₹)	Natural Person	Small Entity	Large Entity
1	Application for registration of Design	Form-1	1,000	2,000	4,000	Application for protecting the unique industrial design of a product
2	Application for the Restoration of Design	Form-4	1,000	2,000	4,000	To restore an expired or lapsed design registration
3	Application for renewal of Design	Form-3	2,000	4,000	8,000	Renewal of design registration to extend its validity
4	Petition for cancellation of registration of a Design	Form-8	1,500	3,000	6,000	Filing for the cancellation of an existing registered design
5	Notice of intended exhibition or publication of unregistered Design	Form-9	500	1,000	2,000	Notifying the intent to exhibit or publish a design before it is registered
6	Application for entry of name of proprietor or part proprietor in the Register	Form-11	500	1,000	2,000	Registering or updating the name of the proprietor or co-owner of the design
7	Request for correction of clerical error	Form-14	500	1,000	2,000	Requesting correction of any clerical or typographical errors in the design documents
8	Request for certified copy	Form-15	500	1,000	2,000	Requesting a certified copy of design-related documents or certificates
9	Application for rectification of Register	Form-17	500	1,000	2,000	Rectifying any errors or inconsistencies in the Design Register
10	Notice of opposition	Form-19	100	200	400	Filing an opposition against a particular design registration or process

10.14. DESIGNS REGISTRATION TREND IN INDIA

The trend of industrial design registrations in India has seen significant changes over the past few years, reflecting the growth in innovation and aesthetics-driven products. Here is a summary of the key statistics related to industrial designs applications filed, examined, and registered, organized year-wise:

1. **Applications Filed:** The number of applications filed has steadily increased, particularly in 2022 and 2023, with a jump from around 12,000 applications in 2019 to over 23,000 by 2023. This indicates a growing interest in design protection in India.

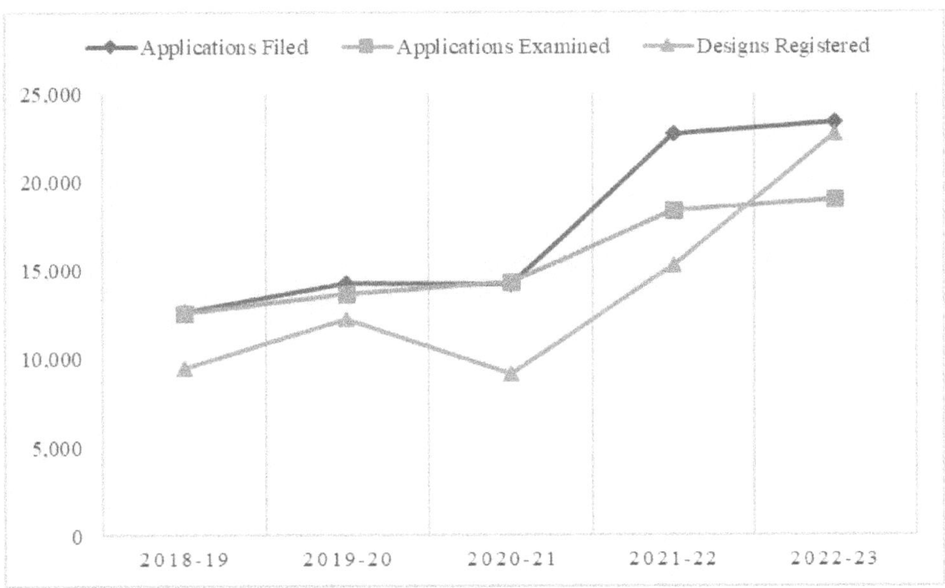

Fig. 10.2. Chart for Design Registration profile of India for the period 2018-23[40].

2. **Applications Examined:** The examination process has also seen a marked improvement. The number of applications examined increased from around 12,000 in 2019 to over 19,000 by 2023. This highlights the increased capacity of the Indian Patent Office to handle design applications efficiently.

3. **Designs Registered:** One of the most significant trends is the rise in the number of designs registered. There has been a sharp increase in 2023, with 22,698 registrations, compared to 9,512 in 2019. This rise can be attributed to reforms in the intellectual property framework and increased awareness about design rights among industries.

The sharp increase in design registrations in 2023 (285% increase compared to 2019) suggests that India is increasingly becoming a hub for design innovation. These trends reflect the rising importance of aesthetics and design in product differentiation and market positioning

10.15. INTERNATIONAL TREATIES

Several international treaties play a significant role in standardizing the processes for industrial design registration. Two of the most important treaties are:

1. **Hague Agreement (1925):** The **Hague Agreement** (accessible at: https://www.wipo.int/treaties/en/registration/hague/) facilitates the **international registration of industrial designs**. It allows an applicant to secure protection for an industrial design in multiple countries through a single application filed with the **World Intellectual Property Organization (WIPO)**.

   Example: A company can register its industrial design in several countries simultaneously under the Hague Agreement, reducing administrative costs and simplifying the process of international protection.

2. **Locarno Agreement (1968):** As mentioned earlier, the **Locarno Agreement** (available at: https://www.wipo.int/treaties/en/classification/locarno/) establishes a **classification system** for industrial designs. It is used globally to categorize designs and maintain a standardized classification system, ensuring consistency in international design registration and search processes.

   Example: A fashion designer creating new apparel designs can use the **Locarno system** to classify their design under the appropriate class for international registration.

10.16. FAMOUS CASE LAW: APPLE INC. VS. SAMSUNG ELECTRONICS CO.

A well-known case in the field of design and patent infringement is the **Apple Inc. vs. Samsung Electronics Co.** lawsuit. This case became a landmark in intellectual property law, dealing with the infringement of both **design and utility patents**.

1. **Overview**: In **2011**, Apple Inc. filed a lawsuit against Samsung Electronics in the **United States District Court for the Northern District of California**. Apple alleged that Samsung had infringed on Apple's design and utility patents, particularly in relation to **user interface features** such as the **screen app grid** and the **tap-to-zoom** functionality.
2. **Evidence and Controversy**: As evidence, Apple submitted **side-by-side images** comparing the **iPhone 3GS** with Samsung's **i9000 Galaxy S** to show the design similarities. However, Samsung's counsel argued that Apple had **tampered with the images** to exaggerate the similarities. This led to **counter-suits** from Samsung in various jurisdictions, including **South Korea, Japan, Germany**, and the **United States International Trade Commission (ITC)** in **Washington D.C.**
3. **Outcome**: After **7 years of litigation**, the case finally settled in **June 2018**. Samsung was ordered to pay **$539 million** to Apple for infringing on its design and utility patents. This case became famous for its lengthy proceedings and the significant amount of damages awarded.
4. **Significance**: The Apple vs. Samsung case highlights the importance of **design protection** and the potential consequences of infringement. It also serves as a reminder of the complexities involved in proving design similarity and the role of evidence in intellectual property disputes.

Questions

1. Briefly explain the overview of Industrial Design (ID). Summarize the Non-Protectable Industrial Designs in India.
2. Define industrial Design. Brirfly explain acts amd laws governs Inductrial design.
3. Discuss the Design registration procedure by using a flowchart.
4. Describe the enforcement of Industrial Design Rights.
5. Explain the classification of Industrial Designs and design registration trends in India.
6. Explain the process of Industrial design registration.
7. Explain the famous case law between Apple Inc Vs Samsung Electronics Co. related with Industrial Design rights.

"Geographical indications are not just markers of heritage and culture, but also give our communities an opportunity to lift up their lives."

: Daren Tang

Module - 5

Chapter 11:
GEOGRAPHICAL INDICATIONS

INTRODUCTION

Geographical Indications (GI) are unique signs used on products that have a specific geographical origin and possess qualities, reputation, or characteristics inherent to that location. In this chapter, we will explore the various acts, laws, and rules related to GI in India, the ownership and rights granted to holders of a registered GI, and the process of GI registration. We will also cover different classes of GI, what qualifies as a non-registerable GI, and the collective marks used for protection. Additionally, we will discuss how GI rights are enforced and examine the GI ecosystem in India.

11.1. GEOGRAPHICAL INDICATIONS

Geographical Indications (GIs) are special names or signs used on products that have a specific geographical origin. These products have qualities, reputation, or characteristics that are essentially due to that place of origin. *For example, Darjeeling tea is famous worldwide, and its unique taste and quality are linked to the region of Darjeeling in India.* In every country, there are certain regions known for their **traditional knowledge and heritage** in producing specialized goods across various sectors, such as:

   a. **Agriculture** (e.g., unique crops)
   b. **Food Products** (e.g., spices, tea, coffee)
   c. **Textiles** (e.g., silk, muslin)

These products are deeply linked to the cultural heritage and practices of specific geographical locations. Historically, people from distant places traveled to these regions to purchase these unique goods. **Example: Christopher Columbus** sailed from Spain to India to import its famous spices, highlighting the global demand for region-specific products.

Example: The **British** traveled to Arabian countries to import Arabian horses, valued for breeding fast-running horses.

   1. **Historical Examples of Famous Heritage Products**

      Some well-known examples of heritage products include:

      a. **China Silk**: Valued for its softness, quality, and durability.
      b. **Dhaka Muslin**: A fine cotton fabric from Dhaka, Bangladesh, known for its lightness and craftsmanship.
      c. These products have been in high demand for centuries, and their reputation was built and maintained by the **experts and masters** of the respective geographical locations.

2. **Transmission of Knowledge Across Generations**

The specialized knowledge involved in producing these heritage products was traditionally passed down from **generation to generation** within specific communities. This ensured the preservation of techniques, quality, and authenticity.

3. **Evolution of Geographical Indications (GI)**

Over time, a strong link between these heritage products and their geographical origins became more defined, leading to the development of **Geographical Indications (GI)**.

Definition: A GI is a sign or label that is used on products that originate from a specific geographical location or region and possess certain qualities, characteristics, or a reputation associated with that place.

Key Features:
 ➢ The product must be produced in a specific **geographical region**.
 ➢ There must be a strong link between the product and its **place of origin**, often due to unique environmental factors, traditional methods, or regional expertise.

Example of GIs:
 ➢ **Darjeeling Tea** (India): Famous for its distinctive flavor and aroma, linked to the Darjeeling region's specific climate and soil conditions.
 ➢ **Kanchipuram Silk** (India): Known for its high-quality silk sarees, produced using traditional methods in the Kanchipuram region.

4. **Reputation and Legal Protection of GIs**

The reputation of GI products is built over time and is often painstakingly maintained by **generations of artisans or producers**. The legal protection of GIs ensures that only products genuinely originating from the specified location can use the name. This helps in preventing **misuse of the product's name** and ensures that consumers receive authentic products.

11.2. ACTS, LAWS AND RULES PERTAINING TO GI

In India, Geographical Indications (GI) were introduced in 2003, with the governing laws and rules established in the following legal frameworks:

1. **Geographical Indications of Goods (Registration & Protection) Act, 1999:** This is a sui generis Act of the Parliament of India for the protection of geographical indications in India. It was enacted to comply with the Agreement on Trade-Related Aspects of Intellectual Property Rights (TRIPS) under the World Trade Organization (WTO).

2. **Geographical Indications of Goods (Registration & Protection) Rules, 2002:** The Geographical Indications of Goods (Registration and Protection) Rules, 2002 were framed under the Geographical Indications of Goods (Registration and Protection) Act, 1999. These rules provide detailed guidelines and procedures for the registration and protection of GIs in India.

11.3. OWNERSHIP OF GI

The ownership or rights of a registered GI can belong to:

1. **Producers**: Individuals or groups responsible for producing the GI-tagged goods.
2. **Associations or Cooperative Societies**: Groups formed to represent producers collectively.
3. **Government Authorities**: In some cases, the government may hold ownership.

These entities are responsible for maintaining the integrity and reputation of the GI product.

11.4. RIGHTS GRANTED TO THE HOLDERS

Registered GI holders are granted several important rights under the law:

1. **Right to Grant Licenses:**
 ➢ GI holders can **gift, sell, transfer, or mortgage** the GI rights.

> They can **grant a license** to others, allowing them to use the GI product. For any arrangement to be **legally valid**, it must be in **written form** and registered with the **Registrar of GI**.

2. **Right to Sue:**
   > GI holders can take **legal action** against any unauthorized person or entity using their GI without consent.
   > This right protects the integrity and exclusive rights of the GI holder.

3. **Right to Exploit:**
   > GI holders can authorize **exclusive users** to produce or sell goods under the registered GI label.
   > This grants economic and commercial advantages to the authorized users.

4. **Right to Obtain Reliefs:**
   > **Registered proprietors** and **authorized users** have the right to seek **legal remedies** for any violations of their GI rights.

11.5. REGISTERED GI IN INDIA

India's GI registration encompasses a wide range of products, including **handicrafts, agricultural goods, foodstuffs,** and **alcoholic beverages.**

Table 11.1. Popular GIs Registered in India[67].

Sl. No.	GI Name	Registration Year	State	Type
1	Darjeeling Tea	2004-05	West Bengal	Agricultural
2	Basmati Rice	2000	Punjab, Haryana, Uttarakhand, Himachal Pradesh, Jammu & Kashmir	Agricultural
3	Mysore Silk	2004-05	Karnataka	Manufactured
4	Kanchipuram Silk Sarees	2005	Tamil Nadu	Manufactured
5	Pochampalli Ikat	2004-05	Telangana	Manufactured
6	Chanderi Sarees	2004-05	Madhya Pradesh	Manufactured
7	Kota Doria	2004-05	Rajasthan	Manufactured
8	Mysore Agarbathi	2004-05	Karnataka	Manufactured
9	Malabar Pepper	2008	Kerala, Karnataka	Agricultural
10	Bikaneri Bhujia	2010	Rajasthan	Manufactured
11	Banarasi Silk Sarees	2005	Uttar Pradesh	Manufactured
12	Kashmir Pashmina	2009	Jammu & Kashmir, Himachal Pradesh	Manufactured
13	Nagpur Orange	2005	Maharashtra	Agricultural
14	Naga Mircha	2009	Nagaland	Agricultural
15	Tirupathi Laddu	2010	Andhra Pradesh	Food stuff
16	Phulkari	2011	India (Punjab, Haryana & Rajasthan)	Handicraft

> **First GI Registered in India:** Darjeeling Tea in 2004.
> **Recent Registrations (as of March 2025):**
>   ❖ Bareilly Zari Zardoji (Handicraft - Uttar Pradesh)
>   ❖ Banaras Tirangi Barfi (Food Stuff - Uttar Pradesh)
>   ❖ Kutch Ajrakh (Handicraft - Gujarat)

- ➢ **Total Registered GIs in India: 643 (as of March 2025).**
- ➢ **Distribution of Registered GIs:**
  - ❖ **Handicrafts:** 58% (e.g., Mysore Silk, Kashmir Pashmina).
  - ❖ **Agricultural Products:** 30% (e.g., Darjeeling Tea, Basmati Rice).
  - ❖ **Other categories:** Foodstuffs, Manufacturing, Natural Goods.
- ➢ **Top States for Handicrafts:**
  - ❖ **Karnataka:** Karnataka has the highest number of registered GIs, with a total of 110.
  - ❖ **Tamil Nadu:** Tamil Nadu comes in second with 90 registered GIs.
  - ❖ **Uttar Pradesh:** Uttar Pradesh has 84 registered GIs.
- ➢ **International GIs Registered in India:** Several international products have also been registered as GIs in India, reflecting their **global recognition** and **commercial value**:
  - ❖ **Champagne** (France): Registered as a GI for wine.
  - ❖ **Scotch Whisky** (United Kingdom): Registered as a GI for alcoholic beverages.

11.6. IDENTIFICATION OF REGISTERED GI

Registered Geographical Indication (GI) products are assigned an official **GI tag**, which serves as proof of:
- ➢ **Authenticity** of the product.
- ➢ **Adherence to production standards** and **location of production** as specified during the GI registration.

Non-registered products are prohibited from using this tag, ensuring that only genuine GI products benefit from the exclusive label. **Example**: Products such as **Darjeeling Tea, Mysore Silk**, and **Tirupathi Laddu** carry GI tags representing their **place of origin** and associated **cultural or historical identity**.

1. **The GI tag plays a crucial role in:**
   - ➢ **Consumer trust**: Ensuring buyers know they are purchasing a legitimate product from a recognized region.
   - ➢ **Protection of the product's reputation**: Preventing misuse of the GI name by unauthorized producers.
2. **Issuance of GI Tags in India**

   In India, the **Geographical Indication Registry** is responsible for issuing GI tags. This body functions under the **Department for Promotion of Industry and Internal Trade** (DPIIT), which is part of the **Ministry of Commerce and Industry**.

   The main office of the **Geographical Indications Registry** is located at: **Intellectual Property Office Building, Industrial Estate, G.S.T Road, Guindy, Chennai - 600032**. The **GI Registry** ensures that products claiming to have geographical significance meet the set standards and come from the specific geographical locations associated with their names.
3. **Global Production and Use of GI Products**

   Although GI products can be grown or produced outside their designated regions, they cannot carry the GI tag unless they are produced in the specific geographical area mentioned in the official GI records. **Example**: The plants for **Darjeeling Tea** can be grown in different regions of India, but tea leaves from these plants cannot be sold as "Darjeeling Tea" unless they are cultivated in the **Darjeeling region** itself. The **climate and soil** of Darjeeling are critical to the product's authenticity.

11.7. CLASSES OF GEOGRAPHICAL INDICATIONS

GI-certified goods in India are categorized under **34 different classes**, which cover a wide variety of products. Each class groups products based on their **type** and **industry**:

1. **Class 1**: Chemicals used in industries such as agriculture, science, horticulture, and forestry. It also includes products like **manures, preservatives**, and **adhesives**.
2. **Class 33**: Alcoholic beverages (excluding beers).
3. **Class 34**: Tobacco, smokers' articles, and matches.

The detailed classification of goods can be accessed from the official website of **CGPDTM** (Controller General of Patents, Designs & Trade Marks): https://ipindia.gov.in/writereaddata/images/pdf/classification-of-goods.pdf [68].

Examples of GI Tag Identification:
1. **Darjeeling Tea**: GI tag representing tea from the **Darjeeling** region of **West Bengal**.
2. **Mysore Silk**: GI tag for silk produced in **Karnataka**.
3. **Tirupathi Laddu**: GI tag for the famous laddu from **Andhra Pradesh**.

11.8. NON-REGISTERABLE GI

Not all geographical indications (GIs) are eligible for registration under Indian law. The **Geographical Indications of Goods (Registration & Protection) Act, 1999,** lays down specific **prohibitions** under **Section 9** that must be met for a GI to be registerable[69].

Conditions that Prohibit GI Registration:
1. **Deception or Confusion**: If the use of the GI is likely to **deceive or cause confusion** among consumers regarding the origin or authenticity of the product, registration will be prohibited.
2. **Violation of Law**: Any GI that is **contrary to existing laws** cannot be registered.
3. **Scandalous or Obscene Matter**: GIs that contain **scandalous or obscene content** are not eligible for registration.
4. **Offensive to Society**: GIs that include material likely to **hurt societal sentiments** or **religious susceptibilities** of any community or section of citizens in India are also prohibited from registration.
5. **Generic Terms**: GIs that have become **generic** (i.e., they are widely used to describe a type of good rather than a specific region) are not allowed. This includes GIs that are no longer protected in their **country of origin** or have **fallen into disuse**.

Example: If a term like "Champagne" becomes generic and is used for sparkling wines globally, it might lose its GI protection, especially if it's not protected in its country of origin.

11.9. PROTECTION OF GI

The protection of GIs is an essential aspect of **Intellectual Property Rights (IPR)**, and GI protection is typically **enforced through the courts** of the respective country where the GI is registered. Proper registration of a GI grants several **benefits**, such as:
1. **Identifying and Preventing Piracy**: Registered GIs help in distinguishing authentic products from **pirated or counterfeit** versions.
2. **Enhanced Commercial Value**: Products with GI protection often enjoy increased **market value** due to their association with a specific region's quality and reputation.
3. **Legal Support**: In the event of a dispute, registered GIs provide strong **legal support** in court, allowing for easier enforcement of rights.

Methods of GI Protection:
- **Sui Generis Systems**: This is a **special regime of protection** that is used in many countries, including India, for the protection of GIs. Under this system, GIs are governed by laws that are tailored specifically for their protection, making it a distinct category under IPR.
- **Certification or Collective Mark Systems**: These systems allow producers within a specific region to collectively hold rights to a GI.
- **India's Choice of Sui Generis System**: After the **TRIPS Agreement** (1995), countries were allowed to choose between adopting **TRIPS standards** for GI protection or following the **sui generis system**. India chose the sui generis system to accommodate its unique **legislative** and **geographical diversity**. This system varies between countries based on their jurisdiction and local legislation.

Example: The **Darjeeling Tea GI** is protected under the sui generis system in India, ensuring that only tea produced in Darjeeling is marketed as "Darjeeling Tea."

11.10. COLLECTIVE OR CERTIFICATION MARKS

Certification Marks and **Collective Marks** play an important role in ensuring **quality control** and **standards** for goods and services. They provide a means to distinguish between certified and non-certified products, enhancing consumer trust and ensuring compliance with agreed standards.

11.10.1. CERTIFICATION MARKS:

- ➢ **Definition**: A certification mark is used to certify that a product meets specific **quality standards** or complies with defined **criteria**, regardless of where it was produced.
- ➢ **Purpose**: Certification marks are primarily used to **distinguish certified goods** from those that are not certified. These marks indicate that a product adheres to specific **quality standards**, including **permitted materials**, **manufacturing methods**, or other regulatory criteria.
- ➢ **Example**: The **ISI mark** in India certifies that products such as electrical appliances meet safety and quality standards laid down by the Bureau of Indian Standards (BIS).
  Key Characteristics:
- ➢ Certification marks are issued by a **third-party organization** or agency.
- ➢ They ensure **consistent quality** across products, irrespective of their geographical origin.

11.10.2. COLLECTIVE MARKS:

- ➢ **Definition**: Collective marks are owned by **associations** (such as cooperatives or unions) and indicate that the goods or services originate from a **member of the association**.
- ➢ **Purpose**: The main function of a collective mark is to signify that a particular product or service is produced by a member of a group that adheres to **common standards**. It ensures **quality compliance** for goods or services that share common characteristics.
- ➢ **Example**: The **Amul** brand in India is a collective mark representing products that are produced by members of the **Gujarat Cooperative Milk Marketing Federation**. All members comply with strict production standards.
  Key Characteristics:
- ➢ Collective marks signify **membership** in a specific association and the adherence to **agreed quality standards**. They are typically used by **cooperating enterprises** that produce goods with **shared features** or characteristics.

11.11. ENFORCEMENT OF GI RIGHTS

The **enforcement of GI rights** is a critical aspect of **intellectual property protection**. Once a GI is registered, the rights associated with it must be protected against unauthorized use or infringement. Enforcement typically involves **legal actions** taken through the court of law.

Methods of Enforcement:

1. **Civil Actions**: The registered GI holder can take **civil legal action** to protect their rights. Some common civil sanctions include:
   i. **Injunctions**: Court orders to **prohibit unlawful acts**, such as unauthorized use of the GI.
   ii. **Damages**: The court may award **monetary compensation** to the GI holder for any losses suffered due to infringement.
2. **Criminal Sanctions**: In some cases, **criminal action** may be taken against individuals or companies that engage in fraudulent or unauthorized use of a GI. This could involve **fines**, **imprisonment**, or **seizure of counterfeit goods**.
3. **Administrative Actions**: **Administrative authorities** (such as the GI Registry) may intervene to stop unauthorized use or issue **warnings** to infringing parties. This method is typically quicker and less costly than going through the courts.

Key Points:
> - GI protection ensures that **only authorized producers** in the designated geographical area can use the GI label.
> - The enforcement mechanisms vary by country but typically involve a combination of **civil**, **criminal**, and **administrative measures** to safeguard the rights of GI holders.

Example: The holders of the **Darjeeling Tea GI** can file a legal case against a company selling tea under the "Darjeeling" label if the tea is not grown in the Darjeeling region, thereby enforcing their GI rights.

11.12. PROCEDURE FOR GI REGISTRATION

The process of registering a **Geographical Indication (GI)** involves a thorough **search**, **scrutiny**, and **approval process** to ensure the protection of unique geographical products. The procedural steps from prior search to registration ensure that the GI is properly authenticated and protected under Indian law.

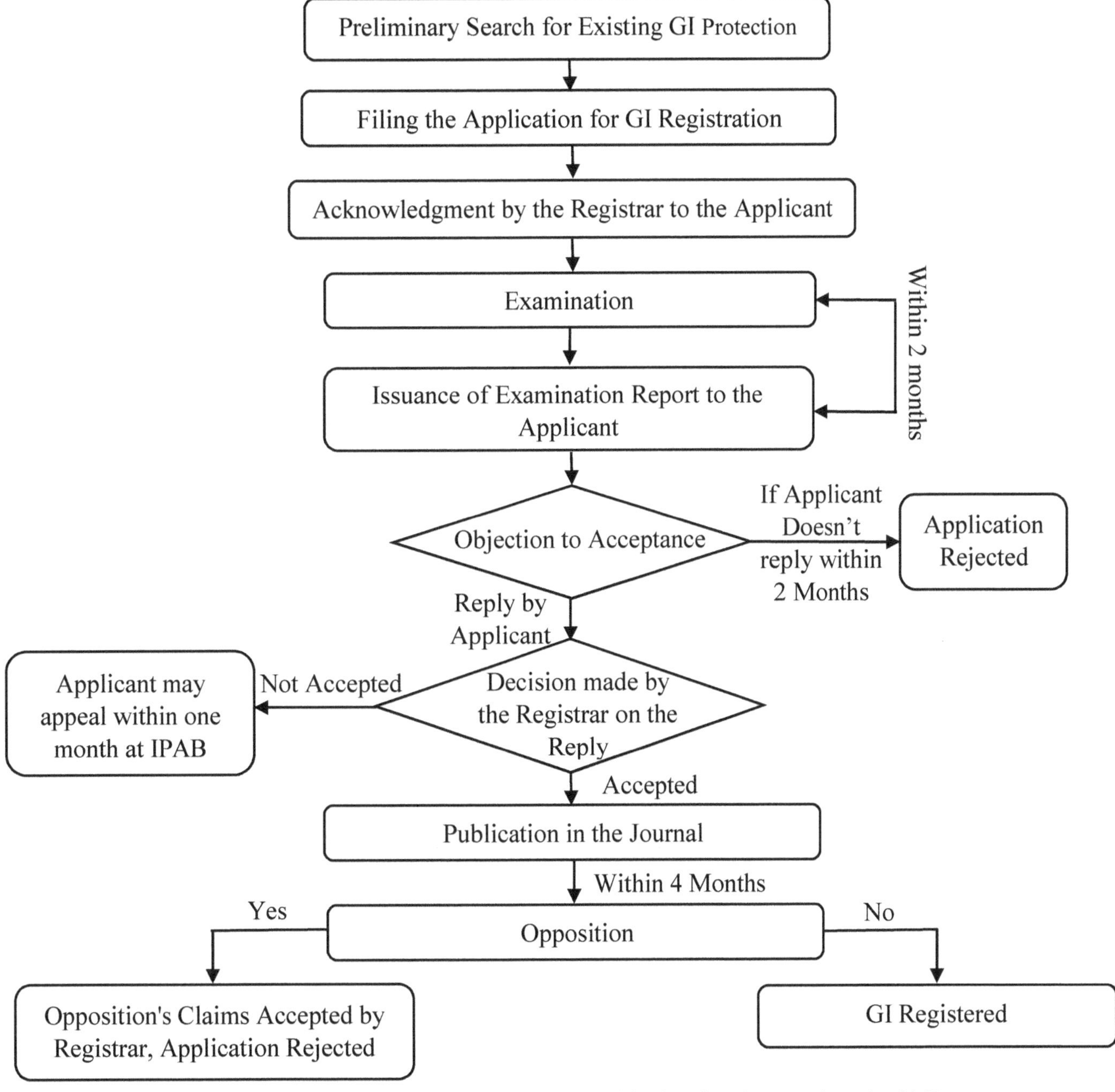

Fig. 11.1. Flowchart of Process for Geographical Indication Registration[16].

1. **Preliminary Search for Existing GI Protection**

   Before filing an application for GI registration, it is important to verify whether the concerned GI is already registered or protected. This step ensures the uniqueness of the application and avoids legal conflicts.

   Search Resources:

   i. **WIPO Search Tools**:

      Appellations of Origin and Geographical Indications: Use the **World Intellectual Property Organization (WIPO)** search engine to check whether a GI or appellation of origin is already protected. The search can be performed at this link: WIPO Search Engine.

   ii. **IP Offices of Member Countries**: WIPO has also created a directory that provides links to the **intellectual property (IP) offices** of member countries. The registered GIs of any country can be accessed via this directory: WIPO Member Country Directory.

   iii. **India-Specific GI Search**: The list of **registered GIs in India** can be accessed from the official website of the **Controller General of Patents, Designs, and Trademarks (CGPDTM)**: CGPDTM Registered GI List.

2. **Filing the Application for GI Registration**

   Once the prior search confirms that the GI is not already protected, the next step is to file an application. The application can be submitted by an individual, an organization, or an authority established under Indian law.

   Application Requirements:

   - ➤ **Prescribed Format and Fee**: The application must be submitted in the **prescribed format** to the **Registrar of Geographical Indications** along with the **prescribed fee**. For more details, refer to the rules on the official website: GI Registration Rules.

   - ➤ **Applicant Details**: The application should include all relevant details of the applicant and clearly mention the interest of the **producers** associated with the product.

   - ➤ **Map Submission**: The submission of **three certified copies** of the **map of the region** where the GI belongs is **mandatory**.

   - ➤ **Signatures**: The application must be **duly signed** by the applicant or their agent. The applicant must also provide details on how the **standards** for the GI will be maintained.

3. **Examination Process**

   Once the application is submitted, it undergoes several rounds of scrutiny to ensure compliance with the required standards.

   Steps in the Examination Process:

   i. **Initial Scrutiny**: An **Examiner** at the GI Registry will review the application to check for any **deficiencies** or **similarities** with existing GIs.

   ii. **Communication of Discrepancies**: If any discrepancies are found, the Examiner will communicate them to the applicant, who must respond within **one month** of receiving the communication.

   iii. **Examination Report**: After receiving a satisfactory response, the Examiner will prepare an **examination report** and submit it to the **Registrar** for further review.

   Final Scrutiny:

   - ➤ **Clearing Doubts/Objections**: If the Registrar finds any further doubts or objections, the applicant must resolve them within **two months**; otherwise, the application will be **rejected**.

4. **Publication and Objection Period**

   Once the Registrar approves the application, it is published in the **official Geographical Indication Journal** for public notification.

   - ➤ **GI Journal**: The application is published to invite objections, if any. The official GI journal can be accessed at this link: GI Journal.

➢ **Objection Period**: Any objections must be filed within **four months** of the publication. If no objections are raised, the GI will be registered.

5. **Registration and Renewal**

   If the application passes the objection period without challenges, the GI is registered.

Key Points:
   ➢ **Registration Date**: The date of **filing the application** is considered the **registration date**.
   ➢ **Initial Registration Period**: A GI is initially registered for **ten years**.
   ➢ **Renewal**: The GI registration can be **renewed** upon payment of the prescribed renewal fee.

11.13. DOCUMENTS REQUIRED FOR GI REGISTRATION

The documents required for Geographical Indication (GI) registration ensure that the product is properly represented and verified before receiving official protection. Each document, from the application form to the affidavit of producer representation, plays a crucial role in safeguarding the authenticity and unique characteristics of the product under Indian law.

1. **Applicant Information:** The first step in the GI registration process involves providing detailed information about the applicant.

   Key Details Required:
   ➢ **Applicant's Name:** Full name of the individual, organization, or legal authority applying for the GI.
   ➢ **Address:** Complete and accurate address of the applicant.
   ➢ **Particulars:** Any additional relevant details about the applicant, including their legal status and role in representing the producers of the concerned product.

2. **Application Form GI-1A:** The GI registration application must be submitted using the **prescribed form GI-1A**, which is designed to collect all necessary information related to the GI. This form ensures uniformity in the application process and includes all required fields to ensure compliance with the law.

3. **Statement on the Designated Goods:** The application must include a **statement** explaining the **designated goods** that the applicant seeks to protect under GI registration. The statement should provide a detailed description of the product, including its unique characteristics that make it eligible for GI protection.

4. **Class of Goods:** The product must be classified under the appropriate **class of goods** as outlined by the GI Registry. The GI Registry uses a classification system to categorize products into different classes, such as agricultural products, textiles, handicrafts, etc. The applicant must clearly indicate which **class** the product belongs to.

5. **Affidavit for Producer Representation:** The applicant must submit an **affidavit** that establishes the claim of **genuinely representing the interests** of the producers of the product. The affidavit acts as a legal declaration that the applicant is authorized to represent the producers and has the right to apply for GI protection on their behalf.

6. **Characteristics of the Geographical Indication (GI):** A comprehensive description of the **characteristics of the GI** must be provided. This description should highlight the product's **unique features** that are tied to the geographical region, such as quality, reputation, or other attributes that distinguish it from similar products.

7. **Special Human Skill (if applicable):** If the production of the GI product involves any **special human skill**, it must be clearly mentioned in the application. **Examples:** Certain traditional handicrafts or artisanal products may require **specialized knowledge** or skills that are passed down through generations. This skill forms an important part of the **cultural heritage** associated with the GI.

Table 11.2. Important application forms related to GI[16].

Sl. No.	Form No.	Title	Requisite Fee (₹)
1	GI-1	Application for the registration of a Geographical Indication for goods included in one class.	5,000
2		Application for the registration of a Geographical Indication for goods included in one class from a Convention country.	5,000
3		A single application for the registration of a Geographical Indication for goods in different classes.	5,000 for each class
4		A single application for the registration of a Geographical Indication for goods in different classes from a Convention country.	5,000 for each class
5	GI-2	Notice of opposition to the registration of a Geographical Indication or an opposition or an authorised user.	1,000 for each class
6		Form of counter-statement.	1,000
7		Application for extension of time for filing notice of opposition.	300
8	GI-3	Application for the registration of an authorised user of a registered Geographical Indication.	500
9		Request for issuance of a registration certificate as an authorised user.	100
10		For renewal of an authorised user.	1,000
11	GI-4	Renewal of the registration of a Geographical Indication at the expiration of the last registration.	3,000
12		Application for restoration of a Geographical Indication or an authorised user removed from the Register.	1,000 plus applicable renewal fee
13		Application for renewal within six months from the expiration of last registration of Geographical Indication.	3,500
14	GI-8	Application for registration of a Geographical Indications agent.	1,000
15	GI-10	Application for cancellation of an entry in the Register or to strike out goods.	300

11.14. GI ECOSYSTEM IN INDIA

The **Geographical Indications (GI) Ecosystem in India** has seen significant growth over the years, playing a crucial role in safeguarding unique regional products, promoting rural economies, and preserving traditional knowledge.

Key Insights

1. **Diverse Range of Products**: GI applications cover various categories like agricultural goods, handicrafts, food products, and natural items. Notable examples include Darjeeling tea, Alphonso mangoes, and Banarasi silk.
2. **Impact on Rural Economies**: GI tags provide premium branding to local products, enhancing income opportunities for rural communities. For instance, Karnataka and Tamil Nadu lead in GI registrations, benefiting local artisans and farmers.
3. **Government Initiatives**: The Indian government has launched programs like "One District One Product" to promote GI products, alongside initiatives such as raising awareness on GI benefits. In addition, Rs. 75 crores (approx. $8.42 million) has been allocated for GI awareness and promotion over three years.

4. **Importance for India**: GIs protect the reputation of Indian products globally, fostering both local employment and exports. The GI ecosystem is tied closely to the **Trade-Related Aspects of Intellectual Property Rights (TRIPS)** agreement, which has set standards for GI protection worldwide.

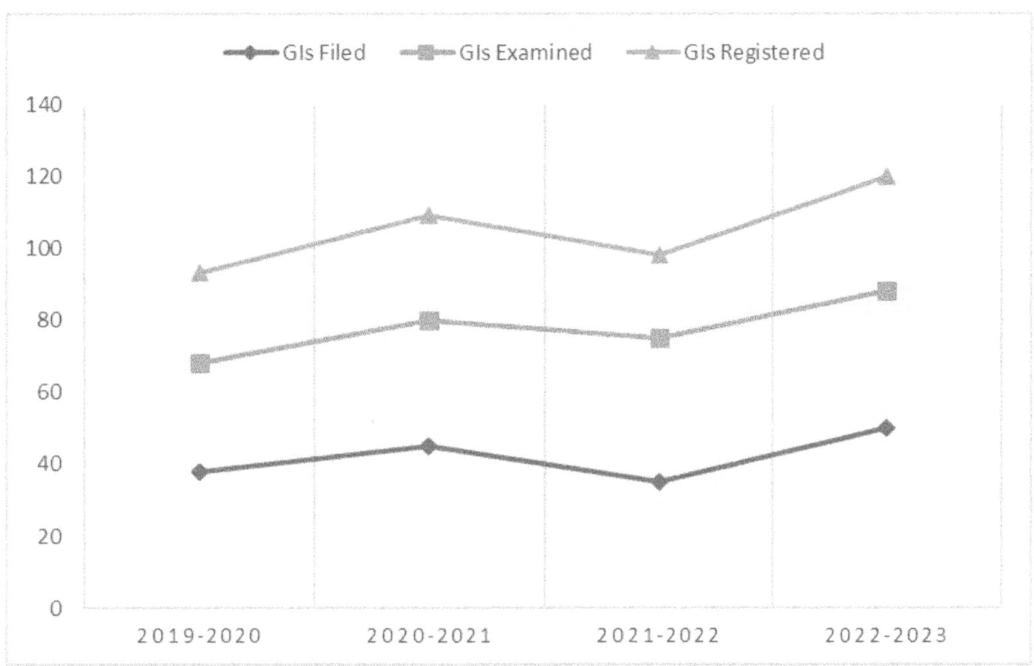

Fig. 11.2. Geographical Indication (GI) Registration Trend in India[67].

Questions

1. Explain registered Geographical Indications (GI) in India with the tabulate of examples.

2. Explain the Identification of Registered Geographical Indications (GI) items. What are the common methods used to project GI in India.

3. Using a flowchart, explain the process of GI registration.

4. Define Geographical Indications (GI) with an example. What are the rights granted to GI holders?

5. Which specific acts, laws and rules govern geographical indications in India? Give some examples of well-known geographical indications registered in India.

6. How would you describe the overall ecosystem and significance of geographical indications in India?

"A Patent is only worth as much as its owner is willing to spend to defend it."

: Eric Halber

Module - 5

Chapter 12:
CASE STUDIES ON PATENTS

INTRODUCTION

In this chapter, we will explore some important case studies related to patents, focusing on well-known examples like the Curcuma (Turmeric) patent, Neem patent, and Basmati patent. These cases highlight how intellectual property rights (IPR) play a significant role in protecting traditional knowledge and innovations. Along with these case studies, we will also discuss key intellectual property (IP) organizations in India and various government schemes and programs that support innovation and patent protection. This chapter aims to help students understand the practical aspects of IPR through real-world examples

12.1. CASE STUDY OF CURCUMA (TURMERIC) PATENT

Curcuma longa, commonly known as turmeric, is a plant native to India and Southeast Asia. It has been used for centuries in traditional Indian medicine (Ayurveda) and cuisine. Turmeric contains an active compound called curcumin, which is known for its anti-inflammatory, antioxidant, and healing properties. Over time, the significance of turmeric has grown beyond traditional uses, attracting attention globally, leading to patent applications related to its medicinal properties. A prominent example of this is the **Curcuma Patent Case**, which highlights issues around **biopiracy, intellectual property rights (IPR),** and the protection of traditional knowledge.

1. **The Turmeric Patent Dispute**

   In 1995, the United States Patent and Trademark Office (USPTO) granted a patent (US Patent No. 5,401,504) to two researchers from the University of Mississippi Medical Center. The patent was for the "use of turmeric in wound healing." The patent claimed the novel use of turmeric powder in healing wounds, specifically as a topical treatment.

   However, this claim faced opposition, particularly from India, where turmeric had been used for thousands of years in traditional medicine for the same purpose. The patent led to concerns about the unfair appropriation of traditional knowledge, a concept known as **biopiracy** wherein corporations or individuals claim patents on traditional practices without recognizing or compensating the original knowledge holders.

2. **Challenge to the Patent**

   The Council of Scientific and Industrial Research (CSIR), India, challenged the turmeric patent in 1996. CSIR provided documented evidence that turmeric had been used for centuries in India for the treatment of wounds and rashes, thus making the patent claim invalid. This documentation was found in ancient texts and medical publications in various languages, including Sanskrit.

   CSIR's argument was based on the premise of "prior art", which refers to any knowledge or practice that has been known publicly before a patent application is filed. Since the use of turmeric for wound healing was part of Indian traditional knowledge, it could not be considered a novel invention under patent law. As a result of this opposition, the USPTO conducted a re-examination of the patent.

3. Outcome of the Case

In 1997, after reviewing the evidence provided by CSIR, the USPTO revoked the patent on turmeric. The case was significant because it was one of the first instances where traditional knowledge was used successfully to challenge a patent. It set an important precedent for the protection of indigenous knowledge systems and emphasized the need for global patent systems to recognize and respect the value of traditional practices.

4. Importance of the Turmeric Patent Case

i. **Biopiracy and Intellectual Property Rights (IPR):** The turmeric patent case brought the issue of biopiracy into international focus. Biopiracy refers to the exploitation of indigenous knowledge without proper authorization or compensation. The turmeric case showed how traditional knowledge, often passed down through generations, could be appropriated by individuals or corporations under patent laws. This led to increased awareness of the need to safeguard traditional knowledge from exploitation.

ii. **Traditional Knowledge Digital Library (TKDL):** In response to cases like the turmeric patent, India established the **Traditional Knowledge Digital Library (TKDL)**. TKDL is a database that compiles information from ancient texts, such as Ayurveda, Unani, and Siddha, to prevent the misappropriation of traditional knowledge by making it accessible to patent offices worldwide. This database plays a crucial role in providing evidence of prior art and ensures that patents are not granted on traditional knowledge.

iii. **Ethical Considerations in Patent Law:** The turmeric patent case also raised ethical concerns about the global intellectual property system. It questioned whether patent laws, which are often based on Western legal frameworks, are suitable for protecting knowledge that originates in indigenous or traditional societies. The case underscored the need for reforms in patent laws to accommodate and protect non-Western knowledge systems.

iv. **Global Awareness and Policy Changes:** The turmeric case and similar cases, such as the **Neem Patent** and the **Basmati Rice Patent**, have led to greater awareness among governments and international bodies about the need to protect traditional knowledge. These cases have influenced policy changes and reforms, particularly within organizations like the **World Intellectual Property Organization (WIPO)**, which now recognizes the importance of protecting traditional knowledge and genetic resources.

5. Lessons for Engineers and Researchers

The turmeric patent case serves as a critical example of how **intellectual property rights** intersect with **ethics** and **social responsibility**. It highlights the importance of respecting and acknowledging the contributions of traditional knowledge in research and innovation. When conducting research, especially in fields related to biotechnology, medicine, or agriculture, it is vital to ensure that proper credit is given to indigenous knowledge holders, and efforts are made to protect such knowledge from exploitation.

Additionally, the case emphasizes the importance of **due diligence** when filing for patents, particularly when the subject matter may have roots in traditional practices. Researchers must ensure that they conduct a thorough literature review, including traditional sources, to verify the novelty of their work.

6. Conclusion

The turmeric patent case is a landmark event in the history of intellectual property rights and the protection of traditional knowledge. It demonstrated that traditional knowledge, like scientific knowledge, has value and should be protected under patent laws. For engineers and researchers, the case serves as a reminder of the ethical responsibilities they bear when working with knowledge that may have cultural and historical significance.

The successful challenge of the turmeric patent was not just a victory for India but for all societies that have contributed to the global pool of knowledge. It has led to important developments in the recognition and protection of traditional knowledge in the global intellectual property framework.

12.2. CASE STUDY OF NEEM PATENT

Neem (Azadirachta indica) is a tree native to the Indian subcontinent, widely known for its medicinal properties and its role in agriculture as a natural pesticide. For centuries, neem has been used in traditional Indian medicine (Ayurveda) and agriculture for its antifungal, antibacterial, and pesticidal properties. The **Neem Patent Case** is a significant event in the history of intellectual property rights (IPR), particularly concerning the misappropriation of traditional knowledge, or **biopiracy**. This case became an international focal point in the debate over patenting naturally occurring substances and the protection of indigenous knowledge.

1. **Background of the Neem Patent**

   In 1994, the European Patent Office (EPO) granted a patent (EP 0436257 B1) to the United States Department of Agriculture (USDA) and a multinational company, W.R. Grace, for the method of producing a neem-based pesticide. The patent claimed that the process of extracting neem oil and its pesticidal application was an invention. This triggered opposition from environmental groups, scientists, and activists from India and other countries, who argued that neem's pesticidal properties had been well-known and used in Indian agriculture for centuries.

   The patent was considered an instance of **biopiracy**, where traditional knowledge from India was being claimed by foreign entities without proper recognition or compensation to the local communities who had been using neem for generations.

2. **The Challenge to the Patent**

   Several organizations, including the **Indian government, environmental groups**, and **non-governmental organizations (NGOs)**, opposed the neem patent. One of the key players in this opposition was Dr. Vandana Shiva, an environmental activist and founder of the Research Foundation for Science, Technology, and Ecology (RFSTE). RFSTE, along with the **International Federation of Organic Agriculture Movements (IFOAM)** and **Magda Aelvoet**, a member of the European Parliament, filed a legal challenge to the EPO, arguing that the neem-based pesticide was not an invention but a form of traditional knowledge that had been used for centuries in India.

   The basis of their argument was **"prior art"**, similar to the turmeric patent case. They presented documented evidence of the traditional use of neem as a pesticide in India, which included ancient texts, local agricultural practices, and oral knowledge passed down through generations.

3. **Outcome of the Case**

   In 2000, after six years of legal battles, the **European Patent Office (EPO)** revoked the patent granted to W.R. Grace and the USDA. The EPO concluded that the claimed process for producing a neem-based pesticide did not meet the requirements for patentability because it lacked novelty and was based on traditional knowledge that had been publicly known for a long time.

   The revocation of the neem patent was seen as a major victory for the protection of traditional knowledge and a significant moment in the global fight against biopiracy.

4. **Importance of the Neem Patent Case**

   i.   **Biopiracy and Ethical Concerns:** The neem patent case brought attention to the issue of biopiracy, where corporations or individuals from developed countries seek to patent traditional knowledge from developing countries. The case highlighted the **unethical appropriation** of indigenous knowledge without recognizing or compensating the local communities that had preserved this knowledge for centuries.

   ii. **Legal and Policy Implications:** The neem case played a crucial role in shaping the international debate on intellectual property rights. It emphasized the need for changes in patent laws to prevent the patenting of traditional knowledge. As a result, countries like India started advocating for the inclusion of provisions in international agreements, such as the **Agreement on Trade-Related Aspects of Intellectual Property Rights (TRIPS),** to protect traditional knowledge.

iii. **Traditional Knowledge Digital Library (TKDL):** Similar to the turmeric case, the neem patent case motivated India to further develop the **Traditional Knowledge Digital Library (TKDL)**. This database compiles traditional knowledge from ancient texts and practices to ensure that patent offices worldwide have access to prior art information. TKDL serves as a valuable tool in preventing biopiracy by providing evidence of the traditional uses of plants like neem.

iv. **Sustainable Agriculture and Biodiversity:** The neem patent case also highlighted the importance of sustainable agricultural practices and the role of biodiversity in traditional farming systems. Neem, as a natural pesticide, has been an integral part of Indian agriculture for centuries, promoting **organic farming** and reducing dependence on chemical pesticides. The case drew attention to the need for protecting biodiversity and traditional ecological knowledge, which are essential for sustainable development.

v. **Global Awareness and Legal Reforms:** The revocation of the neem patent and similar cases brought about significant global awareness regarding the exploitation of traditional knowledge. The case contributed to international discussions on the need for **access and benefit-sharing agreements**, which ensure that indigenous communities are compensated when their knowledge or resources are used for commercial purposes. This led to the development of frameworks such as the **Nagoya Protocol on Access and Benefit-Sharing** under the **Convention on Biological Diversity (CBD)**.

5. **Lessons for Engineers and Researchers**

The neem patent case provides important lessons for engineers and researchers, especially those working in fields related to biotechnology, agriculture, and pharmaceuticals. It underscores the importance of conducting thorough research before filing for patents, including a review of traditional knowledge and prior art. Researchers must ensure that they do not inadvertently claim ownership over practices or knowledge that are already widely known or used.

6. **Conclusion**

The neem patent case is a landmark example of the intersection between intellectual property rights, ethics, and traditional knowledge. The successful revocation of the patent not only protected the rights of local communities but also set an important precedent for the global intellectual property system. It demonstrated that traditional knowledge, which has been passed down through generations, deserves the same level of protection and respect as modern scientific inventions.

12.3. CASE STUDY OF BASMATI PATENT

Basmati rice, known for its unique aroma, long grains, and distinctive taste, has been cultivated in the Indian subcontinent for centuries, particularly in India and Pakistan. It is a staple food and a valuable agricultural commodity with deep cultural and economic significance in these regions. However, in 1997, a patent was granted in the United States for a type of Basmati rice, leading to widespread controversy and discussions about **biopiracy**, **intellectual property rights (IPR)**, and the protection of **geographical indications** (GI).

The **Basmati patent case** is one of the most significant examples of the challenges faced by developing countries in protecting their traditional products and knowledge in the international intellectual property framework.

1. **The Basmati Patent Controversy**

In 1997, the United States Patent and Trademark Office (USPTO) granted a patent (US Patent No. 5,663,484) to RiceTec Inc., a Texas-based company. The patent covered strains of Basmati rice hybrids that the company had developed, as well as the methods for selecting these hybrids. RiceTec marketed this hybrid rice under names that included the term "Basmati." The company also received patents for "novel rice lines" that were claimed to possess traits similar to traditional Basmati rice, such as its unique aroma and long grains.

This patent raised significant concerns in India and Pakistan, both of which considered Basmati to be a product of their cultural heritage and geographical uniqueness. The Indian government and various agricultural organizations argued that Basmati had been traditionally grown in India and Pakistan for hundreds of years, and the patent amounted to **biopiracy** an attempt to appropriate a traditional product without recognition or benefit to the original producers.

2. **Legal and Ethical Issues**

    i. **Geographical Indication (GI):** One of the key issues in the Basmati patent controversy was the use of the term "Basmati" by RiceTec. In international trade, **Geographical Indication (GI)** refers to products that have specific qualities or reputations due to their origin in a particular region. Basmati rice is considered a **GI product** of India and Pakistan, meaning that only rice grown in these regions can rightfully use the name "Basmati." India argued that RiceTec's use of the term "Basmati" was misleading and violated the principles of GI protection.

    ii. **Biopiracy and Traditional Knowledge:** The Basmati patent case was another example of **biopiracy**, where traditional agricultural products or knowledge are patented by foreign entities without proper recognition or compensation to the original producers. Just as in the **Turmeric** and **Neem** patent cases, the Basmati patent raised ethical questions about the exploitation of traditional knowledge and the need for legal mechanisms to protect such knowledge.

    iii. **Impact on Farmers and Trade:** The patent had significant implications for Basmati farmers in India and Pakistan. The use of the name "Basmati" for rice produced outside these regions could potentially reduce the value of traditional Basmati rice in international markets. This could negatively impact the livelihoods of farmers who had been growing Basmati for generations. Additionally, RiceTec's patent raised concerns about the possible restriction of access to seeds or breeding techniques for local farmers.

3. **Challenge to the Patent**

The Indian government, along with various agricultural organizations, challenged the Basmati patent granted to RiceTec. India argued that the patent violated the principles of **prior art**, as Basmati rice had been cultivated in the Indian subcontinent for centuries. India also raised objections to the use of the name "Basmati," which it considered a violation of **geographical indications**. In response to these objections, RiceTec eventually withdrew several key claims of the patent in 2001. The USPTO ruled that RiceTec could not claim exclusive rights to the name "Basmati" and limited the scope of the patent. However, RiceTec was still allowed to market its rice products under different names.

4. **Outcome of the Case**

The partial revocation of the patent was considered a victory for India and the protection of traditional agricultural products. The decision prevented RiceTec from monopolizing the term "Basmati" and ensured that the unique geographical and cultural significance of Basmati rice was recognized.

However, the case also highlighted the need for stronger protections for **geographical indications** and traditional knowledge in the global intellectual property system. It underscored the challenges that countries like India face in protecting their traditional products from misappropriation in foreign markets.

5. **Importance of the Basmati Patent Case**

    i. **Geographical Indication (GI) Protection:** The Basmati case emphasized the importance of protecting products with **geographical indications**. GI products are those that are closely tied to the region in which they are produced, and their quality or reputation is often linked to the specific geographical environment. In the case of Basmati rice, the climate, soil, and traditional farming techniques in India and Pakistan contribute to its unique characteristics.

    ii. **Biopiracy and Intellectual Property Rights (IPR):** The case is a classic example of **biopiracy**, where multinational companies or foreign entities attempt to patent traditional knowledge or products without compensating or acknowledging the original producers. It brought attention to the need for reforms in global intellectual property law, particularly with respect to traditional knowledge and **genetic resources**. The Basmati patent case contributed to the ongoing debate about how to balance the interests of innovators with the rights of indigenous communities and traditional knowledge holders.

iii. **Impact on Trade and Agriculture:** The Basmati patent case had significant implications for international trade, especially for agricultural exports from developing countries like India and Pakistan. Had the patent remained in place, it could have limited the ability of Indian and Pakistani farmers to export Basmati rice under its traditional name. The case underscored the importance of protecting traditional products to ensure fair competition in global markets.

iv. **International Legal Frameworks:** The case also influenced international legal frameworks related to intellectual property and trade. For example, the **Agreement on Trade-Related Aspects of Intellectual Property Rights (TRIPS)** includes provisions for the protection of geographical indications. The Basmati case helped to raise awareness about the need for stronger GI protections in agreements like TRIPS, which are enforced by the **World Trade Organization (WTO)**.

6. Conclusion

The Basmati patent case is a landmark event in the global struggle to protect traditional knowledge and geographical indications from misappropriation. The partial revocation of RiceTec's patent was a significant victory for India and Pakistan, safeguarding the cultural and economic significance of Basmati rice. The case also highlighted the challenges posed by the international intellectual property system, particularly for developing countries, and the need for stronger protections for traditional products and knowledge.

12.4. IP ORGANIZATIONS IN INDIA

Intellectual Property Rights (IPR) play a crucial role in promoting innovation, creativity, and economic growth by granting inventors and creators the exclusive right to use their creations. In India, several organizations work to protect and manage intellectual property, ensuring that innovations and creative works are legally recognized and safeguarded.

1. **Office of the Controller General of Patents, Designs, and Trade Marks (CGPDTM)**

   The **Controller General of Patents, Designs, and Trade Marks (CGPDTM)** is the primary government office responsible for administering the laws related to patents, trademarks, designs, and geographical indications in India. It operates under the Department for Promotion of Industry and Internal Trade (DPIIT), Ministry of Commerce and Industry, Government of India.

Functions:

i. **Patents**: The CGPDTM oversees the administration of the **Indian Patents Act, 1970**, and is responsible for granting patents for inventions. Patents provide exclusive rights to the inventor for a certain period, allowing them to control the use and distribution of their invention.

ii. **Designs**: The office administers the **Designs Act, 2000**, which provides protection to the aesthetic aspects of products, such as their shape, pattern, or configuration.

iii. **Trademarks**: The **Trade Marks Act, 1999** is managed by the CGPDTM, allowing businesses and individuals to register and protect their unique names, logos, and symbols that distinguish their goods and services.

iv. **Geographical Indications (GI)**: The CGPDTM also handles the registration of **Geographical Indications (GI)** under the **Geographical Indications of Goods (Registration and Protection) Act, 1999**. GI protects products that have specific qualities due to their geographical origin, such as Darjeeling tea or Basmati rice.

Offices:

The CGPDTM has several regional offices across India for processing patents, trademarks, designs, and GI applications. The main locations include:

- ➢ Patent offices in **Delhi, Mumbai, Chennai, and Kolkata**.
- ➢ Trademark offices in **Ahmedabad, Chennai, Delhi, Kolkata, and Mumbai**.

2. **Intellectual Property Appellate Board (IPAB)**

   The **Intellectual Property Appellate Board (IPAB)** was established in 2003 to hear appeals against the decisions made by the CGPDTM concerning patents, trademarks, geographical indications, and plant varieties.

However, in 2021, the IPAB was dissolved, and its functions were transferred to **High Courts** in India. Now, IP-related disputes and appeals are handled by the courts.

Role:

The IPAB played a crucial role in resolving disputes related to the granting, cancellation, and revocation of patents, trademarks, and GIs. With its dissolution, IP-related cases are now dealt with by the respective **High Courts** in each state.

3. **National Intellectual Property Rights (IPR) Policy, 2016**

The **National IPR Policy** was launched in 2016 to promote a culture of innovation and creativity in India, ensuring that intellectual property is effectively protected, managed, and enforced. The policy aims to create awareness about IP, strengthen IP administration, and encourage commercialization of innovations.

Key Objectives:

- ➢ **Awareness**: Promote awareness and respect for IPR among all sectors of society.
- ➢ **Generation**: Encourage the creation of IP assets by providing incentives for research and development (R&D).
- ➢ **Protection**: Strengthen the legal and institutional framework to protect IP rights effectively.
- ➢ **Enforcement**: Improve enforcement mechanisms to combat IP infringement and counterfeiting.
- ➢ **Commercialization**: Facilitate the commercialization of IP assets by supporting entrepreneurs and startups.

The **Department for Promotion of Industry and Internal Trade (DPIIT)** is responsible for coordinating the implementation of this policy and working with other government bodies to strengthen India's IPR ecosystem.

4. **Department for the Promotion of Industry and Internal Trade (DPIIT)**

The Department for the Promotion of Industry and Internal Trade (DPIIT) plays a crucial role in shaping and implementing policies related to Intellectual Property Rights (IPR) in India. Its key activities include:

- ➢ **IPR Policy Formulation and Implementation**: DPIIT is responsible for creating and executing policies that foster a robust IPR ecosystem in India, including the *National IPR Policy* of 2016, which aims to strengthen the legal and institutional frameworks for IPR.
- ➢ **Modernizing IP Administration**: DPIIT oversees the modernization of Intellectual Property Offices (IPOs) for efficient management of patents, trademarks, and copyrights. This involves digitizing processes, reducing pendency times, and improving accessibility to IP services.
- ➢ **Capacity Building and Public Awareness**: DPIIT organizes awareness programs, workshops, and training for stakeholders, including businesses, students, and law enforcement agencies, to promote the importance of IPR and how to protect innovations.
- ➢ **International Cooperation and Treaties**: DPIIT represents India in international IPR forums and actively participates in treaties and agreements to harmonize IPR policies globally, ensuring Indian IP rights are recognized and protected internationally.
- ➢ **Enforcement and Compliance**: DPIIT works with law enforcement and judicial bodies to strengthen IP enforcement mechanisms. This includes anti-counterfeiting and anti-piracy initiatives to safeguard IP rights and curb infringement.
- ➢ **Encouraging Innovation and Entrepreneurship**: DPIIT supports start-ups and MSMEs by providing simplified procedures for filing IP applications and offering various incentives for innovation-driven businesses to safeguard their IP.

5. **Indian Patent Office (IPO)**

The **Indian Patent Office (IPO)** operates under the CGPDTM and is responsible for examining and granting patents in India. The IPO plays a crucial role in promoting innovation by providing legal protection to inventors and ensuring that patents are granted according to Indian law.

Functions:

- **Patent Examination**: The IPO examines patent applications to ensure they meet the requirements of novelty, inventive step, and industrial applicability.
- **Granting Patents**: If an invention meets all the criteria, the IPO grants a patent, giving the inventor exclusive rights for 20 years from the date of filing.
- **Patent Information**: The IPO maintains a database of granted patents and published applications, allowing the public to access information about innovations and prior art.

6. **Trademark Registry**

The **Trademark Registry** is part of the CGPDTM and is responsible for the registration and protection of trademarks in India. Trademarks are essential for businesses to distinguish their products and services.

Functions:

- **Registration of Trademarks**: The registry processes applications for trademark registration, ensuring that trademarks meet the requirements of distinctiveness and legality.
- **Trademark Search**: Before applying for a trademark, businesses can perform a search on the Trademark Registry's online portal to ensure that the trademark is not already registered or in use.
- **Protection of Registered Marks**: Once registered, trademarks are protected under Indian law, and the trademark holder can take legal action against unauthorized use.

7. **National Biodiversity Authority (NBA)**

The **National Biodiversity Authority (NBA)**, established under the **Biological Diversity Act, 2002**, plays a key role in regulating the use of biological resources and ensuring that the benefits from their use are shared fairly and equitably. The NBA works to protect India's biodiversity and prevent biopiracy by monitoring the commercial use of biological resources, such as plants and animals, and ensuring that local communities benefit from their use.

Functions:

- **Access and Benefit Sharing (ABS)**: The NBA ensures that businesses or researchers using India's biological resources share the benefits with local communities, in line with the **Nagoya Protocol** on access and benefit-sharing.
- **Preventing Biopiracy**: The NBA plays a crucial role in preventing the misappropriation of traditional knowledge and biological resources by foreign entities.

8. **Copyright Office**

The Copyright Office, part of the Ministry of Commerce and Industry, is responsible for administering the Copyright Act, 1957. Copyright protects original literary, artistic, musical, and cinematographic works from unauthorized reproduction, distribution, and adaptation.

Functions:

- **Registration of Copyright**: The office registers copyrights, providing legal protection to the creators of original works.
- **Issuing Licenses**: The office issues licenses for the use and reproduction of copyrighted works.
- **Copyright Enforcement**: The office works with enforcement agencies to combat piracy and protect the rights of creators.

9. **Protection of Plant Varieties and Farmers' Rights Authority (PPV&FRA)**

The **Protection of Plant Varieties and Farmers' Rights Authority (PPV&FRA)** was established under the **Protection of Plant Varieties and Farmers' Rights Act, 2001** to protect the rights of plant breeders, farmers, and researchers.

Functions:

- **Plant Variety Registration**: The PPV&FRA registers new, distinct, uniform, and stable plant varieties, providing breeders with exclusive rights to commercialize their new varieties.

- ➢ **Farmers' Rights**: The authority also recognizes the contribution of farmers to the preservation of plant genetic resources and protects their rights to save, use, exchange, and sell farm-saved seeds.
- ➢ **Benefit Sharing**: The PPV&FRA ensures that local communities and farmers benefit from the commercial use of plant varieties.

10. **Traditional Knowledge Digital Library (TKDL)**

The **Traditional Knowledge Digital Library (TKDL)** is a collaborative project between the **Council of Scientific and Industrial Research (CSIR)** and the **Ministry of AYUSH**. It aims to protect India's traditional knowledge by documenting it in a searchable digital format and preventing biopiracy.

Functions:

- ➢ **Documenting Traditional Knowledge**: The TKDL contains information about traditional medicinal systems like Ayurveda, Unani, and Siddha, as well as traditional agricultural practices.
- ➢ **Preventing Biopiracy**: By making traditional knowledge accessible to patent examiners worldwide, the TKDL prevents foreign companies from patenting traditional Indian knowledge.

12.5. SCHEMES AND PROGRAMMES

The National Research Development Corporation (NRDC) offers various schemes and programs to support innovation and technology commercialization. Key initiatives include:

1. **IP Consultancies:** NRDC provides consultative services to academia, R&D institutes, and industries on innovation, technology transfer, and IP policy.
2. **Technology Landscaping:** It aids stakeholders in evaluating technologies, market trends, and patent developments to inform decisions on R&D, investments, and patent strategies.
3. **Programme for Inspiring Inventors and Innovators:** Focuses on promoting inventions, facilitating innovation centers, and offering techno-commercial support, patent seminars, and knowledge management programs.
4. **Programme for Development of Technology Inspiring Commercialization:** Includes a digital innovation portal, technology value addition, market surveys, and entrepreneurship programs for rural and backward regions.
5. **ASEAN-India Cooperation:** NRDC has developed a portal for sharing technologies between India and ASEAN countries, fostering collaboration and bridging technological gaps. This platform facilitates innovation sharing and commercialization across sectors such as health, education, and agriculture.

Questions

1. Identify IP Organizations in INDIA. Explain schemes and programs for Intellectual Properties Rights
2. Summarize the IPR-related activities the Department for Promotion of Industry and Internal Trade (DPIIT) undertakes.

REFERENCES

[1]   D. Deb, R. Dey, and V. E. Balas, "Intelligent Systems Reference Library 153 Engineering Research Methodology A Practical Insight for Researchers." [Online]. Available: http://www.springer.com/series/8578

[2]   G. Pólya, How to Solve It : A New Aspect of Mathematical Method. 2014. [Online]. Available: https://www.amazon.com/How-Solve-Mathematical-Princeton-Science/dp/069116407X

[3]   COPE: Committee on Publication Ethics | Promoting integrity in scholarly research and its publication, Available: https://publicationethics.org/.

[4]   "Responsibilities for ethical research, https://www.dmu.ac.uk/research/ethics-and, governance/responsibilities-of-the-researcher.aspx".

[5]   Richard Pears and Graham Shields, *Cite Them Right: The Essential Referencing Guide*, 11th ed. Palgrave Macmillan, 2019.

[6]   H. R. Jamali and M. Nikzad, "Article title type and its relation with the number of downloads and citations," *Scientometrics*, vol. 88, no. 2, pp. 653–661, Aug. 2011, doi: 10.1007/s11192-011-0412-z.

[7]   K. Li, J. Rollins, and E. Yan, "Web of Science use in published research and review papers 1997–2017: a selective, dynamic, cross-domain, content-based analysis," *Scientometrics*, vol. 115, no. 1, pp. 1–20, Apr. 2018, doi: 10.1007/s11192-017-2622-5.

[8]   J. Zhang, H. Wang, and Y. Sun, "Exploring Citation-Based Knowledge Flow in Scientific Research," in *2013 Ninth International Conference on Semantics, Knowledge and Grids*, IEEE, Oct. 2013, pp. 58–65. doi: 10.1109/SKG.2013.22.

[9]   "WIPO - World Intellectual Property Organization." Accessed: Sep. 04, 2024. [Online]. Available: https://www.wipo.int/portal/en/index.html

[10]   A. E. Shamoo and D. B. Resnik, "Responsible Conduct of Research."

[11]   "World Intellectual Property Day 2021 - 'IP and SMEs: Taking Your Ideas to Market.'" Accessed: Sep. 04, 2024. [Online]. Available: https://www.wipo.int/pressroom/en/articles/2021/article_0004.html

[12]   "Traditional Knowledge Digital Library Unit (TKDL) | Council of Scientific & Industrial Research." Accessed: Sep. 04, 2024. [Online]. Available: https://www.csir.res.in/documents/tkdl

[13]   D. Rangnekar, "The Socio-Economics of Geographical Indications A Review of Empirical Evidence from Europe UNCTAD-ICTSD Project on IPRs and Sustainable Development Intellectual Property Rights and Sustainable Development," 2004. [Online]. Available: www.unctad.org

[14]   W. I. P. O. EN, "World Intellectual Property Indicators 2022," 2022, doi: 10.34667/TIND.47082.

[15]   *GLOBAL INNOVATION INDEX 2023 ;innovation in the face of uncertainty*. WORLD INTELLECTUAL PROPER, 2023.

[16]   *Lahinde Pañjāba dī hāsa rasa shāirī*. Pabalīkeshana Biūro, Pañjāba Yūnīwarasiṭī, 2022.

[17]   "1_42_1_Patent_Amendment_Rules_2016_16May2016".

[18]   "The Patents Act, 1970." [Online]. Available: http://www.ipindia.gov.in

[19]   "Section 20(1) in The Atomic Energy Act, 1962." Accessed: Sep. 10, 2024. [Online]. Available: https://indiankanoon.org/doc/1470006/

[20]   "THE SEMICONDUCTOR INTEGRATED CIRCUITS LAYOUT-DESIGN ACT, 2000".

[21]   "Section 100 in The Patents Act, 1970." Accessed: Sep. 10, 2024. [Online]. Available: https://indiankanoon.org/doc/252755/

[22]   "1_70_1_The-Patents-Rules-2003-Updated-till-23-June-2017".

[23]   "https://ipindia.gov.in/writereaddata/Portal/IPOFormUpload/1_12_1/form-1.pdf".

[24]   "https://ipindia.gov.in/writereaddata/Portal/IPOFormUpload/1_13_1/form-2.pdf".

[25] "Jurisdiction of Patent Offices | Administration | Patents | Intellectual Property India | Government of India." Accessed: Sep. 11, 2024. [Online]. Available: https://www.ipindia.gov.in/jurisdiction-of-patent-offices.htm

[26] "indian patenting process flowchart | Invntree." Accessed: Sep. 12, 2024. [Online]. Available: https://www.invntree.com/tag/indian-patenting-process-flowchart

[27] "Rule 80." Accessed: Sep. 12, 2024. [Online]. Available: https://ipindia.gov.in/writereaddata/Portal/ev/rules/pr80.html

[28] W. Intellectual Property Organization, "World Intellectual Property Indicators 2023," 2023, doi: 10.34667/tind.48541.

[29] "MANUAL OF PATENT OFFICE PRACTICE AND PROCEDURE."

[30] "Section 13 in The Copyright Act, 1957." Accessed: Sep. 17, 2024. [Online]. Available: https://indiankanoon.org/doc/4010217/

[31] "Section 17 in The Copyright Act, 1957." Accessed: Sep. 18, 2024. [Online]. Available: https://indiankanoon.org/doc/1404402/

[32] "Section 28 in The Copyright Act, 1957." Accessed: Sep. 18, 2024. [Online]. Available: https://indiankanoon.org/doc/176237/

[33] "India Code: Section Details." Accessed: Sep. 18, 2024. [Online]. Available: https://www.indiacode.nic.in/show-data?actid=AC_CEN_9_30_00006_195714_1517807321712&orderno=14

[34] "Section 57(1) in The Copyright Act, 1957." Accessed: Sep. 18, 2024. [Online]. Available: https://indiankanoon.org/doc/746625/

[35] "India Code: Section Details." Accessed: Sep. 18, 2024. [Online]. Available: https://www.indiacode.nic.in/show-data?actid=AC_CEN_9_30_00006_195714_1517807321712§ionId=14586§ionno=63&orderno=84

[36] "Section 52 in The Copyright Act, 1957." Accessed: Sep. 18, 2024. [Online]. Available: https://indiankanoon.org/doc/1013176/

[37] "Section 2 in The Copyright Act, 1957." Accessed: Sep. 18, 2024. [Online]. Available: https://indiankanoon.org/doc/797096/

[38] "Work Flow :: Copyright Office." Accessed: Sep. 19, 2024. [Online]. Available: https://copyright.gov.in/frmWorkFlow.aspx

[39] "Fee Details :: Copyright Office." Accessed: Sep. 19, 2024. [Online]. Available: https://copyright.gov.in/frmFeeDetailsShow.aspx

[40] "1_114_1_ANNUAL_REPORT_202223_English".

[41] "Section 33(3) in The Copyright Act, 1957." Accessed: Sep. 19, 2024. [Online]. Available: https://indiankanoon.org/doc/7078672/

[42] "Berne Convention for the Protection of Literary and Artistic Works." Accessed: Sep. 19, 2024. [Online]. Available: https://www.wipo.int/treaties/en/ip/berne/

[43] "Ch_XXVIII_01_ap".

[44] "Rome Convention for the Protection of Performers, Producers of Phonograms and Broadcasting Organizations." Accessed: Sep. 19, 2024. [Online]. Available: https://www.wipo.int/treaties/en/ip/rome/

[45] "Universal Copyright Convention | International Law, Berne Convention, Protection | Britannica." Accessed: Sep. 19, 2024. [Online]. Available: https://www.britannica.com/topic/Universal-Copyright-Convention

[46] "WTO | intellectual property - overview of TRIPS Agreement." Accessed: Sep. 19, 2024. [Online]. Available: https://www.wto.org/english/tratop_e/trips_e/intel2_e.htm

[47] "R.G Anand vs M/S. Delux Films & Ors on 18 August, 1978." Accessed: Sep. 19, 2024. [Online]. Available: https://indiankanoon.org/doc/1734007/

[48] "Can the monkey selfie case teach us anything about copyright law?" Accessed: Sep. 19, 2024. [Online]. Available: https://www.wipo.int/wipo_magazine/en/2018/01/article_0007.html

[49] "In the courts: Court confirms legal status of *Happy Birthday to You!*" Accessed: Sep. 19, 2024. [Online]. Available: https://www.wipo.int/wipo_magazine/en/2016/01/article_0009.html

[50] "Amitabh Bachchan miffed at possibility of losing copyright to his father Harivansh Rai's literary works – Firstpost." Accessed: Sep. 19, 2024. [Online]. Available: https://www.firstpost.com/entertainment/amitabh-bachchan-miffed-at-possibility-of-losing-copyright-to-his-father-harivansh-rais-literary-works-4395633.html

[51] "ARRANGEMENT OF SECTIONS".

[52] "Collection of Laws for Electronic Access INDIA".

[53] "Nice Classification." Accessed: Sep. 23, 2024. [Online]. Available: https://www.wipo.int/classifications/nice/en/

[54] "Vienna Classification." Accessed: Sep. 23, 2024. [Online]. Available: https://www.wipo.int/classifications/vienna/en/

[55] "STANDARD OPERATING PROCESS OF TRADE MARKS APPLICATIONS Processing of TM Application in Trade Mark Registry".

[56] "Flowchart of Process for Trademark Registration," https://ipindia.gov.in/workflow-chart.htm.

[57] "rules-2001".

[58] "Visual_Storytelling".

[59] "Section 2 in The Copyright Act, 1957." Accessed: Sep. 26, 2024. [Online]. Available: https://indiankanoon.org/doc/797096/

[60] "The Designs Act 2000 | Intellectual Property India." Accessed: Sep. 25, 2024. [Online]. Available: https://ipindia.gov.in/designs-act-2000.htm

[61] "DESIGN SEARCH." Accessed: Sep. 26, 2024. [Online]. Available: https://search.ipindia.gov.in/designsearch

[62] "WIPO Global Design Database." Accessed: Sep. 26, 2024. [Online]. Available: https://designdb.wipo.int/designdb/en/index.jsp

[63] "WIPO Hague Express." Accessed: Sep. 26, 2024. [Online]. Available: https://designdb.wipo.int/designdb/hague/en/

[64] "Availability - EUIPO." Accessed: Sep. 26, 2024. [Online]. Available: https://www.euipo.europa.eu/en/designs/before-applying/availability

[65] https://allthingspatent.wordpress.com/, "Design registration process in India."

[66] "Section 2(d) in The Designs Act, 2000." Accessed: Sep. 27, 2024. [Online]. Available: https://indiankanoon.org/doc/618466/

[67] "REGISTRATION DETAILS OF GEOGRAPHICAL INDICATIONS".

[68] "THE FOURTH SCHEDULE".

[69] "India Code: Section Details." Accessed: Sep. 30, 2024. [Online]. Available: https://www.indiacode.nic.in/show-data?actid=AC_CEN_11_60_00002_199948_1517807322766§ionId=2624§ionno=9&orderno=9